COLLECTOR BOOKS

A Division of Schroeder Publishing Co., Inc.

The current values in this book should be used only as a guide. They are not intended to set prices, which vary from one section of the country to another. Auction prices as well as dealer prices vary greatly and are affected by condition as well as demand. Neither the Editors nor the Publisher assumes responsibility for any losses that might be incurred as a result of consulting this guide.

Searching for a Publisher?

We are always looking for knowledgeable people considered to be experts within their fields. If you feel that there is a real need for a book on your collectible subject and have a large conprehensive collection, contact Collector Books.

Additional copies of this book may be ordered from:

Collector Books
P.O. Box 3009
Paducah, Kentucky 42002-3009

@ $9.95. Add $2.00 for postage and handling.

Printed by IMAGE GRAPHICS, INC., Paducah, Kentucky

INTRODUCTION

This book was compiled to help put serious buyers in contact with the non-collecting sellers all over the country. Most of us have accumulated things that are not particularly valuable to us but could very well be of interest to one of the buyers in this book. Not only does this book list the prices that collectors are willing to pay on thousands of items, it also lists hundreds of interested buyers along with the type of material each is buying. *Wanted to Buy* is very easy to use. The listings are alphabetically arranged by subject, with the interested buyer's name and address preceding each group of listings. In the back of the book, we have included a special section which lists the names and addresses of buyers along with the categories that they are interested in. When you correspond with these buyers, be sure to enclose a self-addressed, stamped envelope if you want a reply. If you with to sell your material, quote the price that you want or send a list. Ask if there are any items on the list that they might be interested in and the price that they would be willing to pay. If you want the list back, be sure to send a S.A.S.E. large enough for it to be returned.

PACKING AND SHIPPING INSTRUCTIONS

Special care must be exercised in shipping fragile items in the mail or U.P.S. Double-boxing is a must when shipping glass and china pieces. It is extremely important that each item be wrapped in several layers of newspaper. First, put a four-inch layer of wadded newspaper in the bottom of the box. Secondly, start placing the well-wrapped items on top of the crushed newspaper, making certain that each piece of glass or china is separated from the others. Make sure that there are at least four inches of cushioning newspaper or foam between each item. When the box is nearly full, place more cushioning material on top of the contents and then seal the box.

Finally, place this box and contents in a large box cushioned again with at least four inches of newspaper on all four sides, top and bottom. This double-boxing is very important. Our Postal Service and United Parcel Service are efficient; however, we must pack well just in case there is undue bumping in handling.

When shipping coins and precious metals, be sure to register your shipment and request a return slip so that you will know that the buyer received the goods, as well as the date that they were delivered. All material should be insured for full value. Remember, always use strong boxes, lots of packing, and good shipping tape.

ABC PLATES

I collect ABC plates and am looking for any kind except newer braille ones. Send SASE, name, address, phone number, and your price. Other interests include advertising seed catalogues, seed packages, seed boxes or displays. Please see also my listing under Pottery in this book.

Lisa Nieland
1228 W Main St.
Red Wing, MN 55066; 612-388-4027

ADVERTISING

Quality porcelain signs and any company catalogs are wanted on a variety of subjects that were advertised through the years past. Some signs were flat, others used flanges. Diecuts and other shapes are common.

Mike Bruner
6980 Walnut Lake Rd.
W Bloomfield, MI 48323

Signs	We Pay
Adams Express, w/logo	**140.00**
Campbell's Soup, curved	**300.00**
Coca-Cola, diecut	**800.00**
Damascus Ice Cream	**240.00**
Crisco, diecut w/can	**400.00**
Hood's Milk, w/cow, round	**600.00**
Kelly Girl Tires, round	**1,200.00**
Koolmotor, round	**220.00**
Lincoln Paints, w/Lincoln on can	**130.00**
Lincoln Telephone, w/candlestick phone	**350.00**
Mayo's Plug Tobacco	**160.00**
Red Devil Cement	**170.00**
Wadham's Motor Oil	**310.00**
Wards Vitovim Bread Thermometer	**220.00**
Wells Fargo and Company	**260.00**

I collect **old advertising pieces of almost any kind**: bins for grocery items, displays for all manner of goods, vending machines, lighted signs, lighted advertising clocks, door push plates, sewing notion items (from scissors displays to spool cabinets and dye displays), advertising art on cardboard (some came with an attached cardboard easel stand) and old glass globes (gasoline companies and others) used on various displays. If it was used to sell a product, I'm interested! Prices for the items will depend on their condition and rarity.

B.J. Summers
233 Darnell Rd.
Benton, KY 42025

	We Pay
Porcelain or Tin Advertising or Utility Signs, ea	**10.00-60.00**
Soft Drink Machines, ea	**100.00-300.00**
Tobacco Tins or Glass Jars, ea	**5.00-50.00**
Peanut Jars, ea	**10.00-40.00**
Candy Jars, ea	**5.00-30.00**
Advertising Chalkboards, ea	**5.00-25.00**
Glass Globes, ea	**100.00-300.00**

Wanted: **gasoline and advertising globes**. These may be one-piece etched or painted glass, have metal bands with glass faces, or have plastic bands with unusual glass faces. Long-time collector **will pay top prices for quality items**.

Wayne Priddy
P.O. Box 86
Melber, KY 42069
502-554-5619 or 502-444-5915

I am a private collector of **early advertising signs from the turn of the century up to the 1920s depicting phonographs** such as Victor, Columbia, Edison, etc. Below is a small list of signs I am currently looking to buy. Quality is important. Please write, call or fax. Thank you.

Kirk Lahey
70 Collins Gr. Unit 22
Dartmouth, NS
Canada B2W 4E6
3902-434-5699 or FAX 902-435-7886

Advertising

Phonograph Company Signs	We Pay
Pathe, tin	**400.00+**
Pathe, porcelain	**500.00+**
Mandel, tin	**300.00+**
Columbia Records Thermometer, tin	**600.00+**
Victor Records Thermometer, tin	**600.00+**
Columbia Grafonola, tin, shows dancing couple	**400.00+**

I am a non-stop buyer of **British figural biscuit tins**. These second-use tins originally held biscuits (cookies) and were issued by British bakeries whose names are usually found somewhere on the tins, e.g. Huntly and Palmer, Crawfords, Peek Frean, McVitie Price, Carr's, Gray Dunn, etc. They are often mistaken for toys, but always have a part, such as a roof, that opens or comes off completely. **I pay up to $5,000** for those tins shaped as cars, delivery vans, airplanes, boats or other vehicles. I am also looking for stacked books, houses or other buildings, windmills, castles, gypsy wagons, large birds, etc. Also wanted are figural sweet tins, usually toffee tins, and some French and Dutch tins that meet the same criteria as the British biscuit tins.

Condition is important. Non-figural, box-style tins, no matter how ornate or colorful, are not of interest. Tins must be shaped as some recognizable object. All phone calls returned. Photos are always appreciated.

The Butler Did It!
Catherine Saunders-Watson
P.O. Box 302
Greenville, NH 03048-0302
Phone or FAX 603-878-2171

	We Pay
Crawford's Gold Bi-Plane	**2,500.00**
Huntly & Palmer Stacked Books	**200.00-375.00**
Huntly & Palmer Delivery Van, brown & gold	**up to 1,000.00**
Carr's Double-Decker Bus	**up to 750.00**
Peek Frean Castle, one section w/flag	**up to 550.00**
Biscuit Tin Vehicles, ea	**500.00-5,000.00**
Crawford's Circus Wagon, w/lions	**1,000.00**
Crawford's Organ Grinder's Cart	**1,500.00**
Gray Dunn Motorcycle w/Sidecar	**5,000.00**

I am buying products and advertising made by the Fairbank Company. All items must be in excellent or better condition and guaranteed authentic with full return rights if not so. All items *must* be marked with the Fairbank name unless prior approval is given. If you are buying to sell to me, contact me first as I can't buy duplicates and don't want you stuck with an unwanted item. If possible send photographs or photocopies. Please no magazine ads for Gold Dust or Fairy Soap. Other ads may be okay, check with me first. Listed here are some of my wants.

Soaps: Fairy, Santa Claus, Dandy, Glycerine Tar, White Star, PicNic, Copco, Western Star, Clariette, Chicago, Pummo, and Scouring Bar. I need a bar of Fairy Soap in the blue heart box with the girl sitting on top of the bar wearing a bonnet and holding a bouquet of flowers.
Cottolene: Gold label tins, I have five of the red label tins. Lots of items.
Snowhite Shortening: I have a 45-lb. tin, need all other stuff.
Fairbank Family Lard Co.: I have one olive tin, no other information.
Polly Prim: Scouring powder in a round tin, circa 1914.
Gold Dust: A common item, I have 5 sizes of the boxed soap up to a 2-lb 4-oz box.
Fairbank Scales: Only very small ornate countertop sizes are needed.
Paper Ephemera: Most anything relating to a Fairbank Co.

Jim Fairbank
Rt. 4, Box 5428
Clodfelter Rd.
Kennewick, WA 99337
509-627-0933

We collect, buy and trade the **glass jars and counter trays** companies supplied their vendors. These have their company logo or name included in the design of the item. Some would also have paper labels in addition to the embossed name, and later ones have painted names. We are generally only interested in embossed items, not painted or only paper labeled. Below are examples and approximate prices for jars complete with original lids and no cracks or heavy chips and trays that have no cracks or chips. Jars with minor chipping along rim will be only slightly less, but large rim chips or chips on other surfaces will greatly devalue items. Missing lids or trays with any chipping usually bring much less than perfect items.

Always buying very old plain counter jars in unusual shapes and old penny candy jars. Many of these, like those listed below with a * have been reproduced. Original Planters jars were only made in clear glass (none were colored) and are embossed 'Made in USA.'

Advertising

Abalone Cove Antiques
7 Fruit Tree Rd.
Portuguese Bend, CA 90275
310-377-4609 or FAX 310-544-6792

	We Pay
After Dinner Famous Peanuts Jar	**75.00**
Barsam Bros Jar	**80.00**
Beich's Jar	**60.00**
Dad's Cookies Jar	**90.00**
Elephant's Peanuts Jar	**100.00**
Hoffman's Chocolates Tray, vaseline	**40.00**
Nabisco Jar	**50.00**
Nut House Peanut Jars, various styles, ea	**45.00-70.00**
Pitcain Water Spar Jar	**75.00**
Planters Peanuts Jar, corner peanut*	**175.00**
Planters Peanuts Jar, fishbowl*	**50.00**
Planters Peanuts Jar, football	**160.00**
Planters Peanuts Jar, 8-sided, lg*	**75.00**
Planters Peanuts Jar, running Mr Peanut*	**110.00**
Planters Peanuts Jar, sq	**50.00**
Squirrel Peanuts Jar	**75.00**
Teaberry Gum Tray, clear w/pedestal	**30.00**
Teaberry Gum Tray, vaseline or white w/pedestal	**30.00**
Teaberry Gum Tray, amber, low	**35.00**
Water Spar Varnish Jar	**75.00**

We are interested in buying **all unusual Planters Peanuts and Mr. Peanut memorabilia**, especially containers that held Planters products and point-of-sale display items. We are also interested in any material from the many Planters Peanut stores that existed throughout the country. We will always reimburse your postage or UPS and insurance costs. A SASE will guarantee a reply to any query. Please write or call if unsure of any item or if the item is not listed below. Unwanted items include magazine ads, plastic cups, metal dishes, pocketknives, plastic banks, and items made after 1970.

Sherwin Borsuk
80 Parker Ave.
Meriden, CT 06450
203-237-8042

Planters Peanuts **We Pay**

Item	We Pay
Ad, cardboard, for trolley car	**50.00+**
Coloring Book, before 1950, unused	**10.00+**
Product Box, cardboard	**25.00+**
Store Display, cardboard or paper w/Mr Peanut	**50.00+**
Store Display, metal	**250.00+**
Jar, clear glass w/lid, not reproduction	**25.00+**
Jar, clear glass w/paper label(s)	**50.00+**
Letter Opener, Planters Chocolate and Nut Co	**250.00+**
Statue, metal figural Mr Peanut w/crossed legs	**250.00+**
Statue or Hand Puppet, rubber Mr Peanut, ea	**350.00+**
Costume, Mr Peanut	**100.00+**
Figure, papier-mache Mr Peanut	**100.00+**
Figure, papier-mache or composition Mr Peanut on lighted electric base	**1500.00+**
Peanut Butter Pail	**150.00+**
Postcard, Planters stores or factories, ea	**2.00+**
Shipping Crate, wood	**100.00+**
Toy, plastic vehicle w/Mr Peanut as driver	**150.00+**
Tin, pocket size	**250.00+**
Tin, Planters nuts, under 1-lb size	**10.00+**
Tin, Planters nuts, 5-lb size	**50.00+**
Tin, Planters nuts, 10-lb size	**25.00+**
Tin, Planters Products, over 10-lb size	**200.00+**

We buy all unusual and some common **Planters Peanuts** items including toys, old boxes, older displays and jars with paper labels. We are not interested in the new bank that just came out recently or the red, tan or light blue bank. The dishes cannot be cracked and must have the Mr. Peanut logo on it. The matches have to be mint condition. The only advertising from magazines that we are looking for would be full sheets from about 1918. Depending on the item, some flaws may be acceptable. We are always looking for rare and hard-to-find items and pay top prices. Only serious inquires need apply. If you are not sure if the item is old or new, please call. We also buy other types of advertising, especially figural. We reimburse actual UPS and insurance charges.

Marty Blank
P.O. Box 405
Fresh Meadows, NY 11365
516-485-8071 (6:30-9:30 pm EST)

Planters Peanuts	**We Pay**
Alarm Clock	**25.00**
Ashtray, ceramic figural	**40.00**

Advertising

Bank, red, white & blue plastic **90.00**
Bank, orange plastic .... **40.00+**
Bank, other colored plastic **10.00**
Display, tin, old .... **100.00+**
Cruet Set, oil & vinegar, ceramic figurals **40.00**
Dishes, china **40.00**
Doll, bobbin' head **50.00**
Doll, jointed **100.00**
Magazine Ad **10.00**
Matches, figural **35.00**
Night Light, figural **50.00**
Peanut Butter Maker, figural, w/box **10.00**
Playing Cards, mint .... **5.00+**
Radio, can form **20.00**
Radio, figural **30.00**
Salt & Pepper Shakers, older version, ceramic figural **25.00**

I buy *State Farm Insurance promotional items given to policy holders prior to 1965.* I would appreciate either a picture or a photocopy of the item and will pay shipping cost.

Denny Kaufman
5918 S Columbia Ave.
Tulsa, OK 74105
918-747-8211

We Pay

Bumper Tags, brass, oval w/car motif, ea **20.00-50.00**
Cigarette Lighters, ea **7.00-15.00**
Driver's License Tubes, ea **20.00-50.00**
Pencils, bullet type, ea **10.00-15.00**
Pencils or Pens, mechanical, pearlized, ea **15.00-50.00**
Pocketknives, ea **35.00-100.00**
Road Maps, prior to 1960, ea **5.00-20.00**
Tape Measures, celluloid, ea **20.00-35.00**
Watch Fobs, enamel on brass, ea **50.00-125.00**
Other Items, too numerous to mention .... **Call or Write**

Wanted: **Pre-1940 advertising and country store items** such as signs; trays; displays; syrup dispensers; soda fountain items; match holders; pot scrapers; country store items including dye cabinets, vet cabinets, chewing gum packs and boxes; tobacco and coffee tins as well as peanut butter and oyster tins plus most others; cash registers; coin-op;old toys; Coke; Pepsi; beer; and anything else remotely related.

We don't want magazine items, reproductions or junk. We do pay the highest prices, so know how much you want before contacting us. Photos are helpful and will be returned.

House of Stuart
P.O. Box 2063
Jensen Beach, FL 34958-2063
407-225-0900

We are interested in **Monarch Food related items** with the exception of magazine ads. We are interested in 1920-1936 period only. This includes all bottles and jars with labels, paper and cardboard boxes, Teenie Weenie items, sample sizes, and cans.

We are also interested in **advertising stoneware, especially Red Wing and other advertising jars and jugs**. We seek the following items. Please send pictures or lists with prices.

Monarch Food Items Wanted:
Monarch Marshmallow Tin, lg
Monarch Prune Box, cardboard
Monarch Tapioca Box, cardboard
Teenie Weenie Popcorn Tin, w/lid & handle
Teenie Weenie or Regular Peanut Butter Sample w/Label

Stoneware Items Wanted:
Jug, EE Bruce & Co, Wholesale Druggists, Omaha, Nebr in oval, quart w/dome top
Jug, Haarmann's Pure Tomato Catsup, Omaha, Neb in shield, w/bail handle
Jars or Jugs w/Ferris (eg, Fred Ferris, Wholesale Wines & Liquors, Elmira, NY)
Pitcher, Cherryband w/Fern Brand Coffee in oval
Pitcher, w/advertising, sponge band, sm
Refrigerator Jar, w/advertising, lg
Jar, North Star Creamery, 1-lb size
Bowl, #11, paneled, w/advertising, sponge decor
Bowls, #9-#11, w/advertising, sponge decor

Bruce and Nada Ferris
3094 Oakes Dr.
Hayward, CA 94542
510-581-5285

I would like to compile a collection of animal cracker items for my daughter to go with the china child's breakfast set given her at her birth. I have cookie tins and sheet music, but surely there must be other **items with the Barnum and Bailey or Nabisco logo**! What do you have? I'lll pay any reasonable price for excellent condition items. I can't list them because I don't know what's available. Can you help? I also want **advertising refrigerator magnets**. Thanks!

Yvonne Marle Holmberg
7229 Pine Island Dr., NE
Comstock Park, MI 49321-9534
616-784-1715

AMERICAN INDIAN

Museum, private collector, dealer **will pay top prices for old American Indian artifacts — nothing newer than 1940**. Special interests are: beaded and corn husk bags, gloves, belts, vests, shirts, and dresses. Also interested in Indian baskets, pipes, and all types of weapons. Another special interest is black and white Indian photographs, postcards, hard cards and all larger photos. **I will pay $5 to $10,000 and up for individual items mentioned**. I am also interested in buying entire collections. Please send description and photo or call.

Fred L. Mitchell
835 Valencia
Walla Walla, WA 99362
509-529-4672

AQUARIUMS AND PET-RELATED ITEMS

Wanted: aquarium, goldfish bowls, pet-related paper ephemera, and other pet-related items. These include:

Tropical Fish & Aquarium Magazines, all dates
Turtle Magazines

Public Aquarium Broadsides
Pet Catalogs, especially Victorian era through the 1940s
Public Aquarium Guides, up to 1930s only
Aquarium Catalogs
Bird Product & Cage Catalogs
Tropical Fish Food Tins & Boxes
Dog & Cat Product Tins & Boxes
Metal Foundry Catalogs, w/aquariums pictured
Old Aquariums
Old Aquarium Products (ie, air pumps, heaters, etc)
Dog Food Signs
Fish food signs
Terrariums

Send all offers. Also wanted are **P.T. Barnum memorabilia and items**.

Gary Bagnall
3090 McMillan Rd.
San Luis Obispo, CA 93401
805-542-9988 or 805-481-3847

ART DECO AND ART NOUVEAU

We will purchase Art Nouveau and Art Deco items, **originals of the period only** (no reproductions), including but not limited to:

- Bronzes, figurals & vases
- Ceramics, figurals & vases
- Art Glass
- Lighting
- Photo Frames
- Inkwells
- Furniture
- Carpets
- Paintings

Please send a clear photo of the item, including measurements and distinguishing markings — note any damages please. All inquiries will be answered and photos will be returned.

Accent on Antiques
P.O. Box 4516
Boca Raton, FL 33429
407-368-6823

Art Deco and Art Nouveau

Mission oak and hammered copper items wanted. **Furniture by all makers wanted, signed or unsigned**, such as adjustable-back chairs (Morris), settles, benches, couches, beds and dressers, desks and library tables, book stands, cases, cabinets, tables and chairs, sideboards and servers, etc. Looking for square cut-out furniture by all makers.

Metal work items wanted: lamps with mica or glass shades, vases and candlesticks by Roycroft, Van Erp, Jarvie and others; silver by Kalo and others; applied or cut-out square motif metal items by Roycroft and others; metal vases and candle holders with buttresses by Roycroft, etc.

Other arts and crafts items, jewelry, or original catalogs from this circa are always wanted.

Gary Struncius
P.O. Box 1374
Lakewood, NJ 08701
908-364-7580 or 800-272-2529

AUTOMOBILIA

Automobile **books and automobilia of all types** purchased. We will buy hard and soft-bound books, in or out of print, new or used, remainders, surplus stock, large private collections or single copies. Our main interest is in books that deal with auto racing, history of cars and their manufacturers, motorcycles, famous automotive personalities, design, etc. We willingly purchase all automotive books. However, we specialize in European and exotic automobiles such as Ferrari, Maserati, Lamborghini, Mercedes, Porsche, Rolls Royce, etc. We also specialize in domestic manufacturers that are no longer in existence such as Packard, Studebaker, Auburn, Dusenberg, etc. We do not buy ex-library books, sales literature, owners or workshop manuals unless they are appropriate to those types of automobiles previously listed. We purchase automobilia such as race posters, art, period photographs, original design renderings, etc. We are aggressive buyers of top quality items regardless of age and quantity. Prices quoted are for books with dust jackets in top condition.

LMG Enterprises
2500 Newning
Schertz, TX 78154
Phone or FAX 210-658-5207

	We Pay
Annual Automobile Review 1953/54 #1	**100.00**
Annual Automobile Review 1954/54 #2	**160.00**

At Speed (Alexander) **80.00**
Autocourse 1964-65 .... **90.00**
Bentley 50 Years of the Marque (Green) **60.00**
Boyhood Photographs of JH Lartique (Lartigue) **100.00**
British Light Weight Sports Cars 78 (Japanese) **140.00**
Cara Automobile (Pininfarina) **80.00**
Comicar (Bertieri) **50.00**
Delorean Stainless Steel Illusion (Lamm) **40.00**
DMG 1890-1915 (German) **180.00**
Errett Loban Cord (Borgeson) **120.00**
Farrari 80 (2nd Edition - Italian) **100.00**
Farrari Yearbooks, 1949-1970, ea **70.00-400.00**
First Century of Portraits Celebrating Mercedes **200.00**
Grand Prix Car (Vol 1 & Vol 2 - Pomeroy) **160.00**
L'Art et L'Automobile (Poulain) **60.00**
La Targa Florio (Garcia) **80.00**
Les 24 Heures de Mans (Labric) **160.00**
Piloti che Gente (4th Edition - Ferrari) **140.00**
Spirit Celebrating 75 Years of Rolls Royce (Dallison) **60.00**
Ten Ans de Courses (Montaut) **600.00**

We buy **original automobilia but specialize in sports and racing cars** — mostly postwar, but will always consider prewar. Fast replies to all inquiries.

Original Literature
Box 23576
Mandarin, FL 32241-3576
FAX 904-739-3164

We Pay

Racing Posters (Sebring, Lemans, etc) through 1960s, ea .... **100.00+**
Original Sales Brochures, Manuals, Annuals, Etc, mostly postwar Italian cars, ea .... **100.00+**

I buy any quantity of **original gasoline globes or signs** — one piece or collections. Globes or signs need not be perfect but in decent condition. On globes, single sides or inserts only are okay. Just call or write.

Oil Co. Collectibles
Scott Benjamin
411 Forest St.
La Grange, OH 44050
216-355-6608

	We Pay
Glass Globe, glass inserts	**250.00+**
Metal Globe, glass inserts	**300.00+**
Picture-Type Globe, w/airplane, etc	**400.00-2,000.00+**
Sinclair Aircraft, 1-pc	**2,000.00+**
Musgo, 1-pc	**2,800.00+**
Bezol, 1-pc	**1,200.00+**
Other 1-Pc Globes, ea	**500.00-2,000.00+**

I'm an avid collector of **flower vases, i.e, bud vases**, that were used in automobiles from about 1900 through about 1930. Most of the vases were glass, although some were of metal or ceramic. Most vases came to a point or were rounded on the bottom and were attached using metal brackets. Most are found today with their brackets missing. Since prices may vary so much due to condition and manufacturer, it is impossible to quote prices that I will pay. A complete description and photo if possible will be needed for verification. I would especially be interested in vases by **Steuben, Tiffany, Sinclaire, Hawkes**, and others of this quality.

Ms. Dulce Holt
504 Broadway
Chesterton, IN 46304
219-926-2838 or 219-926-4170

Buying **glass auto gearshift knobs** with swirl colors. They look like big marbles. These knobs were after-market, dress up your car accessories in the late 1920s and 1930s that came in all combinations of colors. Average size is 2" round or a flattened oval. They usually have a threaded insert to be screwed onto the gearshift lever. (Sometimes this insert is missing.) Sometimes they are attached to a metal extension which was then screwed onto the gearshift lever.

Condition: Prefer perfect. Will accept knobs with a few pinhead knicks or factory imperfections. OK if threaded insert is missing (has empty socket). Not wanted: Knobs which are cracked, have large chips or major scuffs.

Unless you are willing to shop and sell on approval after my inspection, send a color photo. I will pay all return postage and insurance for the value of the shipment if knobs are sent on approval and not taken. I would like you to send a price on what you have for sale, but I have no problem in making offers if you prefer.

Ed Sprangle
1768 Leimert Blvd.
Oakland, CA 94602-1930

We Pay

Swirled Glass Gearshift Knobs, ea **25.00-70.00**

AVIATION

I buy memorabilia from **commercial airlines (no military)** including chinaware, glassware, playing cards, crew wings and badges, timetables, advertising items, etc. China and glassware from all airlines, domestic and foreign, old and new, wanted. Playing cards from domestic airlines, any era but preferably older sought. Timetables and paper material must be from before 1945. Of special interest are any items relating to Pan Am flying boats and from the German airships Graf Zeppelin and the Hindenburg, as well as **chrome ashtrays with a chrome plane on a pedestal, and large travel agency plane models** in metal or plastic that are twenty-seven inches or larger.

Dick Wallin
P.O. Box 1784
Springfield, IL 62705
217-498-9279

We Pay

American Airlines, cup & saucer, DC3 ....**500.00+**
American Airlines, other dishes, DC3 ....**500.00+**
American Airlines, knife, hollow handle, Flagship ....**20.00+**
American Airlines, knife, flat, Flagship **15.00**
American Airlines, fork, Flagship **15.00**
American Airlines, pickle fork, Flagship ....**35.00+**
American Airlines, pitcher, Flagship Fleet ....**100.00+**
American Airlines, spoon, Flagship **15.00**
American Airlines, tray, Flagship Fleet **100.00**
British Airways, butter pat, Concorde **20.00**

Aviation

British Airways, salt & pepper shakers, Concorde, pr	**20.00**
Pan American, china item, w/winged globe logo	**150.00+**
Pan American, other china or glassware items, ea	**10.00**
Regent Air, china or glassware items, ea	**20.00**
TWA, china item, w/red & gold double globe logo at top	**50.00**
United Airlines, teapot, w/shield logo in circle	**35.00**
Any Foreign Airlines, salt & pepper shakers, china, pr	**15.00+**
Any Foreign Airlines, butter pat, china	**15.00+**
Ashtray, chrome w/plane on pedestal	**100.00+**
Travel Agent Plane Model, 27" or larger	**200.00-2,000.00**

I am buying **commercial aviation items**. I prefer items from the 1920s through the 1970s, whether a single piece or a collection. Listed below are some of the things I am seeking. I also want anything old and unusual.

John R. Joiner
52 Jefferson Pkwy., Apt. D.
Newnan, GA 30263
404-502-9565

	We Pay
Pilot Wings	**25.00+**
Pilot Hat Emblems	**25.00+**
Flight Attendant Wings	**25.00+**
Flight Attendant Hat Emblems	**25.00+**
Timetables	**3.00+**
Playing Cards	**1.00+**
Postcards	**50¢**
Anniversary Pins	**5.00+**
Pilot Manuals	**25.00+**
Maintenance Manuals	**25.00+**
Display Models	**50.00+**
Early Signs	**20.00+**
Dining Service Items	**1.00+**
Posters	**5.00+**

BANKS

These tin (or tin with paper label) **miniature oil-can banks** are usually four ounces in size and represent a specialty within the collectible bank category. Beginning in the early 1940s, these banks were produced as a promotional tool for gasoline and motor oil dealers. In addition to motor oil, many other specialty oils and fluids were promoted with these banks including antifreeze, top oil, and lubricants. There are well over one hundred to one hundred fifty versions known to date. Many oil companies offered five or six different banks representing most, if not all, of their oil products. The most common tin banks are Cities Service with Koolmotor for various grades of oil (HD, 5D, Premium, etc.). Another is Wolf's Head Motor Oil with a number of versions, the most desirable being Wolf's Head Light Duty or Heavy Duty Motor Oils. The Super Duty version is the most common.

Listed below are some of the brands I seek in order to expand my collection of oil-can banks. Please drop me a card with your find and desired price. **Price range is from $5 to $65** based on condition and rarity. I'll respond immediately.

Peter Capell
1838 W Grace St.
Chicago, IL 60613-2724
312-871-8735

Banks From These Companies	We Pay
Freeway Service Stations	**75.00**
Blue Flash Tiolene 'Can Take It'	**75.00**
Pacific Cooperative Heavy Duty Motor Oil	**45.00**
Pure Tiolene Motor Oil, celluloid & tin	**60.00**
RPM Delo Lubricants (Standard Oil California)	**45.00**
Sohio, The Standard Lubricant	**45.00**
Standard, glass block	**60.00**
Wakefield Castrollo Uppper Cylinder Lub	**35.00**

Plastic Figural Gas Pump Banks	We Pay
Pure	**50.00**
Shell	**50.00**
Sunoco	**50.00**

BARBED WIRE

I am interested in buying **antique barbed wires made between 1868 and 1890**. Special interest in any wire using a 'star' as a barb. Persons having any antique barbed wires are invited to send short sample to me for identification and offer.

John Mantz
1023 Baldwin Rd.
Bakersfield, CA 93304
805-397-9572 or FAX 805-831-3491

	We Pay
Hodge's Spur Rowel Wire, 1887	**5.00**
Dodge's Rowel Wire, 1881	**150.00**
Phillip's Cocklebur Wire, 1883	**250.00**

BARWARE

Wanted: **cocktail shakers, vintage cocktail recipe books and barware**. Cocktail shakers of glass and chrome, all kinds including figural, lady's leg, Zeppelin, Penguin, Dumbell, Golf Bag, Roosters, Lighthouse, and those made by Revere, Chase, Manning Bowan are wanted. Enclose photo or sketch and description and write to:

Stephen Visakay
Cocktail Shakers
P.O. Box 1517
W Caldwell, NJ 07007

BASEBALL MEMORABILIA

We buy fine **baseball memorabilia from the turn of the century to 1950**. We only buy items of Hall of Famers (including autograph baseballs), teams and events, and publications such as *Baseball Scorecards* that are in excellent or better condition. We don't buy damaged or lesser-quality items nor autographs that are not or cannot be properly authenticated.

Frank J. Ceresi
3600 N Nelson St.
Arlington, VA 22207
703-522-5450

We Pay

Baseball Scorecard, regular season, 1900-1910, ea..........................**up to 300.00**
Baseball Scorecard, regular season, 1911-1920, ea..........................**up to 200.00**
Baseball Scorecard, regular season, 1921-1930, ea..........................**up to 65.00**
Baseball Scorecard, regular season, 1931-1940, ea..........................**up to 35.00**
Baseball Scorecard, regular season, 1941-1950, ea..........................**up to 25.00**
Baseball Magazine, 1913-1920, ea..**up to 100.00**
Baseball Magazine, 1921-1930, ea..**40.00**
Baseball Magazine, 1931-1940, ea..**30.00**
Baseball Magazine, 1941-1950, ea..**20.00**
Team or Hall of Fame Autographed Baseball, depending on condition & scarcity..**50%+ of book value**
Autographed Hall of Fame Baseball Card, price depends on condition & scarcity..**60%+ of book value**
Advertising Baseball Cards (tobacco, candy, ice cream, etc), in excellent or better condition..**50% of book value**

BELLS

I buy **old table bells**: glass, silver, porcelain, brass figurines, embossed bronze or brass, mechanical with figures (no plain tap). This does *not* include school bells, animal bells, new or modern bells. I also buy figurines with nodding heads made of bronze, brass or porcelain. These are known as **nodders**.

Dorothy Malone Anthony
802 S Eddy
Ft. Scott, KS 66701

BETSY MCCALL

I buy **anything Betsy McCall** including dolls, clothing and accessories. I prefer excellent to mint condition but will consider any item. All prices listed below are negotiable. Please contact me with your Betsy McCall items first!

Marci Van Ausdall
P.O. Box 946
Quincy, CA 95971
916-283-5723

	We Pay
Betsy's Trunk, 14", EX	65.00+
Betsy's Dog Nosey	35.00+
Betsy's Lamb, by Knickerbocker	35.00+
Coloring Books, ea	10.00+
Colorforms, complete	15.00+
Children's Dishes & Silverware Set, w/9" plates	35.00+
Cookie Cutter	15.00+
Doll, nude, 8", EX	75.00+
Doll, nude, 8", poor condition	20.00
Doll, all original, 14"	125.00+
Empty Boxes, cardboard, for clothing or dolls, ea	10.00
Betsy McCall Pattern, by McCall's Pattern Co	8.00+
Paper doll Folder, Whitman	15.00+
Paper dolls, Golden Books	10.00
Paper dolls, Whitman, boxed	20.00+
Outfit, mint in package	25.00+
Magazine, *McCall's*, May 1951	10.00+
Pamphlet, original about Betsy	15.00+
Playhouse, vinyl	50.00+
Playset, Betsy McCall Fashion Shop	25.00+
Playset, Fashion Designer Studio, boxed	200.00+
Playset, At the Ranch, boxed	250.00+
Playset, A Day w/Betsy McCall, boxed	200.00
Puzzles, ea	10.00+
Any Unusual Betsy Item	Call or Write

BILLIARDS

I buy billiard ball racks — the old wooden ones with narrow shelves, also fancy pool cues and pool hall chairs. They must be in good to excellent condition. Please send photos.

Edward Blumenthal
Rt. 2, Box 2365A
Grayling, MI 49738

	We Pay
Racks	100.00+
Cues	50.00+
Chairs	75.00+

BLACK AMERICANA

I buy **all types of Black Americana**, especially salt and pepper shakers, spice sets, cookie jars, clocks, string holders, wall pockets, egg timers, egg cups, head vases, sprinkler bottles, teapots, spoon rests, pie birds, tablecloths, kitchen towels, etc. A favored category is Black Americana advertising, including anything Aunt Jemima, Coon Chicken Inn, Cream of Wheat, Gold Dust Twins (please no magazine advertisements), any premiums, products, or advertising signs with a Black Americana theme or logo. I buy children's books and toys with a Black-American theme (e.g., Little Black Sambo, Nicodemus, pickaninnies, golliwogs, Beloved Belindy, Topsy-Turvy) as well as other folk art or manufactured dolls, toys, games, and puzzles. Other Black-related books bought are literature, poetry (e.g., Dunbar, Weeden) and humor (e.g., *Two Black Crows*). I want vintage entertainment-related minstrel material, Amos 'n' Andy, Josephine Baker, Hattie McDaniel, and various *Gone with the Wind* items. I *do not buy* African artifacts, slave or Ku Klux Klan material.

Judy Posner
R.D. #1, Box 273 HW
Effort, PA 18330
717-629-6583 or FAX 717-629-0521

	We Pay
Book, any Little Black Sambo, various, ea	**35.00-65.00**
Book, *Ten Little Niggers*	**65.00-95.00**
Cheese Shaker, Mammy	**45.00-55.00**
Cookie Jar, Aunt Jemima, hard plastic	**200.00-250.00**
Condiment Set, Mammy & barrels, ceramic	**85.00-95.00**
Doll, Beloved Belindy, Knickerbocker, 1964	**150.00-175.00**
Doll, Topsy Turvy, folk art, various, ea	**45.00-65.00**
Egg Cup, Golliwog	**45.00-60.00**
Plate, child's; golliwog	**45.00-60.00**
Puzzle, Little Black Sambo	**25.00-35.00**
Record, Little Black Sambo	**35.00-40.00**
Salt & Pepper Shakers, Coon Chicken Inn, pr	**200.00-250.00**
Shipping Crate, Cream of Wheat	**55.00-60.00**
Spoon Rest, Mammy (or w/Chef), various, ea	**50.00-75.00**
Syrup Pitcher, Little Black Sambo	**50.00-65.00**

Wanted: **any paper items**, documents, pictures, caricatures, newspapers, postcards, greeting cards, etc., **that depict Negroes from before 1930**. Also store advertising **signs**, as well as restroom signs, and other Negro directional and warning signs.

Walt Thompson
P.O. Box 2541-W
Yakima, WA 98907-2541

	We Pay
Greeting Card	**3.00+**
Newspaper, w/articles on Negros, issued before 1870, complete	**20.00+**
Sign, store advertising	**75.00+**
Sign, restroom	**25.00+**
Slave Ownership Document	**50.00+**
Slave Freedom Papers	**100.00+**
Any Negro Cartoon Character, on paper, before 1900	**Write**

I buy **Black and golliwog items of all types**, including china, ceramic (especially figurals such as cookie jars, tepots, etc.), foot tins, perfume bottles, early Black Sambo, Mammy, minstrels, advertising signs, humidors, food product boxes, etc., with the image of any Black person or character (e.g., Aunt Jemima).

I am known for paying absolute top dollar for older golliwog pieces such as light-up figures, tin toys, hand-painted Vienna bronze miniatures, books, games, complete decks of cards, puzzles, clocks and watches, lamps, tins, shakers, candy containers, vintage Christmas cards — anything shaped like or bearing the image of a golliwog, whether a Robertson's premium or not. I return all phone calls and respond to all correspondence. Photos appreciated. No potty items or repos, please.

The Butler Did It!
Catherine Saunders-Watson
P.O. Box 302
Greenville, NH 03048-0302
Phone or FAX 603-878-2171

	We Pay
Cigarette Lighter, Art Deco Black bartender	**up to 750.00**
Cookie Jar, Mammy	**350.00+**
Figurine, Santa & golliwog, Spode, china	**45.00-350.00**
Golliwog Bank, Carlton Ware, ceramic	**175.00+**
Golliwog Vienna Bronze Miniature (on crocodile, etc), ea	**up to 200.00**
Golliwog Fireworks, boxed	**250.00**
Golliwog Perfume Bottle	**150.00-250.00**
Food Product Boxes, w/Black image	**25.00-350.00**

Humidors, Black head .... **up to 350.00**
Tin, Pickaninny Peanut Butter **350.00-550.00**

I am interested in **Black memorabilia from before 1950**. Items must be in good condition, anything unusual. Send photo for me to bid. Examples of items wanted are listed below.

Arthur Boutiette
410 W 3rd St., Suite 200
Little Rock, AR 72201

We Pay

Advertising Items, ea .... **25.00+**
Book, vintage Black Sambo, ea .... **35.00+**
Book, w/golliwog .... **30.00+**
Doll, Beloved Belindy .... **20.00+**
Game, for Black children .... **20.00+**
Lamp, Mammy .... **75.00+**
Photo, tintype .... **20.00+**
Photo, tintype of Black soldier .... **40.00+**
Salt & Pepper Shakers, Coon Chicken Inn, pr .... **100.00+**
Toy, Amos 'n' Andy, tin .... **150.00+**
Toy, Alabama Coon Jigger, tin .... **150.00+**

I have collected Black memorabilia for the past twelve years. I'm always interested in adding different and unusual items to my collection. I'm interested in **sterling souvenir spoons, kitchen items, matchcovers, ink blotters, and advertising items** such as: boxes, tins, bottles, containers, signs, etc. I am not interested in native-type items or dolls. A photo or photocopy is helpful along with a description and condition, as well as your asking price. See also **Toothbrush Holders** in this book.

Joyce Wolford
1050 Spriggs Dr.
Lander, WY 82520

We Pay

Aunt Jemima Items .... **Write**
Bottle, w/advertising .... **20.00+**

Children's Storybook .... **15.00+**
Coon Chicken Inn Items .... **Write**
Cookie Jars .... **Write**
Cookbooks or Recipe Booklets, ea .... **18.00+**
Ink Blotter .... **9.00+**
Linens, printed, appliqued or embroidered, ea .... **20.00+**
Matchcovers, ea .... **6.00+**
Souvenir Spoon, demi or teaspoon, ea .... **50.00+**
String Holder .... **55.00+**
Salt & Pepper Shakers, unusual pr .... **35.00+**
Tin, advertising .... **25.00+**
Toothbrush Holder, figural .... **50.00+**
Wall Pocket .... **45.00+**

BLUE RIDGE

We buy **all patterns of Blue Ridge china and dinnerware made by Southern Potteries**. We don't buy any crazed, chipped, or cracked pieces. If pattern name is not known a color photo is helpful. Send listing of number and kinds of pieces for sale with prices wanted.

Oscar Hubbert
P.O. Box 1415
Fletcher, NC 28732
704-687-0350

BOOKS

We buy **good condition used and out-of-print reference books on antiques**. Particularly need books on art glass, cut glass, silver, R.S. Prussia, toys, furniture, folk art, shaving mugs, dolls, etc. Buy hardcover or paperback; one book or entire library. Send list with title, author, date, number of pages, condition, your phone number and price wanted. We pay generous shipping allowance. The list is just a fraction of the books we need. Please list all titles you have available.

Antique & Collectors Reproduction News
Box 71174-WB
Des Moines, IA 50325
515-270-8994

Book Title	We Pay
Glass, Art Nouveau to Art Deco; by Arwas	**50.00**
Pairpoint Glass Story, by Avila	**65.00**
French Cameo Glass, by Blount	**50.00**
Wavecrest, by Cohen	**25.00**
Libbey Glass, by Fauster	**50.00**
Pairpoint Glass, by Padgett	**45.00**
All Titles Cut Glass, by J.M. Pearson, ea	**25.00-50.00**
Antique Shaving Mugs of the US, by Powell	**18.00**
Occupational Shaving Mugs, by Powell	**15.00**
Napkin Rings, by Schnadig	**25.00**

I am interested in **pre-1900 leather books**. Individual books on almost any subject are wanted, but they must be in good condition. Also, I am buying sets, but they must be complete. **I pay from between $10 to $50 per book** depending on title and content. See examples here. Send your list and price.

Mr. Arthur Boutiette
410 W 3rd St., Suite 200
Little Rock, AR 72201

	We Pay
The Life of George Washington, by Washington Irving, 3 vols	**120.00**
Children's Stories, by Hans Christian Andersen	**40.00**
Longfellow Poems	**20.00**
Joan of Arc, by Shelly	**25.00**

I am interested in **books that are collections and anthologies of the cartoonists from 1890 to 1960**. No general collections of cartoons (Best of Punch), comic books, recent reprints, or storybooks based on cartoons are wanted.

The marking of first editions varies with different publishers, though a majority of the books by the artists will state a first printing or edition, or have the number one still in the number series. Others will have a date on the title page matching the copyright date. Prices are for books in fine to excellent condition — no tears, coloring, loose pages, bent covers, broken spines. Prices vary greatly with condition. Listed here are some cartoon anthologies wanted. Publishers for these are Cupples & Leon Publishing Co., Star Co., Ball Pub. Co., and Cartoon Reprint Series. **I will pay from $15 to $75** for these books.

Bringing Up Father
Dolly Dimples
Joe Palooka
Dick Tracy
Harold Teen
Keeping Up With the Jones

Books

Little Orphan Annie
Mutt & Jeff
Percy & Ferdie
Smitty
The Gumps
Winnie Winkle
Moon Mullins
Nebs
Regular Fella's
Tillie the Toiler
Toonerville Trolly

Craig Ehlenberger
Abalone Cove Rare Books
7 Fruit Tree Rd.
Portuguese Bend, CA 90275
310-377-4609 or FAX 310-544-6792 (6 am-9 pm PST)

Other Early Artists	**We Pay**
John McCutcheon	**25.00+**
Clare Briggs	**25.00+**
Outcault (Buster Brown)	**35.00+**

Artist's Collections, First Editions Only	**We Pay**
Addams, Charles	**12.00**
Alain	**10.00+**
Arno, Peter	**10.00+**
Corbean, Sam	**8.00+**
Darrow, Whitney Jr.	**8.00+**
Day, Chon (Brother Sebastion)	**6.00+**
Dunn, Alan	**8.00+**
Fisher, Ed	**8.00+**
Giovannetti, Pericle L.	**8.00+**
Hamilton, William	**12.00+**
Hoff, Syd	**8.00+**
Hokinson, Helen	**10.00+**
Kelly, Walt (Pogo) (most are paperback without dust jackets)	**15.00+**
Ketcham, Hank (Dennis the Menace), all say First, no dust jackets	**10.00+**
Key, Ted (Hazel)	**8.00+**
Kovarsky, Anatol	**8.00+**
Partch, Virgil (VIP)	**5.00+**
Petty, Mary	**10.00+**
Price, George	**12.00+**
Segar (Popeye)	**30.00+**
Shafer, Burr	**10.00+**
Stevenson, James	**10.00+**
Syverson, Henry	**5.00+**
Taylor, Richard	**8.00+**
Wilson, Gahan	**8.00+**

I buy the following books providing they are in very good condition (all illustrations present, bindings tight and clean). Prices vary widely, depending on the edition, presence of dust wrapper (if issued), and other points. Postage will be reimbursed as well as insurance (if necessary to insure).

Robert L. Merriam
Rare, Used & Old Books
39 Newhall Rd.
Conway, MA 01341

Authors:
Mary P. Wells Smith: Old Deerfield, Young Puritans & Jolly Good Times Series (I pay $9 each.)
Mary Twain, first and early editions; all criticism
Emily Dickinson, all editions and criticism
Walt Whitman, all editions and criticism
Herman Melville, all editions and criticism
Robert Frost, all editions and criticism
John McPhee, first editions

Illustrators:
Arthur Rackham
N.C. Wyeth
Maud Humphrey
Maxfield Parrish
Schoonover

Subject:
American Revolution and Colonial Americana
Western Massachusetts History
Moral Stories: small editions published by the American Tract Society and other religious groups in the 1880s. (I pay between $2 to $5 each for these.)

I purchase most books **relating to the Black Hills, Mount Rushmore or South Dakota**. Best prices are paid for **county histories or books printed before 1970 relating to persons, families, towns, or companies in South Dakota**. I purchase any books related to Sioux, Lakota, or Dakota Indians published any date; and books related to log cabins, Dungeon and Dragons, or puzzles. I will consider any book printed before 1970 relating to the West, art of the West, pioneers, cowboys, and women of the West. Condition is very important in pricing books. Only books in good condition will be considered for purchase.

James F. Taylor
515 Sixth St.
Rapid City, SD 57701
605-341-3224

Books

Subject	We Pay
South Dakota County History, pre-1950	**50.00+**
South Dakota County History, any date	**10.00+**
Relating to Making of Mount Rushmore	**10.00+**
Indian Non-Fiction, pre-1950	**30.00+**
Log Cabin Construction	**10.00+**
Log Cabin Non-Fiction, pre-1950	**25.00+**
Puzzles	**10.00+**
Women of the West, pre-1945	**50.00+**
Golf, pre-1945	**25.00+**
Fishing, pre-1950	**10.00+**
Dungeons & Dragons, hardcover only	**25% of Cover Price**
Log Cabin Magazine	**50¢+**

Wanted: **miniature, pictorial and humorous books.** Little Leather Library miniature books were initially published with leather covers which were later changed to embossed vinyl. Measuring about 3x4", they were often previously published classical and well-known works. **I pay from $1 to $2 for these.**

Pictorial books both old and new are wanted on art, antiques and collectibles, aviation, photography, architecture, decorative arts, postcards, etc. Time-Life Books and others have published a number of series on many subjects. I will by sets or individual books and will pay up to $5 each. I am also interested in currently published Dover books from the Pictorial Archive Catalog and will pay up to 50% of cover price.

Humorous books wanted are comic strip or cartoon type and may be paperback or hardcover. I prefer large format collections, compilations, and histories. Especially wanted:

- Pogo & Walt Kelly
- Grin & Bear It
- Little Nemo
- The Far Side
- Doonsbury
- Calvin & Hobbs
- They'll Do It Everytime
- Political, Editorial Cartoons & Comics

I will pay up to 50% of the cover price and more for older items based on their conditon. Send title, author, format (paperback or hardcover), number of pages, size, and detailed description of condition. Thank you.

Gary R. Smith
517 Laurel Ave.
Modesto, CA 95351

I am interested in purchasing copies of *The Illustrated Book of Poultry*, by Lewis Wright (L. Wright) with colored plates by J.W. Ludlow. The book was published by Cassell Publishers in 1874. **I will pay up to $500.00 for clean, complete copies with no foxed pages**. I will consider other copies or pages from the same book.

James M. Bennett
Rt. 1, Box 127K
Pleasanton, TX 78064-9724
210-569-6720

Wanted: **a book that shows and tells about every brewery in Germany**. It must be in very good condtion — so I will pay top dollar! **I will pay $100** to start!

Also wanted are **Italian postcards, Napoleon-Gradi, entitled The Martyr**. Must be in very good condition. **I'll pay $25**.

Mike Geffers
1615 Doty St.
Oshkosh, WI 54901

I am looking for a copy of *A Trail Plowed Under*, by Charles Russell. **I will pay up to $25**.

John D. Lamb
10378 Bigtree Ln.
Jacksonville, FL 32257
904-886-0943

I buy books for private people and am finding it very difficult to locate two books. I hope someone will have them for sale: *The Private Character of Queen Elizabeth*, by Frederick C. Chamberlin, published by Lane/Dodd Mead, 1921 (or any edition, any date); and *Visions in Stone: The Scripture of William Edmondson*, by Edmund Fuller, published by University of Pittsburgh Press, 1973. Thank you for your help.

Hilda's Book Search
Hilda Gruskin
199 Rollins Ave.
Rockville, MD 20852
301-948-3181

I am intersted in purchasing **new or modern signed editions** for resale. I am also interested in **Easton Press and Franklin Press** all-leather volumes both signed and unsigned. I collect the signed volumes of Ted De Grazia, a well-known Arizona artist. Some examples of the prices that I pay are listed below. The value of individual volumes is of course dependent on the condition which must be fine or better. I will appreciate any and all quotes. I ask that a complete description of the book and its condition be sent with SASE. Thank you for your help.

AL-PAC, Lamar Kelley
2625 E Southern Ave., C 120
Tempe, AZ 85282-7633
602-831-3121 or FAX 602-831-3193

	We Pay
Easton Press Leather Volumes	**12.00**
Franklin Press Leather Volumes	**12.00**
Easton Press Signed Leather Volumes	**15.00**
Franklin Press Signed Leather First Editions	**15.00-25.00**
First Edition Signed Ted De Grazia	**20.00-25.00**
Modern Signed First Editions	**10.00-40.00**
Other Volumes, older, full leather, by well-known authors	**10.00-1,000.00**

We are interested in **any old books dated before 1874**. We also buy **current editions of fine quality**. We buy first state books that are in as-new condition. Books of interest dated after 1937 should have flawless dust jackets (no tears). Of special interest are first issues, first printings of literary, science or science fiction. No book club editions are wanted. Author signed editions will influence price. Inquiries are welcome. Please send a description of your book or books and the price you are asking. Prices escalate depending on quality and condition of the book and dust cover. Please do not send books without A.B.A.C.U.S.® prior approval. For an example of minimum prices paid for as-new quality collectible books, see listing below.

A.B.A.C.U.S. ®
Phillip E. Miller
343 S Chesterfield St.
Aiken, SC 29801
803-648-4632

Sinclair Lewis — **We Pay**

Ann Vickers...**25.00+**
Arrowsmith...**30.00+**
Cheap and Contented Labor...**75.00+**
Dodsworth...**15.00+**
Elmer Gantry...**100.00+**
Gideon Planish...**16.00+**
God-Seeker...**20.00+**
It Can't Happen Here...**30.00+**
Jayhawker...**15.00+**
Kingsblood Royal...**28.00+**
Mainstreet...**78.00+**
Our Mr Wren...**22.00+**
Storm in the West...**17.00+**
The Job...**80.00+**
The Prodigal Parents...**25.00+**
Work of Art...**17.00+**

Immanuel Velikovsky — **We Pay**

Ages in Chaos...**17.00+**
Earth in Upheaval...**16.00+**
Oedipus and Akhnaton...**20.00+**
Peoples of the Sea...**15.00+**
Ramses II and His Time...**12.00+**
Stargazer and Gravediggers...**16.00+**
Worlds in Collision...**17.00+**

I buy **fine used or old books specializing in biographies, autobiographies, political gossip, memoirs, and histories (not college texts)**. I look for books with dust jackets in very good or better condition. I pay top prices — better than bookstore or flea market offers. I also pay cash and postage on all purchases. Caution: just because a book is old doesn't mean it is valuable. Look at me!

Herb Sauermann
21660 School Rd.
Manton, CA 96059

We are purchasing **children's books having from four to thirty-two pages with color plates by such publishers as Raphael Tuck and McLoughlin**

Brothers. Books must be pre-1920s and not torn. They can be on linen, linenette, or common paper. Send a list of your books for sale to:

Melanie Hewitt
2101 Beechwood
Little Rock, AR 72202

	We Pay
Common Paper	**5.00-75.00**
Linenette	**10.00-85.00**
Linen	**20.00-125.00**
Ethnic or Negro Stories, ea	**30.00-225.00**

We buy **children's and art books from the 1850s through the 1970s**. This includes pop-up, movables, Little Golden, Wonder, Pied Piper, Treasure, Saalfield, Whitman, Cupples and Leon, Goldsmith, Grosset & Dunlap, and Bonnie Books. We also buy **juvenile and series books** published from the 1900s through the 1970s. Condition is a top priority as are dust jackets (if issued with book). Please only quote first editions. We reimburse actual UPS and insurance costs.

Encino Books
Diane Yaspan
5063 Gaviota Ave.
Encino, CA 91436
818-905-7711 or FAX 818-501-7711

Most Uncle Wiggily items were published/produced from about 1912 through 1948. I am looking for the hard-to-find items and thus will accept a book in less than excellent condition if it is one I don't have.

Also wanted are the **Bobbsey Twins series books**. The first three books in the series, published prior to Grosset & Dunlap, are smaller (approximately 4¾x6¾") and show a standing portrait of the twins on their covers. Please see some specific wants listed here.

Audrey V. Buffington
2 Old Farm Rd.
Wayland, MA 01778
508-358-2644

Uncle Wiggily Books — We Pay

Uncle Wiggily at the Lake .... 20.00+
Uncle Wiggily in Fairyland .... 20.00+
Uncle Wiggily & the Birds .... 30.00+
Uncle Wiggily Holidays, copyright 1920 only, Graham .... 20.00+
Uncle Wiggily Surprises, copyright 1937, Blue Ribbon .... 20.00+
The Uncle Wiggily Book, copyright 1927, Appleton .... 20.00+
Dottie & Willie Flufftail .... 15.00+
Dickie & Nellie Fliptail .... 15.00+
Woodie & Waddie Chuck .... 15.00+
Bobby & Billy Ringtail .... 15.00+
Dottie & Willie Lambkin .... 15.00+

Other Uncle Wiggily Items — We Pay

Baby Dish .... 150.00+
Balloon .... 100.00+
Button, vegetable ivory .... 40.00+
Candle .... 50.00+
Coloring Book, copyright 1955 .... 35.00+
Fabric .... 40.00+
Flatware, spoon & fork set .... 100.00+
Handkerchief .... 80.00+
Halloween Costume .... 200.00+
Mug, 2-handle .... 100.00+
Pin-Back Button .... 200.00+
Puzzle, 1968-1970, Parker Brothers .... 30.00+
Puzzle, Put-Together, Jack-O'-Lantern, Graham .... 120.00+
Puzzle, inlaid type, 1953-1966, Milton Bradley .... 40.00+
Record, Uncle Wiggily & Cameo Kid, Records for Children .... 40.00+
Record, Uncle Wiggily & His Friends, RCA .... 30.00+
Tea Set .... 800.00+
Wallpaper .... 40.00+
Anything Unusual .... Call or Write

Bobbsey Twins — We Pay

The Bobbsey Twins, Mershon Pub., copyright 1904, gray w/orange & white or gray w/red & yellow cover, ea .... 500.00+
The Bobbsey Twins in the Country Mershon Pub., copyright 1904 .... 800.00+
The Bobbsey Twins, Stitt Publishing Co, copyright 1906 .... 1,000.00+
The Bobbsey Twins in the Country, Stitt Pub. Co, copyright 1906 .... 1,000.00+
The Bobbsey Twins, Chatterton-Peck, copyright 1907, brown (tan) w/yellow cover .... 500.00+

The Bobbsey Twins in the Country, Chatterton-Peck, copyright 1907, brown (tan) w/yellow cover .... **800.00+**

The Bobbsey Twins at the Seashore, Chatterton-Peck, copyright 1907, brown (tan) w/yellow .... **800.00+**

The Bobbsey Twins, same size & cover as Chatterton-Peck, except Grosset & Dunlap at bottom of spine, title & copyright pages list Mershon or Chatterton-Peck only .... **400.00+**

The Bobbsey Twins, by Hope (not full name) on spine, w/paper applique on front cover, 5¼x7⅝" .... **200.00+**

The Bobbsey Twins in the Country or *The Bobbsey Twins at the Seashore*, Hope (not full name) on spine, w/paper applique on front, 5¼x7⅝", ea ...... **200.00+**

I am interested in buying **Uncle Wiggily** and **Raggedy Ann and Andy books** as well as **color-illustrated children's books from before 1940 and pop-up books. I will pay $10 and up** depending on condition and title. I prefer bindings to be in excellent shape and color illustrations to be untorn and unmarked. Pop-up books must be in excellent condition.

Jacquie Henry
Antique Treasures & Toys
P.O. Box 17
2240 Academy St.
Walworth, NY 14568
315-968-1424

As a dog lover and collector of dog toys, I seek a book by Alfred Koehn entitled *Royal Favourites at the Lotus Court*, Peiping, China, 1948. There is no text in this quarto volume. It consists of a series of seventeen colored plates of the Pekingese dog.

Elenore D. Chaya
4003 S Indian River Dr.
Ft. Pierce, FL 34982
407-465-1789

We buy **children's serial books** including Hardy Boys, Nancy Drew, Bobbsey Twins, etc. Any book series for children, youth or young adults is wanted. If you open the book and it lists a series, we are interested. Books must be in good to better conditon. Dust jacketed books are preferred but not necessary.

Bob and Gail Spicer
R.D. 1 Ashgrove Rd., Box 82
Cambridge, NY 12816
518-677-5139

	We Pay
Hardy Boys	**1.00-3.00**
Nancy Drew	**1.00-3.00**
Cherry Ames	**1.00-3.00**
Tom Swift	**1.00-4.00**

Wanted to buy: **Raggedy Ann and Andy books by Johnny Gruelle**. These were published by M.A. Donohue and Company. Price will depend on condition.

Carole Jemison
Rt. 1, Box 73
Wann, OK 74083
918-534-2129

We buy and sell new and out-of-print **books on antiques and collectibles**. Wanted are older references or price guides pertaining to specific subjects on antiques and collectibles. Send list of titles with condition, year, size, and price.

Collector's Companion
Perry Franks
P.O. Box 24333
Richmond, VA 23224

We buy **books on all types of edged weapons**: pocketknives, swords, cutlasses, dirks, custom knives, daggers, fixed blades, oriental types, switchblades, etc. Books don't have to be in A-1 condition as long as all the pages are intact and in readable condition. For books not listed below, please state price you want.

Knife Readables
1115 Longfellow Blvd.
Lakeland, FL 33810
813-666-1133

	We Pay
History of John Russell Cultery Company	20.00+
A Boy's Book of Switchblade Knives	25.00+
Sunday Knives	20.00+
Best of Knife World Vol I and Vol II	12.00+
Knife Makers of Old San Francisco	29.00+
Knifemakers Who Went West	35.00+
Second Scrimshaw Connection	40.00+
A History of Cultery in the Connecticut Valley	25.00+
The House of Wostenholm 1745-1945	30.00+
Remington, reprint catalogs, ea	10.00+
Nippo-To: The Japanese Sword	45.00+
Collector's Pictorial Book of Bayonets	12.00+
The Indian Sword	10.00+
Italian Fascist Dagger	8.00+
Napanach: A White Man's Knife With a Red Man's Name	15.00+
The Old Knife Book	15.00+
Classic Bowie Knife	30.00+

We buy **used and out-of-print and paperback books on all subjects**. Original dust jackets are preferred whenever possible. We do not buy college textbooks, books in poor condition, or books whose illustrations have been removed. We also buy **antique pens and clocks**.

Norma Wadler
The Whale's Tale
P.O. Box 1520A
Long Beach, WA 98631
360-642-3455

	We Pay
Books	1.00-500.00+
Clocks	40.00-300.00+
Pens	1.00-100.00+

BOTTLE OPENERS

I buy **any figural bottle opener** that is a standing figure, three-dimensional figure, or wall-mount figure that I do not already have. And I'll buy a second one, if it is in better condition than mine, so that I can upgrade my collection.

Charlie Reynolds
2836 Monroe St.
Falls Church, VA 22042
703-533-1322

	We Pay
Bear Head, wall mount, 2 holes under chin	**1,500.00**
Boots, brass	**50.00-75.00**
Boy w/Books, cast iron	**2,000.00**
Cardinal, cast iron	**325.00**
Chess Horse Knight, brass	**200.00**
Dragons, cast iron	**125.00**
Drunk on Lamppost or Signpost, aluminum	**200.00**
Eagle Head, wall mount, 2 holes under chin	**1,500.00**
Elephant, w/raised trunk, cast iron, 3¼"	**350.00**
Eskimo Holding Bottle, pot metal	**350.00**
Knight, Syroco Wood	**450.00**
Lady w/Harp, cast iron	**450.00**
Monk, Syroco Wood	**350.00**
Nudes, brass or cast iron, ea	**40.00-75.00**
Rhino, cast iron, Japan	**350.00**
Roadrunner, opener in beak & tail	**350.00**
Turtle, brass, opener at bottom	**200.00**

BOTTLES

Applied color label soda bottles (commonly known as painted bottles) are becoming increasingly popular collectibles. Until about the 1930s soda bottles had embossed names or paper labels. Then in the mid-1930s nearly all bottles produced had painted-on (pyro-glazed) lettering with company logos or pictures often added. Wanted are examples not currently found in my collection for further research. A photo would be most helpful. Collectors, dealers — anyone with an interest in these bottles — is invited to contact me about information concerning my books on this subject.

Thomas Marsh
914 Franklin Ave.
Youngstown, OH 44502
800-845-7930 or 216-743-8600

Bottles

Before 1900 all bottles were handmade. These can usually be distinguished from modern, machine-made bottles by looking at the seams on each side. On a machine-made bottle they go all the way to the top of the lip. If they end lower, if there are perpendicular seams, or if there are no seams at all, the bottle is handmade and may be collectible.

I will consider purchasing **almost any type of handmade bottle, except fruit jars**. The most desirable have one or more of the following characteristics:

Embossed lettering, design, or picture
Pontil mark (round, rough gouge on underside of bottle where glass-blowing rod was broken off)
Cure or Bitters bottles
Unusual shape, color, or shade (most are aqua, clear or amber)

Bottles without any of the above are probably of no value, even if they are handmade. Presence of a label adds to the value, but presence of contents usually does not. Condition is critical. I will not purchase bottles with cracks, scratches, chips, bruises, iridescence, or with a condition known as 'sick glass' (a milky haze that will not clean off). On the other hand, bubbles or other factory-made imperfections are desirable.

Please send me a full description with a drawing or photo if possible of whatever you have, one bottle or hundreds. I will respond to all communications (include a reply postcard). If I don't buy it, I will give you an informal appraisal. The huge variety of collectible bottles makes it hard to estimate prices without seeing a specific item, but the listing below will give you a general idea. The prices are the minimums for the more collectible bottles in each category (add at least $10 for pontiled varieties). Most bring considerably less — but give me a chance to make an offer in any case.

Michael Engel
29 Groveland St.
Easthampton, MA 01027
413-527-8733

Type	We Pay
Bitters	20.00+
Cosmetics (hair, perfume, cologne)	5.00+
Dairy	30.00+
Food or Household	3.00+
Inks	5.00+
Medicines (especially cures)	10.00+
Peppersauce/Pickle (elaborate shape or design)	20.00+
Poisons	10.00+
Sodas or Beers	5.00+
Whiskey	10.00+

We buy **perfume bottles of all kinds**. We avidly seek commercial perfume bottles, for example: Elizabeth Arden, Schiaparelli, Guerlain, Patou, Dior, and many others. It is best if this type of perfume has its original label and especially its box. Fine De Vilbiss atomizers are also desired. We buy Czechoslovakian perfume bottles of all varieties, but we especially are looking for bottles with larger figural stoppers, in unusual colors, or with jewels. We also buy: Lalique, Baccarat, and also even miniature sample bottles. Send a photo of what you have and we will respond. Sample prices are listed here.

Monsen and Baer
Box 529
Vienna, VA 22183
703-938-2129 or FAX 703-242-1357

	We Pay
Elizabeth Arden, It's You, w/box	**750.00**
Schiaparelli, Zut, w/box	**350.00**
De Vilbiss, gold & black, 8"	**250.00**
Lalique, Camille, blue	**1,000.00**
Czechoslovakian, pink crystal w/nude figural stopper, 7"	**500.00**
Czechoslovakian, w/parrot top, 6"	**350.00**

Looking for **milk bottles embossed Geo C. Cilley, Concord, New Hampshire. Paying current market value.**

M. Pearce
30715 Cove Rd.
Tavares, FL 32778
904-343-6341

BOXES

We collect **Victorian era boxes** which held collars and cuffs; gloves; brush, comb, and mirror sets; shaving sets; neckties; etc. Also wanted are photograph albums and autograph albums. The items we collect have lithographs usually affixed to the front or top of the piece. The lithographic prints usually show scenes or people. We prefer those which show close-up views of children or ladies, but will consider others. The print (or in some cases the entire album) is covered with a thin layer of clear celluloid. In other instances, part of the box or album will be covered with an abstract or floral print paper or colorful velvet material.

Boxes

We are interested only in pieces in top condition: no cracked celluloid, split seams, or missing hardware. Condition of the interior of these boxes and albums is not as important as the condition of the outside. We are *not* interested in French Ivory celluloid boxes or solid celluloid dresser sets. If you see an exceptional celluloid box or album, but are uncertain about buying it for resale, please put us in touch with the owner. If we can buy it, we will pay you a finder's fee.

Mike and Sherry Miller
303 Holiday Dr.
Tuscola, IL 61953
217-253-4991

	We Pay
Autograph Albums, ea	**25.00-75.00**
Boxes, sm, ea	**40.00-75.00**
Boxes, med, ea	**50.00-100.00**
Boxes, lg, ea	**85.00-200.00**
Photograph Albums, ea	**50.00-175.00**
Photograph Albums, musical, ea	**100.00-250.00**

BRASS

Ever since my cat knocked over a rare piece of porcelain, I've concentrated my collecting non-perishables — especially **brass, bronze, and wood objects from China**. I'm especially fond of round bowls and plates and small figurines of animals and people. I'm not interested in items from India, Taiwan, Hong Kong or Japan, but will consider anything else. I will pay a fair price plus postage for an interesting artifact and would appreciate a description of the item before making a decision. **Items must be marked China, Made in China, or have a chop mark.**

Edward Falick
Box 455
Nevada City, CA 95959
916-265-2784

BREWERIANA

Specializing in **old beer advertising from New Jersey**. I pay the best prices for Union (or United) Brewing Co. of Newark, Lyons & Sons, Orange Brewery, or rarer New Jersey Brewery items. Condition is everything. Also interested in all old, ball-type, beer tap knobs; collections or box lots; complete items or parts.

Paul E. Brady
32 Hamilton St.
Newton, NJ 07860
201-383-7204

Pre-1920	**We Pay**
Calendars	**up to 50.00**
Coasters	**up to 10.00**
Foam Scrapers	**up to 25.00**
Signs, tin	**up to 100.00**
Trays	**up to 200.00**
Tip Trays	**up to 50.00**

BRIDAL AND WEDDING COLLECTIBLES

I collect old **bridal items prior to circa 1940s**. The price I pay is totally dependent on the condition of the item. Even old deteriorating dresses have some value for their lace trims and buttons. Please send me a list, pictures if possible, and approximate age of the item(s).

Marilyn Finitz
220 W Olympic Pl. #203
Seattle, WA 98119

	We Pay
Bridal Dresses	**up to 100.00**
Bride's Baskets (silverplate or w/glass inset)	**up to 50.00**
Cake Toppers	**up to 25.00**

Bridal and Wedding Collectibles

Candlesticks....................**up to 100.00**
Cherubs, any type....................**up to 75.00**
Fans....................**up to 50.00**
Frames, suitable for wedding photos....................**up to 85.00**
Gloves....................**up to 10.00**
Head Pieces....................**up to 75.00**
Linen or Lace, suitable for repairs or to create items....................**up to 25.00**
Purses....................**up to 50.00**
Personal Gifts (exchanged between bride & groom)....................**up to 100.00**
Photos, through the 1920s....................**up to 50.00**
Rosary....................**up to 15.00**
Roses (pictures, boxes, dishes & silver)....................**up to 50.00**
Wedding Books & Planners....................**up to 15.00**
Wedding Memorablia....................**1.00-5.00**
Wedding Favors....................**1.00-5.00**
Wedding Albums....................**up to 25.00**

BRONZES

I am buying all **bronze figurals of people and animals, vases, inkwells, and lamps made before 1940**. I would like single bronzes or an entire collection. Please send photos and your price to:

Melanie Hewitt
2101 Beechwood
Little Rock, AR 72207

We Pay

Bookends, pr....................**20.00-150.00**
Statues, 24" or taller, ea....................**500.00-2,500.00**
Statues, 24" or less, ea....................**150.00-1,500.00**
Animals, lg, ea....................**500.00-7,500.00**
Animals, sm, ea....................**100.00-1,100.00**
Vases, ea....................**50.00-3,500.00**
Figurines, ea....................**100.00-300.00**

BUTTONS

We buy **buttons of all sorts, especially old buttons of metal and glass**. The better their condition, the more their value. **Old Lovakian, Venetian, and**

African trade beads are desired. We buy collectons both small and large. Call for more information. Exceptional buttons or beads will be bought on a piece-by-piece basis.

Melanie R. Kadair
Ivy Ridge Plantation
8534 Old Tunica Rd.
St. Francisville, LA 70775
504-655-4696 or 504-655-4646

	We Pay
Glass Buttons, colored or jet, ca 1800-1930, ea	**1.00-4.00**
Gay '90s Buttons, ea	**10.00-30.00**
Opera Buttons, metal, ea	**2.00-30.00**
Metal Buttons, ca 1800-1920, ea	**1.00-4.00**
Metal Pictorial Buttons, ea	**5.00-50.00**
Czechlosovakian Glass Beads, ea	**50¢-4.00**
Venetian Glass Beads, ea	**50¢-4.00**

Collecting **antique and vintage buttons dating back to the 1800s** — metal, picture, Bakelite from the '30s, large carved mother-of-pearl, black glass with gold or silver lustre, Victorian actresses (pin-backs), and old cuff link studs. Please send on approval.

BBB
1931 Laurel Hill
Kingwood, TX 77339

CALCULATORS AND SMALL ADDING DEVICES

We collect **hand-held electronic calculators made between 1970-1980.** Millions were made and they are still easy to find at thrift stores and flea markets. New pocket calculators sell for $5 to $10, so you can usually get used ones for $1 to $2. Calculators made after 1980 have liquid crystal displays (LCD) and most are solar-powered. We *do not* collect these. We collect LED (light emiting diode) pocket calculators. How do you tell them apart? The display (part where you read the answer) is usually covered with colored plastic (red, green, etc.) on the type we collect. Also, they always have a hole (socket) for an adapter plug. At least 100 companies made LED calculators, and we only have room to list a few below. No Texas Instruments, Rockwells, or Unisonics, please (we've got too many of these already!). In addition to the prices below, we also pay shipping.

Bruce and Janice Flamm
10445 Victoria Ave.
Riverside, CA 92503
909-353-1326 (no collect calls please)

Company	We Pay
Bomar	**5.00-10.00**
Brother	**4.00-10.00**
Busicom	**15.00-75.00**
Craig	**5.00-10.00**
HP	**5.00-15.00**
Omron	**5.00-15.00**
Panasonic	**10.00-20.00**
Sanyo	**10.00-20.00**
Summit	**10.00-45.00**
Others	**Call or Write**

Hand-Held Adding Devices	We Pay
Mechanical, old, any smaller than shoe box size	**5.00-50.00**
Metal or Wood Slide Rules	**5.00-15.00**

CALIFORNIA PERFUME COMPANY

In New York City, New York, in 1886, Mr. D.H. McConnell, Sr., founded the California Perfume Company (C.P.C.). These toiletries continued to be manufactured with the C.P.C. label until 1929 when 'Avon Products Inc.' was added. Both names appeared on the label until about 1939 when 'C.P.C.' was removed, and the labeling continued as 'Avon Products.' The name 'Perfection' was used on the household products issued by these companies.

Other products distributed by C.P.C. are: Goetting & Company, Savoi Et. Cie, Gertrude Recordan, Hinze Ambrosia, Easy Day Automatic Clothes Washer, and Marvel Electric Silver Cleaner. Some of these products were packaged in a C.P.C.-labeled container when they were issued and will command better prices with this packaging. I am interested in buying these items and certain C.P.C. items from circa 1900 period. I am particularly interested in the Natoma Rose fragrance and will pay good prices for such items. *I do not want anything bearing the Avon name.* When writing, please send a complete description, including condition, and any note of importance. A self-addressed stamped envelope is required if you are seeking information only. Please, no collect calls.

Mr. Richard G. Pardini
3107 N El Dorado St.
Stockton, CA 95204-3412
209-466-5550 (7 am to 11 pm PST)

	We Pay
Goetting & Company	**20.00+**
Savoi Et Cie	**20.00+**
Gertrude Recordan	**5.00+**
Hinze Ambrosia	**5.00+**
Easy Day Automatic Clothes Washer	**25.00+**
Marvel Electric Silver Cleaner	**25.00+**
Natoma Rose Fragrances	**40.00+**
Natoma Fragrances	**40.00+**
C.P.C. Gift Sets, circa 1900	**50.00+**
C.P.C. Paper Items	**5.00+**
C.P.C. Bay Rum, w/126 Chambers St, New York USA address	**30.00+**

CALIFORNIA RAISINS

I have a special interest in all California Raisin collectibles. Of particular interest are the PVC's made by Applause consisting of their seventh series — Meet the Raisins II. Any other series or types will be considered. Other interests include **advertising items, fast-food collectibles, and toys**.

Delores Lawson
6129 Misson Dr.
Orlando, FL 32810
407-298-4749

California Raisins

We Pay

AC Raisin .... **20.00+**
Mama Raisin........ **20.00+**
Cecil Thyme (the carrot)........ **20.00+**
Leonard Lima Bean (manager)........ **20.00+**
Raisin Man, turquoise (blue) sunglasses & shoes, eyes open under glasses, version 1........ **5.00+**
Raisin Man, turquoise (blue) sunglasses & shoes, version 2........ **5.00+**
Raisin Man, blue & yellow movable surfboard, orange sunglasses & shoes ...**5.00+**
Raisin Man, blue & yellow stationary surfboard, orange sunglasses & shoes, version 2........ **5.00+**

CAMERAS

I buy classic, collectible, and usable cameras of many types; prices paid range from ten dollars to thousands for some rare editions. Send list with descriptions of cameras, or call for estimate or information. We *do not* buy Polaroid cameras or modern point and shoot type cameras. We are primarily collectors of cameras of yesteryear that are in good usable condition. A few examples of both the classic cameras and the more recent vintage cameras and prices paid are listed here. We pay UPS charges for all cameras purchased.

Gene's Cameras
2603 Artie St., SW Suite 16
Huntsville, AL 35805
205-536-6893

Classic/Collectible Cameras **We Pay**

Kodak Retina I, II, IIIC, Reflex........ **25.00-200.00**
Agfa Karat, Isolette, Silette........ **12.00-50.00**
Asahi & Asahiflex........ **100.00-300.00**
Balda & Balda Super........ **25.00-50.00**
Canon Rangefinder, by Canon, Inc, many models........ **100.00-300.00**
Rolleiflex & Rolleicord........ **45.00-500.00**
Exakta, Exa, & other Ihagee Kamerwerk models........ **25.00-250.00**
Minolta Rangerfinder, early folding type or 35mm........ **50.00-300.00**
Nikon Rangerfinders & Other Models, by Nippon Kogaku........ **200.00-3,000.00**
Pentacon/Contax Models, D, E, F, FB, FM, S, etc........ **30.00-300.00**
Alpa, by Pignons AG........ **100.00-1,000.00**

Sears Tower, Types 3, 16, 19, 22, 26, 29, 32, 33, 34, 45, 46............**30.00-200.00**
Voightlander & Sohn, many models **30.00-200.00**
Zeiss Ikon, models such as Contaflex, Contax, Contessa, Ikonta....**25.00-400.00**
Leica Cameras & Leitz Lenses ....**100.00-5,000.00+**
Others; models such as Konica, Olympus, Lordomat, Zorki, Expo, Mamiya, Ernemann **25.00-200.00**

Modern or User Cameras **We Pay**

Canon Series A, F, T, EOS; many models.......................................**25.00-300.00**
Minolta SR, SRT Series, X-Series, Maxx AF Series.........................**25.00-300.00**
Nikon F, F2, F3, F4, FE, FG, FA, FM, FT, EL, S, S2, SP **100.00-500.00**
Nikkormats, Nikomats, Nikkorex..**35.00-125.00**
Olympus OM-1, OM-2, OM-3, OM-4, OM-10, OM-G, OM-P6 ....**50.00-200.00**
Pentax Spotmatic, ME, K1000, Program, LX, KX, A3000, P5, P3, P30 ....**40.00-300.00**
Contax II, III, 137, 159, 167, RTS **100.00-300.00**
Fujica AX Series & AZ Series...**40.00-125.00**
Mamiya C33, C220, C330, other Mamiya **20.00-200.00**
Rolleiflex, Roleicord, Rollei SLR **50.00-500.00**
Yashicamat A, C, D, EM, LM, 124, 124G, 44 ....**25.00-125.00**
Subminiatures: Minox, HIT, Steky, Gami, Expo, Atoron, etc.........**10.00-200.00**
Others: Konica, Topcon, Ricoh, Hasselblad, some novelties..........**10.00-500.00**

CANDLEWICK

Buying Candlewick pattern glassware by Imperial. Special wants are serving pieces, dinner plates, condiment sets, and a birthday cake plate. Please, no chipped, cracked or worn pieces wanted. Also buying other elegant glass of the Depression and postwar period.

David Paulsen
P.O. Box 759
Ontario, OR 97914
503-889-7117

We Pay

Dinner Plate, 10"..**up to 20.00**
Birthday Cake Plate...**200.00**
Serving Bowl...**10.00-60.00**
Oil & Vinegar Cruets, pr...**30.00**

CANDY CONTAINERS

For over fifteen years I have been buying glass candy containers. I have connections to sell top pieces throughout the country. I will buy one piece or an entire collection. Special preference is for rare and unusual pieces with good paint and metal parts where needed. Prices paid vary depending on condition and paint but they will always be near the top of the current market. Examples are listed here.

Jeff Bradfield
90 Main St.
Dayton, VA 22821
703-879-9961

	We Pay
Amusu Theatre Building	400.00
Boob McNutt	Call
Dolly's Bathtub	Call
Flossie Fisher Bed	600.00
George Washington	450.00
Pumpkinhead Policeman, good paint	550.00
Rabbit Family, w/paint	700.00
Rabbit in Eggshell, gold paint	65.00
Spirit of St Louis Airplane	325.00
Statue of Liberty	1,000.00
Swan Boat	600.00

CANES AND WALKING STICKS

Canes and walking sticks are wanted, especially dual-purpose ones that also serve as a container, weapon, or gadget; also fancy-carved canes made of ivory, gold, silver or glass that has something enclosed or attached to the shaft for purposes other than support is of interest. Any well-executed hand-carved cane is sought as well.

Beaver Bros. Antiques
1637 Market St.
San Francisco, CA 94103
415-863-4344

We Pay

Glass, end-of-day 65.00-210.00
Glass Container 85.00-145.00
Gold Plated 135.00-300.00
Gold Rolled 135.00-300.00
14K Gold 300.00-500.00
Gold Quartz 300.00-625.00
Folk Art 100.00-250.00
Scrimshaw 225.00-450.00
Sword 125.00-300.00
Ivory Handle 125.00-300.00
Root 85.00-145.00

CAPE COD

Cape Cod pieces made by Avon are wanted to add to my niece's and my collections. These pieces are made of ruby red pressed glass. Items need not have original contents (cologne, candle, etc.) or boxes to be of interest. Plates, bowls of all sizes, bells, pie plates, and serving pieces are examples of pieces that have been made by the company since the seventies. Please note only Avon Cape Cod items are wanted — no other kinds of Avon bottles are of interest. Other **odd pieces of ruby glass, dinnerware or accessories other than Cape Cod** may be of interest also. (I originally began collecting Cape Cod to go along with some ruby Depression glass.) Below are some examples of prices I have paid.

Linda Holycross
1202 Seventh St.
Covington, IN 47932

We Pay

Bell 4.00
Bowl, serving, 8¾" dia 7.00
Bowl, dessert, 5" 2.50
Bowl, soup or cereal, 7½" dia 4.00
Cake Plate, 3½x10¾" dia 16.00
Candle Holder, hurricane type only, w/clear straight-sided chimney 8.00
Champagne Glass, footed, 9-oz, 5¼" 6.00
Cup & Saucer Set 4.50
Cruet 2.50

Dessert Server, wedge-shaped stainless steel w/red plastic handle, 8"........**5.00**
Goblet, water; 6"........**4.00**
Mug, pedestal base, 5"........**2.50**
Napkin Rings, set of 4........**8.00**
Pie Plate Server, 1½x11"........**7.00**
Platter, 10¾x13½"........**8.00**
Plate, bread & butter, 5¾"........**2.50**
Plate, dessert, 7½"........**3.00**
Plate, dinner........**5.00**
Tumbler, footed, 3¾"........**3.00**
Tumbler, straight sided, 5½"........**4.00**
Vase, footed, 8"........**6.50**

CARNIVAL CHALK PRIZES

I buy old carnival chalkware prizes that were produced to be given away at carnivals from about 1915 to 1950. I am not interested in animals unless they were in the comics, such as Felix the Cat, Spark Plug the Horse, or Disney's Pluto. Some of the early prizes were Kewpie types while others have mohair wigs and dresses. I buy **old radio lamps made of plaster**. Examples of lamps would be Art Deco nudes or cowboys on bucking horses. The radio lamp was the ultimate carnival prize. I reimburse for UPS and insurance.

Tom Morris
P.O. Box 8307
Medford, OR 97504
503-779-3164

We Pay

Alice the Goon, from Popeye, 6" or 10", ea........**45.00+**
Amos & Andy, 12" or 7½" on ashtray, ea........**95.00+**
Betty Boop, 14½"........**125.00+**
Eugene the Jeep, from Popeye, 14"........**175.00+**
Felix the Cat, 12½"........**120.00+**
Hula Girls, various sizes, ea........**35.00+**
Kewpie, 1920s, w/wig or dress, ea........**85.00+**
Ma & Pa Yokum, 12½", pr........**150.00+**
Mae West, 13" to 14"........**45.00+**
Maggie & Jiggs, 8½", ea or pr........**100.00+**
Moon Mullins, from Barney Google, 7"........**45.00+**
Nudes or Semi-Nudes, various sizes, ea........**35.00+**
Nude Art Deco Lamp, various sizes, ea........**85.00+**

Popeye, 9" or larger, ea .... **35.00+**
Sailor Boy, 9" or larger, ea .... **35.00+**
Sea Hag, from Popeye, 8", ea .... **35.00+**
Shirley Temple, 9" or larger, ea .... **45.00+**
Spark Plug, from Barney Google, 7" .... **150.00+**
Superman, 15" .... **110.00+**
Soldier, 13" .... **40.00+**
Uncle Sam, 15" .... **50.00+**
Wimpy, from Popeye, 13½" or 16", ea .... **40.00+**

CARNIVAL GLASS

We buy any good piece of carnival glass. We like old carnival glass in perfect condition with no chips, cracks, or breaks. No reproductions wanted. Any good piece in red, aqua opalescent, ice blue, ice green, some white, electric blue, carnival on moonstone, and carnival on milk glass are wanted. Desired patterns include Peacocks, Peacock at Urn, Orange Tree, and Millersburg. Large vases, punch bowls and plates are especially wanted. Use great caution when buying carnival glass as it can have an inside crack that can be very hard to detect. Other wants include **hand-painted Nippon and R.S. Prussia**. No damaged pieces or reproductions are wanted.

Robert Greenwood
201 E Hatfield St.
Massena, NY 13662
315-769-8130

CAST IRON

We want to buy **old cast-iron cookware** by Wagner, Griswold, W.C. Davis, G.F. Filley, Martin, Favorite, Lodge, etc. We especially want pieces by Wagner Ware and also buy some Wagner cast aluminum. Let us know what you have for sale and your asking price, and we will get back with you as soon as possible.

Randy and Jane Wright
Jane's Collectibles and Stuff
Rt. 2, Box 372 I, Hill St.
Erin, TN 37061
615-289-4068 or 615-289-4096

I collect **cast-iron skillets, muffin pans, broilers, and any unusual items made of cast iron**. I am mainly interested in Griswold, but I also buy Erie, G.F. Filley, Wapok, Waterman, and sometimes Wagner. Because I am a collector, I often can pay more than a dealer.

As I am a collector of almost everything, I buy antiques, collectibles, and nearly anything. Items do not have to be really old to be valuable to me. Help me with my collecting and make some extra money. Write or call and tell me what you have. Chances are good that you will have something that I will want to buy. I pay fair market prices for items I like.

Ronald Fitch
315 Market St.
Suite 2G
Portsmouth, OH 45662
614-353-6879

	We Pay
Griswold Skillet, #1, #2, #11, #13, #14, #20, ea	**up to 800.00**
Griswold Skillet Cover, #13, #14, #20, ea	**up to 300.00**
Griswold Dutch Oven, #11, #12, #13, ea	**up to 300.00**
Griswold Oval Roaster, #3, #5, #7, #9, ea	**up to 450.00**
Griswold Waffle Iron, #0, #00, #1, #2, #6, #8, ea	**up to 400.00**
Griswold Waffle Iron, #18 or #19, hearts & star, ea	**up to 300.00**
Griswold Cake Mold, rabbit, Santa or bundt, ea	**up to 800.00**
Griswold Toy, ea	**up to 250.00**
Griswold Pup, ea	**up to 300.00**
Griswold or Erie Muffin Pans #270, #272, #282, #280, or #2800, w/corn or wheat-stick pattern, ea	**up to 750.00**
Griswold or Erie Muffin Pan, #50 or #100, w/hearts & star pattern, ea	**up to 650.00**
Griswold or Erie Double Loaf Pan or Single Loaf Pan, ea	**up to 1,200.00**
Griswold Vienna Bread Pan, #1, #4 or #957, single or 4-section, ea	**up to 800.00**
Griswold or Erie #26 Double Loaf Pan or #28 Single Loaf Pan, ea	**up to 1,200.00**
Griswold Muffin Pan, #13, #14, or #20, turk head,	**up to 450.00**
Griswold Muffin Pan, #240, #140 or #130, turk head,	**up to 450.00**
GF Filley Muffin Pan, #1, #2, #4, #6, #7, #8, or higher, ea	**up to 350.00**
Wapok Muffin Pan, any number, ea	**up to 250.00**
Wagner #1 Gem Pan, w/handle	**up to 600.00**
Waterman Muffin Pan, any 3-section, ea	**up to 400.00**

Heart Pattern Muffin Pan, any, ea	**up to 1,000.00**
Cast Iron Bank, still, ea	**up to 200.00**
Cast Iron Bank, mechanical, ea	**up to 1,000.00**
Other Cast Iron Items, ea	**up to 1,000.00**

Other Wants	**We Pay**
Art Pottery	**up to 200.00**
Banks	**up to 500.00**
Badges	**up to 200.00**
Bottles	**up to 250.00**
Bronzes	**up to 300.00**
Cameras	**up to 500.00**
Character Collectibles & Toys	**up to 200.00+**
Cookie Jars	**up to 175.00**
Fountain Pens	**up to 1,000.00**
Lamps	**up to 250.00**
Limited Edition Items	**up to 200.00**
Lunch Boxes & Thermoses	**up to 500.00**
Marbles	**up to 200.00**
Paperweights	**up to 500.00**
Postcards	**up to 25.00**
Prints	**up to 200.00+**
Quilts (old & handmade)	**up to 200.00**
Radios & Televisions	**up to 500.00+**
Weathervanes	**up to 500.00**
Watches	**up to 1,000.00**
Many Others	**Call or Write**

I will buy **cast-iron cookware** — especially pieces marked Wagner, Griswold, Filley, Davis, or other manufacturers (also want unmarked items). Unusual pieces are preferred, and items must be in good or better condition with no damage.

Craig Dinner
P.O. Box 4399
Sunnyside, NY 11104
718-729-3850

	We Pay
Buster Brown Waffle Iron	**250.00**
Filley Muffin Pan	**400.00**
Griswold Muffin Pan, #13	**500.00+**

Griswold Muffin Pan, #2800 .... **1,000.00**
Griswold Muffin Pan, #2700 .... **100.00**
Griswold Muffin Pan, other numbers **50.00-1,000.00**
Griswold Skillet, #20 .... **300.00**
Griswold Vienna Roll Pan .... **450.00+**
Griswold Waffle Rack, 3-tiered **600.00**
Griswold or Wagner Skillet Rack, ea **175.00**
Wagner Muffin Pan **75.00**

I want to buy **cast-iron figurals made in the early 1900s from Northern Kansas**.

Mrs. R.C. Miller
4436 Petit Ave.
Encino, CA 91436

CAT COLLECTIBLES

I buy older **limited edition cat plates** and will pay prices as listed in the Bradford Plate Exchange as well as postage. I also buy **crystal cat figurals**.

Glenna Moore
440 Lewers St., #205
Honolulu, HI 96815-2445
808-924-2226

Series/Title **We Pay**

Canada, Killman Wild Kittens, Adorable Ocelot or Bashful Babies, 1985-86, ea **39.00**
Germany, Gobel Wildlife, 1985 Lynxby Calvert **49.50**
Germany, Royale Mother's Day 1975 Lynx Family, by Poluszynski **26.00**
Italy, Veneto Flair Mother/Child: 1981 Lions, by Gialletti **95.00**
United Kingdom, Royal Doulton, Jungle Fantasy, by Novoa; 1979 Ark, 1980 Compassion or 1983 Refuge **75.00-95.00**
United States, American Heritage Kitty Kats, by Kari, 1984 Pansy or 1984 Sammy, ea **19.50**
B & J Country, 1985 Laurel, by Hagara **42.50**
Celebrity Impressions, The Volks Cats, 1988 The Anniversary, by Volks .. **39.50**
Farmont Group, 1983 I'll Be Loved, by Herschenburgh **29.95**

Hackett Little Orphans, 1984 Furry Surprise, by Franca **35.00**
Hackett Crazy Cats, 1982 Primping Time, by Frybach................................**42.50**
Hamilton Collection Garden Verses, 1985 I Love Little Kittens, by Wilcox-Smith **24.50**
Hamilton Collection Fond Memories, 1988 Lap Full, by Grimball **24.50**
House of Global Art English, 1983 James, Henry, Lucy, & Lilly, by Jervis, set of 4 ....**35.00**
Hoyle Remember When, 1983 Playing Grandmother, by Humphrey..........**30.00**
Kern Special, 1984 Champ, by Jansen **39.50**
Lenox Nature's Babies, 1984 Bengal Tigers, by Chase **70.00**
Modern Masters Floral Felines, 1983 Her Majesty, 1984 The Dutchess, or 1985 His Lordship, by Shearer, ea **55.00**
Pemberton Oaks Girls, 1985 Curious Kitten, by Anderson..........................**29.00**
Pickard Lockhart Wildlife, 1978 American Panther, by Lockhart.............**175.00**
Rhea Silva Porcelain Felines, 1984 Abyssinian Playmates or 1985 Tom Is in the Garden, by Oxenham, ea **47.00**
Rockford Editions Little Mothers, 1983 Love Is Blind, by Gutmann...........**29.95**
Roman Cats, 1984 Grizabella, Mr Mistoffelees, Rum Tum Tugger, etc by Doney, series of 8, any...**29.50**
Royal Cornwal Alice in Wonderland, 1979 Cheshire Cat's Grin, by Whitaker...**45.00**
River Shore Single, 1982 Grandpa's Treasures or Grandpa's Guardian, by Rockwell, ea **80.00**
Royal Orleans Christmas, 1982 Pink Panther Midnight Ride, by Depatie ..**25.00**
Southern Living Gallery Forest Friends, 1985 Bobcat, by Barlow...............**39.50**
US Gallery of Art Single, 1984 Innocence, by Woodson **19.50**

CATALINA ISLAND POTTERY

I buy all **unusual and rare pottery made from the factory between 1927 and 1937** on Catalina Island. These are marked either Catalina Island, Catalina, or Catalina Isle and marks can be either handwritten in the clay or ink stamped. Pieces vary from vases to tiles to souvenirs to dinnerware. We only buy mint condition pieces, however we have been known to relax these standards when the very rare pieces are available. We will reimburse actual UPS and insurance charges and will immediately get back to you with receipt of your written or faxed submittal. We also have a phone number by which you can contact us directly and we will accept telephone charges. We pay more than anyone else in the country for Catalina Island pottery.

Walter S. Sanford
3700 E Seventh St.
Long Beach, CA 90804
310-434-7253

Catalina Island Pottery

	We Pay
Frog Bookends	1,500.00+
Dual Seal Candelabra	1,000.00+
Nautilus Shell Vase	1,000.00+
Bird Tile Table	1,500.00+
Floor Vase	1,000.00+
Single Tile	50.00+
Souvenir Ashtray	200.00+
Casino Scene Tile	2,500.00+
Planter, lg	200.00+
Airplane Plate	3,000.00+
Glazed Picture Plate	750.00+
Hand-Painted Plate	400.00+
Teapot	300.00+
Giant Clam Shell	1,500.00+
Lamp	750.00+

I buy pieces marked **Catalina Pottery** made by Gladding McBean, shells, and some pieces marked with blue ink Made in USA. **G.M.B., Franciscan, Catalina Pottery advertising items, and price lists** as well as **some Franciscan dinnerware** pieces are wanted. All pieces must be in excellent condition. Send description or photo and price of your item or call and leave message.

Alan Phair
P.O. Box 30373
Long Beach, CA 90853
310-438-9395

CATALOGS

We buy **catalogs and brochures from wholesalers, importers and manufacturers making or selling antique reproductions**. These include A.A. Importing, Koscherak Bros., L.G. Wright (glass), L.E. Smith, J. Wright (cast iron), Summit Glass, etc. Send list with company name, date, number of pages, condition, your phone number and price wanted. We pay generous shipping allowance.

Paying about $5 for most circa 1970s catalogs; more for hard-to-find ones, less for common ones. Catalogs on all reproductions of interest: glass, metal, furniture, museum recreations, etc. Please list what you have.

Antique & Collectors Reproduction News
Box 71174-WB
Des Moines, IA 50325
515-270-8994

A.A. Importing	**We Pay**
1975 through 1985, ea	**2.50**
1970 through 1974, ea	**4.00**
1965 through 1969, ea	**5.00-10.00**
Pre-1965, ea	**10.00-20.00**

Koscherak Bros.	**We Pay**
Full Color Flyer, ea	**2.00-5.00**
1970s Brochures, ea	**10.00-20.00**
Pre-1970s Catalogs, ea	**20.00+**

Wanted: **catalogs from the 1920s through the 1950s** with information on any of the following **companies that produced silhouettes on glass**:

Art Publishing Co, Chicago, IL
Baco Glass Plaques
CE Erickson Co, Des Moines, IA
Benton Glass Co, Benton Harbor, MI
Bilderback's Inc, Detroit, MI
Buckbee-Brehm Co, Minneapolis, MN
Deltex Products Co, Newton, IA
Ohio Art Co, Bryan, OH
Reliance Products, Chicago or New York
C & A Richards, Boston, MA
The Photoplating Co, Minneapolis, MN
Stanwood-Hillson Co, Brookline, MA
The Volland Co, Joliet, IL
Peter Watson's Studio, Detroit, MI
West Coast Picture Co, Portland, OR
Any other catalogs or old advertisment with information about silhouettes

Shirley Mace
P.O. Box 1602
Mesilla Park, NM 88047
505-524-6717

I collect **seed catalogs issued by American companies since 1817**. I am especially interested in completing my collection of Burpee Company catalogs. My interest is primarily academic; I belong to several organizations that grow and preserve endangered or heirloom vegetables. Seed catalogs enable us to identify varieties which are no longer offered by companies and initiate a search for them.

I like catalogs in excellent condition, but they are seldom found that way. Therefore I am open to offers of catalogs in any readable condition. I also collect **ruby-flashed glass with writing indicating that it came from a state, county, or agricultural fair**.

George Belden
1224 N Mantua
Kent, OH 44240

	We Pay
Burpee Catalogs, pre-1900, ea	**30.00+**
Ruby-Flashed Fair Glass	**20.00+**

We are interested in purchasing original **catalogs from companies such as Heywood-Wakefield, Royalchrome, Lloyd Manufacturing, Herman Miller, and others**. **We will pay $5 to $10 per catalog** depending on desirability and condition.

An Antique Store
1450 W Webster
Chicago, IL 60614
312-935-6060 or FAX 312-871-6660

CATTAIL DINNERWARE

Cattail was a dinnerware pattern popular during the late 1920s until sometime in the 1940s. The dinnerware was made primarily by Universal Potteries of Cambridge, Ohio. It was sold for years by Sears Roebuck & Company. The pattern is unmistakable — a cluster of red cattails with black stems on creamy white.

We are looking for all unusual pieces of Cattail such as cookie jars, tumblers, two-piece casserole (1 1/2-quart, 8¼" in diameter), glass pitcher, linens, glass shaker set in metal rack, etc. Also looking for pantryware: step-on trash can, oval wastebasket, cake cover and tray, double- and single-compartment bread boxes, and four-piece canister set. We buy only pieces in good condition. We don't buy chipped, cracked or crazed, pieces. We will reimburse actual shipping and insurance charges.

Ken and Barbara Brooks
4121 Gladstone Lane
Charlotte, NC 28205
704-568-5716

We Pay

Shaker Set: salt, pepper, sugar & flour; black lids, all same size ....**25.00+**
Shaker Set: short salt & pepper shakers, tall flour & sugar, red lids w/red metal rack ....**30.00+**
Liner, for gravy boat ....**15.00+**
Tablecloth ....**75.00+**
Iced Tea Tumbler, red & black design on clear glass ....**30.00+**
Tumbler, marked Universal Potteries ....**35.00+**
Pitcher, red & black design on clear glass ....**80.00+**
Casserole, 8¼", w/lid ....**25.00+**
Batter Jug ....**65.00+**
Salad Fork & Spoon Set ....**25.00+**
Cookie Jar ....**75.00+**
Jug, w/side handle & cork stopper ....**25.00+**

CERAMIC ARTS STUDIO

Wanted: Ceramic Arts Studio (Madison, Wisconsin), made from 1940s to 1955. I buy Ceramic Arts Studio items both for my collection and resale and will by one piece or collections. I pay top dollar for items that I need to complete my collection and buy all color variations so please send a picture or full descriptions of items for sale.

Vera Skorupski
P.O. Box 572
Plainville, CT 06062
203-828-4097

	We Pay
Adam & Eve	500.00+
Ashtray, Hippo	40.00+
Bank, Tony	40.00+
Black Sambo & Tiger	200.00+
Boxer Pups	65.00+
Camels, pr	125.00+
Dachshunds, pr	50.00+
Dem & Rep	150.00+
Figurines, many others not mentioned here, ea	20.00-500.00+
Fire Man & Woman, gray	300.00
Goosie Gander & Mary	150.00+
Hamlet & Orphelia	300.00+
Neptune	125.00+
Plaques, ea	25.00-300.00+
Red Devil Imp Trio	250.00+
Salt & Pepper Shakers, pr	15.00-200.00+
Santa & Evergreen	100.00+
Tembino & Tembo Elephants, pr	150.00+
Metal Accessories, ea	20.00-40.00

CHARACTER AND PERSONALITY COLLECTIBLES

We buy all types of **Beatles memorabilia but specialize in toy or 3-D type**. We are basically interested in original '60s items. There are many reproductions out there, so give us a call if you have any questions on any item. We aren't really interested in records or paper items unless they are out of the ordinary. **Yellow Submarine items from 1968** are of special interest, so please give us a call or drop a line. All prices below are for excellent to near-mint items, and we are seldom interested in good or lower quality items unless rare. Remember these are just a *few* examples.

BOJO
P.O. Box 1403
Cranberry Twp., PA 16066
412-776-0621

Beatles	We Pay
Apron, white paper w/black & white pictures	**125.00**
Ball, black rubber w/white photo	**350.00**
Banjo, complete only	**500.00+**
Binder, vinyl, various colors	**80.00**
Bongos, by Mastro	**600.00+**
Bubble Bath, Paul or Ringo (condition is important), w/original box	**150.00**
Clutch Purses, various styles, ea	**120.00+**
Colorforms, complete only	**300.00+**
Concert Ticket or Ticket Stubs, if complete w/photo & name (other than Suffolk Downs)	**40.00+**
Corkstopper, ea	**100.00**
Disk-Go-Case, plastic 45rpm record carrier, many colors, ea	**80.00+**
Doll, Remco, Ringo or Paul, w/instrument & life-like hair, 4", ea	**30.00+**
Doll, Remco, George or John, ea	**55.00+**
Dolls, Remco, set of 4	**210.00**
Doll, blow-up style, set of 4 (must hold air well)	**70.00**
Doll, bobbin' head, set of 4, mint condition	**250.00**
Doll, bobbin' head, set of 4, mint condition in original box	**450.00**
Drinking Glasses, many styles, ea	**50.00+**
Drum, by Mastro (hardest to find)	**600.00**
Drum, other manufacturers	**Wanted**
Guitars, many styles, ea	**250.00+**
Hair Bow, on sealed original card	**200.00+**
Hair Spray	**500.00+**
Halloween Costume, mint in box	**300.00**
Halloween Costume, mint, missing box	**130.00**
Handbags, different styles & sizes available, ea	**180.00+**
Lamps, wall or table styles, ea	**300.00+**
Lunch Boxes, metal or vinyl, prices vary widely, mint condition	**230.00+**
Models, plastic, sealed in original box	**150.00+**
Paint by Number Kit, 4 portraits, unused	**400.00+**
Pencil Case, various styles & colors	**80.00+**
Pennants, felt, many styles & colors (many fakes)	**25.00+**
Pillows, any of 3 different styles, w/tag, ea	**90.00+**
Puzzles, ea	**70.00+**
Record Player, mint condition	**1,000.00**
School Bag	**450.00**
Tennis Shoes, unused w/paper insert, mint in box	**350.00**
Thermos, for lunch box	**100.00**
Wallets, various styles & colors, complete	**60.00**

We are collectors of **Beatles memorabilia** from the early 1960s and 1970s. Vast amounts of items featuring the Beatles' name and likenesses such as instruments, dolls, puzzles, lunch boxes, and games were produced during this time. The movie, *Yellow Submarine*, also produced its own line of varied merchandise. Although we are interested in picture sleeves for 45rpm records, we do not need any LP albums. And, please, no reproductions wanted.

Michael and Deborah Summers
3258 Harrison
Paducah, KY 42001
502-443-9359

As a collector of **TV show collectibles and Baby Boomer-era items (1948-1972)**, I am interested in endless numbers of items and toys produced as promotions for TV shows. I am looking for children's lunch boxes and thermoses, Beatles and Elvis items, rock 'n' roll memorabilia, Super Hero and other character dolls, cartoon character items, robots and space toys, cloth items (western motif and character related), cap guns and sets, original boxes (even if empty), and much more. Below is a listing of some of the items I am searching for and the prices I am willing to pay for items in excellent condition. Mint in box items would be higher. Please keep in mind that this is only a small sampling of items; any toys, personality related, advertising, or TV show-related items will be considered for purchase or trade. Please send photos if possible and an SASE for a reply. I would like an opportunity to purchase your items. Thank you.

Terri's Toys & Nostalgia
Terri Ivers
1104 Shirlee Ave.
Ponca City, OK 74601
405-762-8697 or 405-762-5174

Beatles	**We Pay**
Airflite Bag, vinyl	**200.00**
Alarm Clock	**100.00**
Brunch Bag or Kaboodle Kit, ea	**250.00**
Drinking Glass	**25.00**
Drums	**200.00**
Guitar	**200.00**
Hat	**25.00**
Lamp	**100.00**
Record Player	**500.00**
Scrapbook	**100.00**
Shoes	**50.00**
Thermos	**65.00**

Elvis Presley Enterprises Items	We Pay
Decanter	**20.00+**
Dolls, ea	**20.00-300.00**
Guitar	**300.00**
Overnight Case	**125.00**
Pillow	**45.00**
Record Player	**300.00**
Scarf	**35.00**
Scrapbook	**100.00**
Any Other Items	**20.00-50.00+**

Other Wants	We Pay
Cap Guns or Gun & Holster Sets, from TV westerns or detective shows	**up to 150.00**
Hopalong Cassidy Items, w/Hoppy name	**50.00+**
Kiss or Monkees Items (no records)	**10.00+**
Playsets (Flintstones, Blue & Gray, etc)	**40.00+**
Figures & Horses marked Hartland or Breyer	**20.00+**
Advertising Items & Signs	**20.00+**
Promotional Vehicles, plastic or plastic w/metal, 8" to 10"	**30.00+**

We buy all toys depicting **the Kiss rock group** in full-painted faces and costumes. We stay away from most paper and records but may be interested in tour programs or picture discs. Most of the items we are looking for were licensed by Aucoin and are from the 1977 to 1980 period. We are only interested in excellent or better condition items as they are not that old and are not that hard to find in this condition. All prices below are given for excellent to mint condition only. Please call if you have any questions. Thank you.

Bob Gottuso
BOJO
P.O. Box 1403
Cranberry Twp., PA 16066
412-776-0621

Kiss	We Pay
Costume Jewelry	**2.00-18.00**
Backpack, mint condition	**40.00**
Backpack, sealed in original package	**65.00**
Bedspread, sealed in original package	**80.00**
Colorforms, complete	**40.00**
Halloween Costume, w/original box, ea	**30.00**

Cup, 7-11, by Majik Market, ea....**10.00**
Cup, Megaphone-Scream Machine....**35.00**
Curtains, sealed in original package....**80.00**
Doll, Paul or Gene, complete clothing, ea....**45.00**
Doll, Paul or Gene, mint condition in original box, ea....**80.00**
Doll, Ace or Peter, complete clothing, ea....**55.00**
Doll, Ace or Peter, mint condition in original box, ea....**95.00**
Game, On Tour, complete....**30.00**
Guitar, plastic....**50.00**
Guitar, in original package....**100.00**
Halloween Make-Up Kit, Kiss Your Face, sealed in package....**60.00**
Jacket, paper w/flames....**55.00**
Lunch Box w/Thermos....**60.00**
Microphone, in original box....**50.00**
Model, Kiss Van, 100% complete in opened box....**40.00**
Model, Kiss Van, sealed in original box....**60.00**
Notebook, various photos on cover, ea....**15.00**
Pencils, set of 4, sealed in package....**16.00**
Pencil, any group member, sealed on card, ea....**20.00**
Poster Art, sealed in package....**40.00**
Puzzles, group photo, mint & sealed in package, ea....**20.00**
Puzzles, group photo, 100% complete, opened package, ea....**10.00**
Puzzles, any group member photo, mint & sealed in package, ea....**35.00**
Puzzles, any group member photo, 100% complete, opened package, ea .**20.00**
Radio, mint in original box....**60.00**
Radio, mint, missing box....**40.00**
Record Player, mint in box....**180.00**
Record Player, mint, missing box....**100.00**
Remote-Control Van, mint in box....**100.00**
Remote-Control Van, mint, missing box....**50.00**
Rub 'n' Play Set, unused....**40.00**
Sleeping Bag, mint in original package....**100.00**
Sleeping Bag, mint, missing package....**50.00**
View-Master Reel Set, w/booklet....**20.00**
View-Master Double-View on Card, ea....**30.00**
Wastebasket....**60.00**

As a boy I was caught up in the **Davy Crockett** craze of 1955 and 1956. Now I collect the memorabilia of my boyhood hero. Disney copyrighted items with Fess Parker as Davy are my preference. As there is no definitive reference book about Davy Crockett collectibles, there are probably many more items I need than those listed. Please submit all offers, and I promise to answer all letters.

As an advanced collector, condition has become a top priority. Photos and detailed descriptions would really be appreciated. Prices listed are my offers for a near-mint example with the original packaging. Catalogs with strong Davy Crockett reference are also desired. I would enjoy correspondence from fellow collectors. I have hundreds of items to trade. I look forward to hearing from you.

Joey Pinocchio
457 Barretta St.
Sonora, CA 95370
209-533-8873

Davy Crockett	We Pay
Activity Kit, Pixie Dust Set, Glitter Products	100.00
Activity Kit, Pencil Craft Painting Set, Hassenfield #3707	100.00
Activity Paint Set, Marx #3534, #3539 or #3544, ea	400.00
Bow & Arrow Set, Withington #303, #310 or #324, ea	150.00
Canteen & Powder Horn Set, Daisy #2126	100.00
Construction Set, Alamo, Practicole #DC200, #DC300 or #DC500, ea	150.00
Construction Set, Frontierland, Halsam	150.00
Curtains, Drapes or Bedspread, Covington, ea	100.00
Chaise Lounge, Hettrick #5693	250.00
Drinking Glass, Canadian, any of 8, ea	25.00
Game, Indian Scouting Game, Whitman #4654 198	75.00
Game, Electric Quiz, Jacmar	100.00
Game, Adventures, Gardner Games #G226	100.00
Gum Card Display Box, Topps	300.00
Gum Card Wrapper, Topps	50.00
Frontier Game Hunt, Daisy #905	200.00
Frontier Rifle Outfit, Daisy #943	150.00
Smoke Rifle Outfit, Daisy #968	150.00
Play Suit, Ben Cooper #575	100.00
Hunter Outfit, LM Eddy #407	200.00
Thermos, Liberty	100.00
Lunch Pail, Aladdin (Canadian)	200.00
Magic Slate, Strathmore	50.00
Marionette, Peter Puppet Playthings #385, box only	100.00
Shoes, Boots or Moccasins, Trimfoot	150.00
Soap, Cussons (English)	100.00
Tent, Hettrick #181	150.00
Theatre Standee, Buena Vista	200.00
Table & Chairs, Hettrick #5942	350.00
Toy Box, Hettrick #5764	200.00
Tricycle, Hettrick #5685	300.00
Toy, Ge-Tar, Mattel #527	150.00

Character and Personality Collectibles

I am always interested in purchasing good quality ***Lone Ranger*** items that I do not already have in my collection. I would like to have early items from the late 1930s through the early 1950s, but sometimes a brand-new item is needed for my collection. I do not care if the item is a newspaper article about some Lone Ranger/Tonto facts or a premium from some cereal company. I am after puzzles, pin-backs, toy guns, watches, etc., of our hero.

The Silver Bullet
Terry V. Klepey
P.O. Box 553
Forks, WA 98331
360-327-3726

The Lone Ranger	**We Pay**
Book, *The Lone Ranger Rides*, Putnam Publishing	**100.00**
Cereal Box, any company (Kix, Cheerios, Wheaties)	**125.00**
Cereal Box Back, Cheerios, Frontier Town #2	**35.00**
Doll, Lone Ranger or Tonto, early, 1938	**Call or Write**
Gum Cards, 1948, #28 through #48	**20.00**
Gum Cards, ca 1939, lg	**100.00**
Newspapers, early	**25.00**
Pulp Magazines, 1938-1938, ea	**100.00**
Premium, charm bracelet, 1938	**200.00**
Premiums, Lone Ranger Bread, paper, cards, letters, envelopes, ea	**25.00**
Premium, ring, Lone Ranger Ice Cream Cone	**150.00**
Pocket Watch, 1940	**150.00**
Lone Ranger Ice Cream Cone Mold or Box	**Call or Write**

This long-time **Neil Diamond** fan has recently received several collectible items and would like to add to her collection. I would like to purchase concert books, photographs, 33⅓rpm or 45rpm records, tapes, fan club newsletters or materials, record store promotionals — all items will be considered. I would especially like concert items from Atlanta shows, December 1978. Send description of item(s) and asking price.

Karen Geary
5178 US Hwy. 60 W
Paducah, KY 42001

I am buying **Disney children's china dishes, planters, cookie jars, salt and pepper shakers, etc.**. Especially wanted are items listed below.

Calvin L. Hackeman
8865 Olde Mill Run
Manassas, VA 22110
703-368-6982

Disney Ceramics **We Pay**

Cookie Jars, early non-turnabout, Disney characters, ea..............**45.00-100.00+**
Planter, Dumbo ....**25.00+**
Planter, frog character..**35.00+**
Salt & Pepper Shakers, unusual, pr...**10.00-25.00+**
Children's China, sets or individual pieces, Mickey/Minnie, Three Little Pigs, or Snow White & 7 Dwarfs...**Call or Write**

Classic Endeavors is a secondary market brokerage service. Dee Brandt, the owner, also publishes a secondary market, independent newsletter, *Animation Fascination*, which **specializes in the Walt Disney Classics Collection and Disneyana Conventions**.

Although Classic Endeavors does not buy outright, we do accept items on consignment and will list them in our bimonthly newsletter. We also keep a 'Wish List' and are able to often match up buyer and seller. Our fee is 10% of the total sale.

Some specific items wanted are Field Mouse poster, WDCC champagne glass #1 and #2, and Walt Disney Classics Collection videos no longer available to the public such as Crocodile with Clef, Delivery Boy, and Symphony Hour. Videos must be in original wrappings and sleeves. Many items wanted were found only at gift shows and are limited editions.

Animation Fascination/Classic Endeavors
424 Apollo Dr.
Joliet, IL 60435

Disney **We Pay**

Disney Charm, Lucky the Dalmation, sterling silver.............................**250.00+**
Disney Charm, Mrs. Potts & Chipp, sterling silver.................................**200.00+**
Disney Video, Walt Disney Classics Collection, Crocodile w/Clef, Delivery Boy, or Symphony Hour...**35.00+**

My interest in **Smokey Bear** items came from my Dad who worked for the US Forestry for many years. I am interested in Smokey toys, paper goods, or advertising items produced from 1950 to 1970. Prices will depend on the condition of the items. A photograph or complete description would be very helpful along with your price.

B.J. Summers
233 Darnell Rd.
Benton, KY 42025

I buy **all Walton memorabilia**: games, paper dolls, lunch boxes, etc. Also wanted are books by Earl Hamner Jr., TV and movie scripts, posters, etc.

Trudy Menzzentto
2100 Catoe Ct.
Randleman, NC 27317
910-674-0263

The Waltons	**We Pay**
Book	**10.00**
Game	**8.00**
Lunch Box	**10.00**
Magazine, McCall's, Dec 1973	**10.00**
Paper Dolls	**8.00**
Poster	**10.00**
Record	**5.00**
Script	**25.00**

The classic comedy of **The Three Stooges** (Moe, Larry, Curly, and Shep) has entertained generations. As the Midwest's number one Stooge collector and owner of 'Soitenly Stooges' mail-order catalog, I am looking for unique Stooge toys, autographs, photos, original movie posters, comics, and promotional giveaways from the 1920s through the 1970s.

Soitenly Stooges Inc.
P.O. Box 72
Skokie, IL 60076
708-432-9270

The Three Stooges	**We Pay**
Animation Cel	**75.00+**
Autograph	**50.00+**

Bank, ceramic....................100.00+
Book, *Stroke of Luck*....................25.00+
Cancelled Check....................50.00+
Gum Card Set, Fleer, 1959....................250.00+
Hand Puppet Set....................100.00+
Lobby Card, original....................10.00+
Movie Poster, original....................25.00+
Wine Bottle, figural Stooge....................50.00+

I collect **Winnie the Pooh items**. No item too big or small — I collect it all. I am particularly interested in books, porcelains, tins, toys, dishes, and fast-food collectibles. Please send information and asking price.

Tiffany Lininger
2205 2nd Ave. W
Seattle, WA 98119

CHARGE CARDS

Seeking **all old charge-related cards**, airlines credit cards, hotel, restaurant, oil company, bank, specialty store, and gambling credit cards. Almost any card from before 1970 made of paper, plastic, metal, celluloid or fiber is wanted. Credit account cards are not new; some go back to the early 1800s and maybe earlier. I will purchase all undamaged non-plastic charge cards or letters of credit issued before 1960 and will pay all shipping charges on accepted purchases. Also looking for **telephone cards from before 1980**. All cards must be original and unaltered. For other interests see Black Americana and Railroadiana in this book.

Walt Thompson
P.O. Box 2541-W
Yakima, WA 98907-2541

We Pay

American Express, test card, pre-1958....................800.00+
American Express, cardboard, 1958....................100.00+
American Express, before 1971....................15.00+
Any Airline, before 1970....................4.00+
Any Entertainment Credit Card, before 1960....................25.00+
Any Business Credit Card, paper, before 1950....................5.00+

Charge Cards

Diners' Club Credit Booklet, before 1960 .... **20.00+**
Diners' Club Card, before 1950 .... **1,000.00+**
Hotel Credit Card, paper, before 1900 .... **100.00+**
Hotel Credit Card, before 1960 .... **3.00**
Metal Charge Card, before 1920 .... **24.00+**
Metal Charge Plate or Token, ea .... **3.00+**
Oil Company Credit Card, before 1920 .... **30.00+**
Oil Company Credit Card, paper, before 1930 .... **10.00+**
Oil Company Credit Card, plastic, before 1980 .... **2.00+**
Playboy Card, metal .... **5.00+**
Playboy Club Key, metal w/bunny logo .... **8.00+**
Retail Merchant Credit Card, before 1970 .... **2.50+**

CHATELAINS

Chatelains were made in various shapes and sizes and from an assortment of metals. The various items which are generally found on chatelaines are powder compacts, lipstick holders, coin receivers, perfume containers, writing slates and flat pencils; and occasionally needle case holders and similar sewing items. The items were suspended on chains and held together by a hook or clasp that could be attached at the waist. These were quite popular during Victorian times.

I am interested in **chatelains with original matching pieces**. There usually will be at least three pieces on a chatelaine, and often as many as six. They should be in reasonably nice condition. No reproductions wanted, please.

Elizabeth Baer
P.O. Box 266
Perry, IA 50220

We Pay

Chatelaines, non-precious metal .... **100.00+**
Chatelaines, sterling .... **250.00+**
Chatelaines, gold .... **500.00+**

CHINA AND PORCELAIN

I am looking for **Blue Willow pieces in all colors, especially pink**. Also looking for **other dishes with pictures** and will consider anything. Other interests include **ceramic teapots, glass and metal Coca-Cola items (new or old), metal toys, children's furniture, kitchen salesman's samples and especially a special oak-finished Hoosier cabinet**. Please send SASE and your asking price for a reply. Also photographs are helpful.

T. Rodrick
R.R. #2, Box 163
Sumner, IL 62466

I am interested in items from the following companies and patterns. **I would pay 90% of book price and postage. No chips or cracks please.**

Crooksville China Co:
Trellis

Harker:
Ruffled Tulip
Red Apple
Rose Spray
English Countryside
Countryside
Ivy Vine

Hall:
Basket
Bittersweet
Teapots, solid colors w/gold trim

Paden City:
Morning Glory

Universal
Iris

Kathy Chitty
14 Union St. S
Concord, NC 28025
704-786-4296

China and Porcelain

I buy **English china with an all-over floral decoration** — like fine-patterned cloth or wallpaper. Some of the companies that made this are:

Aynsley	Crown Ducal
James Kent	Royal Tudor
Royal Winton	Lord Nelson
Shelley	Other makers wanted

Bruce E. Thulin
P.O. Box 121
Ellsworth, ME 04605
207-667-5225

	We Pay
Tea Set, service for 4 or 6	**250.00-350.00+**
Luncheon Set, service for 4 or 6	**200.00-300.00+**
Serving Bowl	**35.00-75.00+**
Butter Dish, w/lid	**50.00-80.00+**

I buy **English china by T.G. Green and others**. It is light blue and white stripe, dark blue and white stripe, or white dots on blue background. Dinnerware pieces were made as well as accessory items such as canister sets, rolling pins, spice jars, etc. Please, send photos; mint-conditioned items only. We will pay postage.

Deborah and James Golden
3182 Twin Pine Rd.
Grayling, MI 49738
517-348-2610

	We Pay
Canister, w/content's name in black letters	**25.00-50.00**
Canister, plain	**20.00-40.00**
Cup & Saucer Set	**20.00**
Mug w/Saucer	**20.00**
Plate, dinner	**15.00**
Plate, 8"	**10.00**
Rolling Pin	**50.00**
Spice Jar	**15.00**

We buy **Porcellier Mfg. Co. products and literature**. Some of the items that Porcellier manufactured were coffeepots, teapots, sugar and creamer sets, canister sets, milk and syrup pitchers, and ceramic appliances for the kitchen (percolators, electric urns, toasters, waffle irons, etc.). The company also made light fixtures. Most of their wares were marked 'Porcellier' in script. We are looking for items in excellent to mint condition. We pay more for items in original boxes. Please call or write with description of items. Photograph may be required. We will reimburse actual UPS and insurance charges. This is only a partial list. Again, prices depend on pattern and condition. Some items may be substantially higher.

Susan Grindberg
6330 Doffing Ave. E
Inver Grove Hts., MN 55076
612-450-6770

	We Pay
Canister, ea	**30.00+**
Coffepot or Teapot	**20.00+**
Creamer	**8.00**
Light Fixtures, ea	**10.00+**
Percolator, electric	**40.00+**
Pitcher	**25.00+**
Sales Literature	**8.00+**
Sandwich Grill	**75.00+**
Sugar Bowl	**8.00+**
Toaster	**300.00+**
Waffle Iron	**75.00+**
Urn, electric	**45.00+**
1939 New York World's Fair Piece	**100.00+**

I am looking to buy **objects and dinnerware pieces with violets on them**. I prefer fine china such as Limoges, Bavarian, German, Austrian, Nippon, etc. I like hand-painted pieces, but others will do if they are good quality. I only want pieces in perfect condition. Some examples of pieces I would like and prices I'll pay are as follows. Please price, describe, and enclose SASE for reply.

Ellen R. Rubell
48 Kingsland Ave.
Wallingford, CT 06492
203-284-9090 or FAX 203-265-0069

	We Pay
Cup & Saucer Set	**7.00+**

China and Porcelain

Butter Pat .... **7.00+**
Hatpin Holder .... **20.00+**
Plate .... **5.00+**
Pin Tray .... **12.00+**
Toothpick Holder **10.00**
Vase, sm .... **10.00+**

We are interested in purchasing **sets and partial sets of fine china** manufactured by the following companies:

Lenox
Oxford
Royal Copenhagen
Shelley
Wedgewood
Minton
Picard
Rosenthal/Continental
Spode
Others considered

All china must be in like-new condition — free from cracks, chips, crazing or wear on patterns or trim.

Wanda Romine
637 Nancy Dr.
St. Charles, MO 63301-4863

Wanted: **restaurant ware** — my own term — the heavy-bodied, vitrified table/dinnerware generally used in restaurants, cafeterias, hotels, railroad dinning cars, hospitals, schools, air and ship lines from the 1800s to the 1950s. A myriad of designs and colors were used from very plain to very ornate. I am *most interested* in Art Deco or Art Nouveau designs, transportation themes, military, and items naming specific locations. Blue on white items are a plus. Usually the older the item the better; no cracked pieces are wanted but small chips will be considered. Most pieces were marked on the bottom by manufacturer. Manufacturers include (but are not limited to): Shenango, Tepco, Syracuse, Grindley, Johnson Bros., Buffalo, McNichol, Jackson, Hall, and K.T. & K (Knowles, Taylor & Knowles). Send description of pieces, including any damage or stains. Photos are helpful. Sample prices paid are below. Other interests include **Flow Blue, stamps, hand-tinted photos, and postcards**.

Gary R. Smith
517 Laurel Ave.
Modesto, CA 95351

	We Pay
Creamer, red & green striped on white, 4" tall by 3" wide	**up to 3.00**
Demitasse Cup & Saucer Set, anchor & blue stripe on white	**up to 4.00**
Gravy Boat, multicolored intricate design/trim, any color	**up to 2.00**
Plate, green stripe on white, w/divided sections	**up to 1.00**
Plate, Union Pacific Railroad, green on white	**up to 25.00**
Plate, The Shadows, blue on white w/silhouette	**up to 5.00**
Vegetable Server, Sphinx design, oval, 16x10"	**up to 30.00**

CHRISTMAS AND OTHER HOLIDAYS

We buy select old Christmas lights, ornaments, and decorations to use and add to our collection. We especially like the **pre-1920 ornaments and Christmas decorations made in Germany**. Quality, condition, and rarity are important to us. We want lights to work but remember that many of the old ones are 15-volt, so it is not wise to plug them into 110. Use a 15-volt battery to test them. Please describe fully, and photographs are very helpful. What do you have?

J.W. 'Bill' and Treva Courter
3935 Kelley Rd.
Kevil, KY 42053
Phone or FAX 502-488-2116

	We Pay
Belsnickle	**100.00+**
Bubble Lights, Royal, Paramount, Noma, Glolite, Etc	**3.00-5.00**
Bubble Lights, these 'pour' slowly, usually w/clip	**10.00-25.00**
Bulb, Santa, Japan, lg	**50.00+**
Doll, Father Christmas	**25.00-500.00**
Lamp, Santa Claus, sm, complete	**500.00+**
Light Cover, Dresden (condition very important!)	**35.00-100.00**
Lights, Matchless Wonder-Star, sm, single row	**12.00-30.00**
Lights, Matchless Wonder-Star, lg, double row	**35.00-85.00**
Ornaments, pre-1940 glass such as Noah's Ark, Indian, doll head, baby in cradle, ea	**75.00+**
Postcard, hold-to-light, die-cut Santa	**100.00+**
Postcard, hold-to-light, die-cut angels	**15.00-25.00**
Postcard, transparency w/color or black & white Santas, ea	**20.00+**

Christmas and Other Holidays

We are actively seeking **older Christmas items from the 1880s through the 1940s**. If you have one item or a collection of older Christmas to sell, please contact us. We love it all! Condition, size, color, and country of origin are important to note because prices paid vary greatly. Generally, pieces marked Germany bring higher prices than those marked Japan. Due to the vast amount of Christmas produced over the years, it is most helpful if you include a photo and description of items you are selling. Please call us any time you prefer.

We are also buying **other older holiday-related collectibles produced before 1945**. If you have one item to sell or a collection, we would like to hear from you. Again, prices vary greatly on holiday collectibles and are determined by condition, size, country of origin, and scarcity. Therefore, a scarce item in poor condition may bring $20 while the same item in mint condition could bring $200. The following prices listed may not accurately reflect the actual price we may pay for a specific item you are selling. When writing about any of your items, it is best if you send a photo along with a complete description. If you wish to call and we are not available, please leave a message. We return all calls.

The Murphy's
216 Blackhawk Rd.
Riverside, IL 60546
708-442-6846

Christmas	**We Pay**
Ornament, figural glass	**35.00+**
Ornament, wire-wrapped figural	**30.00+**
Ornament, Italian glass	**22.00+**
Ornament, Dresden paper	**45.00+**
Bubble Lights	**4.00+**
Matchless Star Wonder Lights	**22.00+**
Feather Tree, marked Germany	**95.00+**
Tree Stand, revolving & musical, antique only	**250.00+**
Santa Lantern	**25.00+**
Santa-Related Items, ea	**35.00+**
Clock-Work Santa, w/reindeer	**500.00+**
Candle Holder	**5.00+**
Candle Clip	**4.00+**
Light Sets, ea	**10.00+**

Other Holiday Items	**We Pay**
Halloween Candy Container, papier-mache	**20.00+**
Black Cat Collectibles, ea	**5.00+**
Jack-O'-Lantern	**10.00+**
Thanksgiving Turkey, papier-mache	**20.00+**
4th of July Items, ea	**5.00+**

Holiday Postcard .... 2.00+
Holiday Items, lithographed paper, ea .... 20.00+
Holiday-Related Paper Goods, ea .... 6.00+
St. Patrick's Day Leprechans, ea .... 15.00+
Valentines, ea .... 2.00+

We want to buy all types of **old Christmas items from the 1880s through the 1950s**! We buy figural Christmas tree light bulbs, old German figural glass ornaments, German feather trees, old Santas, Belsnickles, cotton batting ornaments, early Santa Claus storybooks, old light sets in original boxes, bubble light trees, bubble lights, German nativity sets, German stick-leg animals, celluloid figures and toys, lithographed scrap ornaments, papier-mache items and candy containers, hard plastic Santas and toys from the 1940s and 1950s, all types of lighted decorations, and any other unusual old Christmas items. Sample prices are below. We answer *all* letters. Please see our listing under Halloween in this book.

Bob and Diane Kubicki
R.R. #1
W Milton, OH 45383
513-698-3650

We Pay

Light Bulb, standing Indian .... 250.00+
Light Bulb, green Father Christmas .... 100.00+
Light Bulb, milk glass army tank .... 175.00+
Light Bulb, Uncle Sam .... 300.00+
Ornament, glass Indian's head, German, old .... 125.00+
Ornament, figural cotton girl w/scrap face .... 75.00+
Ornament, spun cotton fruit, 3" .... 15.00+
Feather Tree, green, German, 6-ft .... 300.00+
Father Christmas Clockworks Nodder .... 1,500.00+
Belsnickle, German, 8" 250.00-450.00
Santa Claus Storybook, 1905 .... 20.00+
Boxed Light Set, early 1920s .... 10.00+
Wooden Box, for early Christmas light set .... 100.00+
Porcelain Socket Light String 30.00
German Nativity Set 35.00-75.00
Bubble Light Tree, green, 18-socket .... 100.00+
Plastic Bubble Light Santa 15.00
German Santa, w/rabbit fur beard, 8" .... 200.00+
Glass Santa-on-Chimney Lamp, black glass base .... 500.00+

Christmas and Other Holidays

Holiday decorations once sold in five-and-ten-cent stores were elegant in their simplicity in comparison with today's mass-market products advertised on television. Other holiday memories of my childhood prompt me to recall items made of paper, papier-mache, and glass that bring back smiles such as a Halloween Jack-o'-lantern or a Coney Island tattoo (see also Coney Island in this book).

My main collecting interests are **Christmas, Halloween, and Easter memorabilia**. Listed here is only a partial listing of items wanted. Jack-o'-lanterns with original tissue faces are worth more (as are all holiday items worth more) if marked Germany.

Rick Scott
49 Mersereau Ave.
Staten Island, NY 10303
718-981-2514

	We Pay
Candy Container, papier-mache rabbit	**10.00+**
Candy Container, papier-mache Santa	**15.00**
Christmas Tree, cellophane or paper, fits over bulb, sm	**15.00+**
Easter Egg, papier-mache	**7.00+**
Easter Egg, w/scene viewing spring, flowers, etc., hard plastic	**15.00+**
Egg Holder, papier-mache rabbit	**10.00+**
Jack-O'-Lantern, papier-mache cat, skull, or witch face, ea	**30.00+**
Jack-O'-Lantern, papier-mache pumpkin face	**15.00+**

I want to buy **glow-in-the-dark plastic animal ornaments from the 1950s**. A plastic hook is attached for hanging on the tree. The series includes a lion, a penguin, an elephant, a donkey, a toucan, and several others. **I will pay up to $10.00** each for these. A photo is appreciated.

Diane Rapson Gabil
1031 N Jones
Essexville, MI 48732

CIGARETTE LIGHTERS

We buy **American- and European-made cigar and cigarette lighters**. Of particular interest to us are lighters with the word(s) cigar, lamp, or match on them; those that have a metal match stick; or those that incorporate something else (i.e., a watch, cane, whistle, pen, pencil, compact, or camera). Also wanted are lighters with hard glass enamel, geometrically-painted lighters, and figurals. We will also purchase display cases, sample cases and other sales-related items. We *do not* buy Japanese lighters or those that use butane gas. We will gladly pay all actual shipping and insurance costs.

Terry Cairo
c/o Lighters
P.O. Box 1054
Addison, IL 60101
708-543-9120

	We Pay
Abdulla	25.00+
Carlton	20.00+
Clark	25.00+
Douglas	15.00+
Dunhill	25.00+
Elgin Otis	30.00+
Eterna	100.00+
Evans Pocket	10.00+
Evans Fruit & Egg	30.00+
Hermes	100.00+
Kum-A-Part	15.00+
Lancel	20.00+
Lincoln	25.00+
Marathon	25.00+
Napier	25.00+
Pall Mall	100.00+
Ritepoint, w/advertising	5.00+
Ronson Pocket	15.00+
Ronson Table (no silver-plated wanted)	45.00+
Scripto, w/advertising	5.00+
Tiffany	100.00+
Zippo Pocket	15.00+
Zippo Table	30.00+
Sterling Silver	50.00+
9K Solid Gold	150.00+
14K Solid Gold	250.00+
18K Solid Gold	400.00+
Solid Platinum	550.00+

I am an avid collector of **Zippo cigarette lighters and case knives**. Below is a list of items I need and the prices I will pay. I also will pay a finder's fee for locating these items. Please call or write with your information or questions.

Clayton V. Vecellio
Box 298
Lewis Run, PA 16738
814-368-5294

Zippo Lighter	**We Pay**
1932, plain	**500.00+**
1933, w/diagonal lines	**700.00+**
1944, black crackle	**20.00+**
1979, w/elephant	**75.00+**
1979, w/donkey	**75.00+**
1969, moon landing	**75.00+**
1970, Bush-Gorbachav	**80.00+**
1970, Regan-Gorbachav	**80.00+**
1971, w/Donald Duck	**75.00+**
1972, w/Mickey Mouse	**100.00+**

CLOCKS

We **buy, sell, repair, and restore antique and collectible hanging, mantel, kitchen, and floor clocks in any condition**. We buy **American and foreign clocks with any kind of case**. We prefer pre-1920s clocks. We *don't buy* or repair cuckoo, electric-cord, quartz, or anniversary clocks. We reimburse actual UPS and insurance charges.

Steve G. Gabany, Ph.D., The Clock Doctor
585 Woodbine
Terre Haute, IN 47803-1759

	We Pay
Ansonia Regulator A	**120.00+**
French, woman w/tambourine	**130.00+**
Gustav Becker, walnut, wall type	**185.00+**
Hamburg-American Plate Clock	**70.00+**
Jerome, split-top mantel	**75.00+**
Ingram Corona, black wood, round top	**100.00+**
Junghans Mantel, Westminster chimes	**90.00+**
Seth Thomas Office #3	**125.00+**
New Haven Miniature Banjo	**65.00+**
SC Spring Triple-Decker	**300.00+**
Seth Thomas, figural	**275.00+**
Seth Thomas, round top w/Westminster chimes	**200.00+**

Seth Thomas Behive Inlaid ....125.00+
Seth Thomas White Adamantine ....125.00+
Seth Thomas Yale Kitchen ....150.00+
Vienna Regulator, 2 weights 275.00
Waterbury, hanging ....125.00+
Waterbury Short-Drop Calendar ....200.00+
Waterbury Duluth, black wood, flat top ....50.00+
Welch & Osborne Cameo A ....100.00+

I collect and will purchase the following **novelty clocks by Lux, Keebler, Westclox, Columbia Time, Mi-Ken, and small German wall pendulette clocks**. Also I'm interested in **Oswald moving-eye clocks**. Prices shown are for clocks in excellent condition. Only original clocks are wanted, *no reproductions, bobbing or swinging bird models.*

Also purchasing pressed wood items by Syrocowood, Ornawood, Durawood, etc. Price depends on item and condition.

Carole Kaifer
P.O. Box 232
Bethania, NC 27010
910-924-9672

We Pay

Lux, Sally Rand 325.00-350.00
Lux, nursery rhyme character 400.00-500.00
Lux, clown w/tie 300.00-400.00
Keebler, Fort Dearborn 300.00-325.00
Columbia Time, Woody Woodpecker 300.00-350.00
Mi-Ken (Japan), wood 20.00-25.00
Mi-Ken (Japan), plastic 15.00-20.00
German, wood 25.00-35.00
German, porcelain 30.00-35.00
Oswald, moving eye ....150.00+

CLOTHING AND ACCESSORIES

I buy old **vintage clothing from the Victorian era to the 1940s as well as Art Deco or other old jewelry**. Clothing must be in excellent condition (no holes). Other wants include **old paper dolls and cranberry glass** (no new Fenton wanted). Send SASE for reply.

Rhonda Hasse
566 Oak Terrace Dr.
Farmington, MO 63640

	We Pay
Camisole, Victorian	35.00-40.00
Child's Dress, Victorian	30.00-60.00
Lady's Dress, Victorian	50.00-125.00
Petticoat	20.00-35.00
Shoes, high top, pr	35.00-50.00
Other Items	Write

COCA-COLA

We are collectors interested in purchasing **older advertising memorabilia pertaining to the Coca-Cola and Pepsi-Cola Companies**. Areas of interest include cardboard, paper, tin, and porcelain signs; die-cut displays; calendars; clocks; trays; playing cards; toys and trucks; light-ups and neons; games; radios; thermometers; salesman samples and miniatures, etc. We are always looking for rare and unusual items made before 1960. The increased popularity of Coca-Cola and Pepsi collecting has created a large market of reproduction and fantasy items. Beware of these items. If you are not sure of an item's authenticity, don't make a mistake, call us first. Using our many years of collecting experience as a knowledge base we write a monthly column which appears in several antique journals. In this column we answer questions and provide informative articles about soda-pop collectibles. So if you have a question regarding Coca-Cola, Pepsi-Cola, or other soft drink collectibles or are wanting to sell an item (or items), please feel free to contact us. It is helpful to send a clear photo with your letter. If you wish the photo to be returned, please include a self-addressed stamped envelope.

Craig and Donna Sifter
511 Aurora Ave., #117
Naperville, IL 60540

Coca-Cola	We Pay
Calendar, bottle version, 1915	2,000.00+
Calendar, 1927	500.00+
Display, sm cardboard Santa, 1950	100.00+
Festoon, shows bathing beauties, 1940s	500.00+

Playing Cards, w/original box, 1909, ... **1,200.00+**
Radio, cooler, Bakelite, 1950 .... **300.00+**
Salesman's Sample Floor Cooler, 1939 .... **1,500.00+**
Pretzel Bowl, aluminum w/bottles as legs, 1935 .... **125.00+**
Sign, flanged w/bottle & button, Drink Coca-Cola, Ice Cold, 1950s .... **200.00+**
Sign, cardboard, 1937 .... **250.00+**
Sign, fountain dispenser, porcelain, 1950s .... **300.00+**
Sign, self-framed cardboard, girl w/violet background, 1940s .... **350.00+**
Sign, counter top w/light, Pause and Refresh w/waterfall, 1948 .... **350.00+**
Thermometer, Masonite, 1944 .... **175.00+**
Tray, pictures Francis Dee, 1933 .... **250.00+**

Pepsi-Cola **We Pay**

Calendar, 1920 .... **1,200.00+**
Folding Chair, 1950s .... **85.00+**
Toy, hot dog wagon, w/orginal box, 1950s .... **225.00+**
Vending Machine, Vendorlater Model 3D-33, 1950s .... **300.00+**

I am buying Coca-Cola **calendars, trays, and trolley car signs**. Also **English/French-Canadian tin or porcelain signs**. Color photos including price and a brief description is my preferred way of dealing. Listed below are some of the specific items I am looking for and the range of prices I would pay.

I am looking for pre-1940 calendars which are difficult to find in mint condition. Condition is very important when determining the value of a calendar. The value of pre-1940 calendars drops dramatically if the pad or pages are trimmed or missing. I am looking for trays in excellent or better condition, although I will consider pre-1910 trays in any condition. Prices vary depending on year and condition of tray.

The standard size for a trolley car sign (made of flexible cardboard) is 11" by 20½". Trolley car signs are difficult to find in excellent condition, mainly due to the materials used to construct them. There are too many dates to be listed, and depending on the year and condition, prices paid range from $50 to $2,000. I will consider advertising trolley card signs other than Coca-Cola if they are in excellent or better condition. I also want **Pepsi-Cola items and memorabilia**.

Kelly Wilson
P.O. Box 41006
Winnipeg, Manitoba
Canada R3T 5T1
Phone or FAX 204-275-6438

	We Pay
Calendar, pre-1914, ea	**100.00-10,000.00**
Calendar, 1914-1922, ea	**50.00-1,500.00**
Calendar, 1923-1940, ea	**25.00-850.00**
Calendar, 1940-1966, ea	**10.00-125.00**
Serving Tray, pre-1910, ea	**25.00-5,000.00**
Serving Tray, 1910-1925, square, ea	**25.00-1,000.00**
Serving Tray, 1926-1942, square, ea	**25.00-1,000.00**
Tip Tray, pre-1907, round	**25.00-2,000.00**
Tip Tray, 1907-1920, oval, ea	**25.00-400.00**
Trolley Car Signs, flexible cardboard, 11x20½", ea	**50.00-2,000.00**

I am an avid collector of **Coca-Cola glasses**. I will buy any glass that is put out by and/or produced by Coca-Cola. I am willing to buy glasses in sets, pieces of sets, and single glasses. Examples of such glasses include: character, promotional, sporting and sporting events, foreign, American, old, nice or funny looking, and glasses commemorating events such as anniversaries and holidays. I am also looking for drinking glasses with pitchers that go along with them — either as sets or just partial sets. If it says Coca-Cola on the glass, I am willing to buy it. I will not buy any glass that is faded, chipped, cracked, peeling, or scratched. Please send a list of descriptions and prices.

Robert J. Bodendorf
379 Market St.
Rockland, MA 02370

COFFIN PLATES

The most desirable metal coffin plates are those with elaborate designs (e.g., trees, flowers, and other symbols of grief or new life), and personalized writing, especially name and age or date. Small coffin plates that say 'Our Darling' are common, and so are those that say 'At Rest,' 'Mother,' or 'Father.' A rubbing, xerographic copy, or photo would be appreciated. The following are typical prices I will pay for metal coffin plates in reasonable condition (not rusted; but a little tarnish is okay).

Adrienne Esco
4448 Ironwood Ave.
Seal Beach, CA 90740
310-430-6479

	We Pay
Our Darling, 4" to 4½"	**5.00**
At Rest, Mother or Father, w/good border design, ea	**5.00-7.50**
Personalized, w/plain border	**7.50-10.00**
Personalized, w/elaborate border	**10.00-15.00**

COIN-OPERATED MACHINES

Coin-operated machines including **jukeboxes, pinball machines, soda machines (especially Pepsi, Dr. Pepper, 7-Up, and off brands), slot and arcade machines, as well as any advertising signs or related memorabilia relating to these items are wanted**. Other soda advertising and collectibles of any sort relating to anything previously mentioned or anything pertaining to Coca-Cola, Pepsi-Cola, Dr. Pepper, Tiny Grape, Nehi, or still others such as Gunther Beer are wanted. I also collect **Catalin radios**.

Richard O. Gates
P.O. Box 187
Chesterfield, VA 23832
804-748-0382 or 804-794-5146

Wanted: **coin-operated slot machines, trade stimulators, gum machines, music boxes, jukeboxes** or anything you may have that a coin went into to operate. Please see Advertising in this book for other interests.

House of Stuart
P.O. Box 2063
Jensen Beach, FL 34958-2063
407-225-0900

COINS

I am a serious collector and have been for the past forty-two years. I pay top prices for coins and can purchase any amount from $5 to $1 million dollars! My real interest is **silver dollars made from 1794 to 1935**, but I buy every other types of coins too.

Examples listed are buying prices for coins in extra-fine condition. Of course, I pay much more for higher quality and rare dates. I need half cents, large cents, Indian cents, two- and three-cent pieces, half dimes, twenty-cent pieces — call or write.

Jay and Peggy McBride
222 E International Speedway Blvd.
Daytona Beach, FL 32118
904-252-5775 or 904-252-7222

Coin Denomination	We Pay
$20 Gold, 1849-1933, ea	**380.00+**
$10 Gold, 1795-1933, ea	**180.00+**
$5 Gold, 1795-1929, ea	**110.00+**
$4 Gold, 1879-1880, ea	**110.00+**
$3 Gold, 1854-1889, ea	**350.00+**
$2 1/2 Gold, 1796-1929, ea	**110.00+**
$1 Gold, 1849-1889, ea	**110.00+**
Silver Dollar, before 1936, ea	**5.00+**
Silver Half Dollar, before 1965, ea	**1.50+**
Silver Quarter, before 1965, ea	**75¢+**
Silver Dime, before 1965, ea	**30¢+**

Wanted: Rare coins, coin collections, accumulations, hoards, old currency. We buy it all. We also need **anything in gold or silver**: jewelry, sterling flatware, pocket watches, gold wristwatches, old fountain pens, etc.

You may ship insured or bring to our shop for our high cash offer. If not delighted, we will return postpaid. If you would like to discuss your holdings first, just write or call. Sample buying prices for coins in good collectible condition are listed here.

Old Mayfield Coins & Collectibles
Mayfield Shopping Plaza
1102 Paris Rd.
Mayfield, KY 42066

	We Pay
Indian Head Cents	**50¢+**
Buffalo Nickels	**25¢+**
Silver Dollars, prior to 1935	**5.00+**
All Denominations Silver Coins, prior to 1964	**Wanted**

I'm interested in buying your coins. I've been a coin collector/dealer for over fifteen years. If you ship me your coins (insure and package securely), I will send you my offer in the form of a check. If you accept my offer, just cash the check; if you decide not to accept, just return my check and I will return your coins and refund your postage costs. So it will not cost you anything. If you prefer, you can describe what you have including year, mint marks (if any), denomination (i.e., 1¢, 5¢, etc.), and condition. I will do my best to give you a price. Please include a stamp for my reply. Below is a sampling of coins wanted. Others wanted including **odd coins and gold coins**. I am also interested in buying **silver items** such as flatware, thimbles, and candlesticks. See also my listing under Silver in this book.

B - 4 Your Time
Attention: Phil Townsend
15 Tabar Ave.
Lee, MA 01238

	We Pay
5¢, 1943 to 1945, ea	**25¢-10.00**
10¢, pre-1916, ea	**35¢-1,000.00+**
10¢, 1916 to 1964, ea	**30¢-1,000.00+**
25¢, pre-1932, ea	**85¢-1,000.00+**
25¢, 1932 to 1964, ea	**75¢-1,000.00+**
50¢, pre-1947, ea	**1.70-1,000.00+**
50¢, 1948-1964, ea	**1.50-100.00+**
50¢, 1965-1970, ea	**60¢-10.00**
$1, pre-1878, ea	**10.00-1,000.00+**
$1, 1878-1904, ea	**4.85-1,000.00+**
$1, 1921-1935, ea	**4.60-1,000.00+**

COMIC BOOKS

I am interested in buying and selling comic books of all kinds. For a reply call or send a self-addressed stamped envelope.

David Ledford
211 Hilldale Ave Apt. 907
Hardin, KY 42048
502-437-3013

COMPACTS

I am interested in purchasing **compacts and vanities of unusual shapes** for my collection. As a general rule, no rounds, squares, oblongs or ovals other than what are listed below are wanted. All compacts must be in nice condition with no dents, dings, discolorations, and no broken mirrors; compacts should be complete with no missing parts.

Elizabeth Baer
P.O. Box 266
Perry, IA 50220

	We Pay
English Royal Commemoratives, by Stratton, ea	25.00+
Gwenda, ea	15.00+
Stratonoids, ea	20.00
Unusual Shapes, ea	25.00-250.00

Collector seeks **all types of old powder compacts**. Also sought are purses/handbags which include compacts as part of the bag or as an attachment. **Vanity bags, carryalls, and cigarette cases with compacts** included are also wanted. Please send a complete description of the items, including maker's marks and description of any damage (if present). Photos of the items would be greatly appreciated. All offers will be replied.

Jette Bellew
15243 Profit Ave.
Baton Rouge, LA 70817
504-756-4875

I buy compacts in Art Deco styles, enameled metals, novelties, figurals, compacts with gadgetry, and especially compact and purse combinations. **I will pay $200 and up for compact and purse combinations made before 1940**.

Lori Landgrebe
2331 E Main St.
Decatur, IL 62521
271-423-2254

We collect ladies' compacts with cases in the shape of other objects (**figural compacts**). We are also very interested in **compacts and mesh purse combinations. Mesh bag vanities** by Whiting & Davis, Evans, Napier-Bliss, R.&G. Co., and F.&B. Co. are wanted. All compacts by J.M. Fisher with Art Deco designs are wanted. (See Ettinger's *Compacts and Smoking Accessories*, pages 55 and 56.)

Only mint or near-mint pieces will be considered. Highest prices are paid for compacts in mint condition complete with puff and original box. Sometimes the mirror will be discolored from age, but that usually does not detract from the compact's desirability.

Below are some of the figural compacts we are seeking for our collection. There are many other figural compacts and mesh vanities not listed that we would also like to find.

Sherry and Mike Miller
303 Holiday Dr.
Tuscola, IL 61953
217-253-4991

Figural Compacts	**We Pay**
Air Balloon	**125.00-150.00**
Bear, by Schuco	**300.00-375.00**
Beetle	**125.00-150.00**
Camera, by Fillkwik	**45.00-60.00**
Drum, by Charbert	**125.00-150.00**
Fan, by Wadsworth	**45.00-60.00**
Flower Basket, by Zell	**60.00-80.00**
Globe, by Kigu	**225.00-300.00**
Guitar, by Samaral	**125.00-150.00**
Military Cap	**35.00-50.00**
Monkey, by Schuco	**225.00-300.00**
Padlock	**45.00-60.00**
Roulette Wheel	**60.00-80.00**

Vanity Compact Bags	**We Pay**
Whiting & Davis Co	**160.00-450.00**
R&G Co	**300.00-500.00**

Buying **Ladies' compacts** from the early 1890's to the present. All types such as, but not limited to: enamels, compacts, (shaped like suitcases, walnuts, ladybugs, pistols, flower baskets, 8-balls, Charlie McCarthy, monkeys, bears) chatelaines, and cloisonnes. Also interested in purses with compacts, walking sticks with compacts, hatpin compacts, bracelet compacts, and Avon Lincoln penny compacts. I am interested in purchasing compacts that are in mint or near-mint condition. The condition of the mirror is not critical. If you see an unusual compact for my collection, but are uncertain about purchasing it for resale, please put me in touch with the owner. If I buy it, I will pay you a finders fee! Also I buy **old Teddy Bears, pre-1940 dolls, old lace, and old jewelry.**

Sue Murphy
29668 Orinda Road
San Juan Capistrano, CA 92675
(714) 364-4333

CONEY ISLAND

My collecting interests are quite varied with a heavy emphasis on both Coney Island and holiday memorabilia (see Christmas in this book). Such collectibles are becoming things of the past. Growing up in the 1950s in New York, I have always had a fondness for the beautiful bizarreness of Coney Island. It still amazes me that I became a high school English teacher, considering the number of days I cut out of school to visit Steeplechase Park, the beach, and the boardwalk. But Coney Island may soon be a ghost town. The gaudy glamour of Coney's old rides and attractions has been neglected and left to rot; the gaudy glamour has taken on the look of a haunted graveyard. Visitors are now forced to watch for broken glass, daytime and nighttime muggers, and the homeless beggars that have replaced the sun-tanned kids looking for beer and soda bottles for their return desposits to earn them another ride on the Cyclone.

I am interested in buying original Steeplechase Park, boardwalk, Nathan's, bathhouse, ride, and freak show memorabilia. Below is a partial listing of memorabilia wanted.

Rick Scott
49 Mersereau Ave.
Staten Island, NY 10303
718-981-2514

	We Pay
Banner, freak show	**50.00+**
Beach Chair, marked Coney Island	**20.00+**
Beach Umbrella, marked Coney Island	**40.00+**
Penny Arcade Machine	**125.00+**

Photo, Coney Island, old	**5.00+**
Photo, freak show	**5.00+**
Postcard, freak show	**5.00+**
Ride Ticket, unused	**5.00+**
Sign, bathhouse	**15.00+**
Sign, freak show	**50.00+**
Sign, for food or drink (Nathan's, etc), ea	**15.00+**
Sign, neon	**50.00+**
Sign, penny arcade	**125.00+**
Sign, subway, old/original only	**10.00+**
Steeplechase Clown Face	**60.00+**
Toy, Wonder Wheel, working	**40.00**

For those who grew up in or ever visited Brooklyn, New York, there was one place designed to make dreamers' fantasies come true. Coney Island was the stuff of which dreams were made. I buy souvenirs of Coney Island, New York's amusement showplace of yesteryear. I am particularly interested in acquiring memorabilia related to Steeplechase Park, a beloved memory of my childhood. Almost anything is of interest to me, except postcards. (I am, however, looking for real photo 'paper moon' postcards.) Please send a photo or photocopy of items you wish to sell along with a SASE, and I promise a speedy response. The prices below are only samples. Of course, condition is always the primary determining factor in pricing. Please see listing here for other areas of interest.

Judith Katz-Schwartz
222 E 93rd St. 42D
New York, NY 10128
212-876-3512

	We Pay
Souvenir Toasting Cup	**10.00-50.00+**
Steeplechase Admission Ticket	**5.00-15.00+**
Steeplechase Artifacts, ea	**25.00-1,000.00+**
Coney Island or Steeplechase Photograph	**5.00-50.00+**
Miscellaneous Souvenirs	**1.00-500.00+**

Other Wants:

- Black Americana
- Children's Dishes
- Dolls and Dollhouses
- Hatpins and Hatpin Holders
- Marbles
- Napkin Rings
- Costume Jewelry
- Disney
- Fans
- Jewelry
- Miniatures
- Ocean Liner

Coney Island

Paper
Photographica
Postcards
Railroadiana
World's Fair
Paper Dolls
Political
Purses
Tramp Art

COOKIE JARS

I buy **all novelty cookie jars**, mostly old ones, although I do buy some newer ones such as Fitz & Floyd, advertising, etc. Other wants include **novelty salt and pepper shakers** (especially fruit and vegetable people, comic characters, and Black memorabilia). **I pay up to $900 for Austrian Goldscheider figurines**.

Gene A. Underwood
909 N Sierra Bonita Ave., Apt 9
Los Angeles, CA 90046-6551
213-850-6276

	We Pay
American Bisque, Cookie Time Clock	**55.00**
American Bisque, Churn Boy	**70.00**
American Bisque, Cow Jumped Over Moon	**130.00**
Brush, Happy Squirrel, w/top hat	**60.00**
Brush, Elephant, w/ice cream cone	**100.00**
Brush, Pumpkin, w/lock on door, elf finial	**100.00**
F&F	**up to 150.00**
National Silver, Mammy	**up to 180.00**
Robinson Ransbottom, Jocko Monkey	**65.00**
Robinson Ransbottom, Peter Peter Pumpkin Eater	**65.00**
Walt Disney, Advertising, McCoy	**Write or Call**

Other Wants	We Pay
Shakers, Mary & Lamb	**15.00**
Shakers, Mother Goose	**18.00**
Shakers, Red Riding Hood	**10.00**

We are buying anything made by **American Bisque Pottery Company** that operated in Williamstown, West Virginia, from 1919 to 1979. This company produced various items and many cookie jars. Also interested in items made by the **American Pottery Company** of Marietta and Byisville, Ohio. Items made from 1942 to 1965 are of interest. Other companies include **A.P. Donagho** of Parkersburg, West Virginia (from 1866 to 1908), and **Terrace Ceramics** of Marietta, Ohio (from 1961 to 1975). Prices paid vary; we are also accepting donations to use in a museum. We are also wanting to buy photos of products.

Laurence Koon
1033 Lynn St.
Parkersburg, WV 26101
304-485-8636

American Bisque	**We Pay**
Casper the Friendly Ghost	**200.00**
Davy Crockett, coming out of forest	**100.00**
Indian Boy, unmarked	**75.00**
Little Audry	**200.00**
Pinkey Lee, unmarked	**75.00**
Policeman	**25.00**
Popeye the Sailor Man, unmarked	**200.00**
Wilma Flintstone, marked USA	**200.00**

Other Companies	**We Pay**
American Pottery, Girl Lamb (two faces), unmarked	**40.00**
American Pottery, Bull (reverse side is Girl Lamb)	**40.00**
American Pottery, Bay Pig (two faces, reverse side is Lady Pig)	**50.00**
AP Donagho, anything	**Write**
Terrace Ceramics, anything	**Write**

We buy **Fruit Kids cookie jars and chalkware figurines** made by Pitman-Dreitzer & Company. Most of the items are marked Pee-Dee 1942 FKR or FKR 1942 PD and Co. Inc. There are two cookie jars, Albert Apple and Stella Strawberry, and six chalkware figures: Stella Strawberry, Priscilla Pineapple, Lee lemon, Charlie Cherry, and Billy Banana. I would like most pieces to be in near-mint to mint condition. We also buy **figural salt and pepper sets** — one set to whole collections. Special interests are fruit and vegetable people, insect people, flower people, anthropomorphic and character sets. Prices paid depend on the item and condition. We pay for shipping, handling, and insurance. Please write or call anytime.

Michelle Carey
2512 Balmoral Blvd.
Kokomo, IN 46902
317-455-3970

We Pay

Cookie Jar, Stella Strawberry or Albert Apple, ea .... **75.00+**
Figurine, Stella Strawberry or Albert Apple, ea .... **30.00+**
Figurine, Charlie Cherry or Priscilla Pineapple, ea .... **30.00+**
Figurine, Lee Lemon or Billy Banana, ea .... **30.00+**

I am a cookie jar lover interested in buying your cookie jars. I especially like **Black Americana or figurals**. Some damage is okay. Call or write. Prices vary according to jar. Other wants include one-of-a-kind handmade folk art. The older, the better; carvings and rugs are especially wanted. Also old **tapestries of animals and interesting subjects (no religious ones, please)**.

Joyce Stratton
RFD #4, Box 550
Augusta, ME 04330
207-622-1001

COUNTRY STORE COLLECTIBLES

We buy most anything connected with the old country stores which operated many years ago. Some still operate today but are becoming a thing of the past. Country stores carried just about anything you could possibly think of during their prime. Listed are items in which we have an interest. Please, if there is something that is not listed, check with us, because there are too many items to be listed here.

Bill Shaw
801 Duval Dr.
Opp, AL 36467

We Pay

Advertising Clocks, Coke, Nehi, NuGrape, etc, ea .... **40.00+**
Advertising Items, paper, metal, plastic, cardboard, tin, etc, ea .... **5.00+**
Calendars, old, ea .... **5.00+**
Candy Jars, old, ea .... **10.00+**
Churns, glass, ea .... **30.00+**
Cookie Jars, old, ea .... **10.00+**

Fountain Pens, old, ea .... **3.00+**
Fishing Lures, old, ea.. **3.00+**
Fishing Reels, old, ea .... **10.00+**
Fishing Rods, bamboo, old, ea.. **10.00+**
Gum Containers, paper, glass, metal, etc, ea .... **10.00+**
Gum Vending Machines, ea.. **25.00+**
Lamp Parts, old, ea.. **2.00+**
Old Store Stock, per item .... **1.00+**
Peanut Vending Machines, ea .... **25.00+**
Shotgun Shell Boxes, cardboard, ea.. **5.00+**
Showcases, counter top or floor models, ea .... **100.00+**
Tins, old, ea.. **5.00+**

I am seeking country store items. Listed below are a few wants. Especially wanted is a **National Mazda light bulb counter display**. I will pay current book price for this depending on condition.

B.J. Summers
233 Darnell Rd.
Benton, KY 42025
502-898-3097

We Pay

Porcelain or Tin Advertising Signs, ea **10.00-60.00**
Soft-Drink Machines or Boxes, ea **100.00-300.00**
Tobacco Tins or Glass Jars, ea **5.00-50.00**
Peanut Store Jars, ea **15.00-65.00**

COW COLLECTIBLES

Wanted: ceramic purple cows. They must have yellow horns, pink noses, and black freckles. These were probably a Japanese product made in the 1950s.

Judy Prout
7852 Sloewood Dr.
Mt. Dora, FL 32757
904-383-6664

We Pay

Condiment Holder **10.00-20.00**
Bank .... **20.00+**
Pitcher .... **20.00+**
Cookie Jar .... **Write or Call**

COWAN

Interested in purchasing Cowan pottery, with a special interest in **figural flower frogs (nudes) and any of the pottery with the beige coloring**. However, would be interested in any and all Cowan pottery. Would ask that the items be in excellent condition: no repairs, chips, or cracks. Would be happy to reimburse actual UPS and insurance charges. I am **willing to pay current book value**.

Laura L. Walker
3907 N Blvd.
Tampa, FL 33603
813-229-6332

CRACKER JACK ITEMS

I am an advanced Cracker Jack collector looking for **all early marked Cracker Jack items**. I look for pre-1940s prizes, boxes and display signs and salesman's promotional items. I also look for the same items in Checkers. I am *not* interested in plastic items or items marked Borden.

Phil Helley
629 Indiana Ave.
Wisconsin Dells, WI 53965
608-254-8659

We Pay

Advertising Mirror **50.00**
Bank, tin book **35.00**
Baseball Card **20.00-75.00**

Baseball Score Keeper **55.00**
Calendar, paper, 1928, round **55.00**
Cracker Jack Box, 1930s **65.00**
Jack at Chalkboard, arm moves, paper **35.00**
Jigsaw Puzzle, paper w/zepplin, 1930s **75.00**
Train Engine, No 512 ..... **65.00**
Train Car, any of 3 circus animals, ea **85.00**
Horse-Drawn Wagon, pot metal **125.00**
License, Model T Ford, 1916 ..... **250.00**
Orphan Annie Stand-Up, tin, oval **45.00**
Pencil Clip **130.00**
Pin-Back Button, w/Cracker Jack Boy, tin **100.00**
Pin-Back Button, celluloid **35.00**
Sign, Cracker Jack, cardboard, 1920s **300.00**

CUFF LINKS

I buy **cuff links circa 1875 through 1935 only**. I do *not* buy modern cuff links under any circumstances. I don't buy any mother-of-pearl cuff links. I don't buy cuff links with advertising, logos, monograms, or initals on them. Condition can be fair except with enamels; they must be in good shape, no cracks or pitting. I reimburse all UPS and insurance charges and return package or send check via Federal Express the same day!

Daryl Price
7804 S Wabash
Chicago, IL 60619
312-846-0965 (evenings only, all day Saturday)

We Pay

Gold 10K, 14K or 18K ..... **35.00+**
Gold Filled ..... **8.00+**
Sterling ..... **15.00+**
Enameled ..... **15.00+**
Crystal ..... **15.00+**
Snap-a-Parts ..... **8.00+**
Dress Sets (no mother-of-pearl) ..... **20.00+**
Boxes ..... **5.00+**
Singles ..... **1.00+**

CZECHOSLOVAKIAN COLLECTIBLES

At the close of World War I, Czechoslovakia was declared an independent republic and developed a large export industry. The factories produced glassware, pottery and porcelain until 1939 when the country was occupied by Germany. I am especially interested in **Peasant Art pottery**.

Delores Saar
45 Fifth Ave. NW
Hutchinson, MN 55350
612-587-2002

Peasant Art Pottery	We Pay
Bowl, 4¼"	40.00
Box, 3"	30.00
Candle Holder	25.00
Chocolate Pot, 8¼"	50.00
Lamp	100.00
Pitcher, w/lid, 7"	50.00
Pitcher, milk; 5½"	45.00
Plate, 12"	30.00
Salt & Pepper Shakers, 2½", pr	30.00
Teapot, 6½"	45.00
Vase, 7½"	45.00

DECOYS

We want to buy **old wooden decoys of any type in any condition**. Broken bodies and/or heads are wanted as long as they are wooden. Close-up side-view pictures are a must for an accurate buying price. Decoys wanted include any duck, goose, swan, shorebird, crow, fish, or owl. Also wanted are **old wooden fishing lures**.

Art Pietrasfewski, Jr.
60 Grant St.
Depew, NY 14043
716-681-2339 (4 pm to 10 pm)

DELFT

I'm interested in buying both **old and new blue Delft** — one piece or a whole collection. Must be blue Dutch Delft, no English or German wanted. I will pay premium for de Porcelyne Fles (Royal Delft) mark and am interested in all old pieces with any mark. Items must be in fine condition with no chips, cracks, or repairs, but some crazing is okay. I am *not* interested in tiles, shoes, jewelry, spoons or advertising (liquor) pieces. Send note with photo (sketch or picture of mark would be greatly appreciated).

Diane D. Granville
28 E Branch Rd.
Patterson, NY 12563

	We Pay
Candle Holder, DPF, round base, 3"	25.00+
Cup & Saucer	15.00+
Ink Stand, w/2 ink pots	60.00+
Mustard Pot, floral, 2½"	15.00+
Pitcher, OED, floral, 7"	40.00+
Plate, floral, 7"	22.00+
Plate, DPF, scenic, 8½"	45.00+
Plate, OED, portrait, 10"	55.00+
Sugar Shaker, floral, 4½"	18.00+
Vase, DPF, floral, 3"	25.00+
Vase, scenic, 5"	15.00+
Vase, floral	725.00+

DEPRESSION ERA GLASSWARE

I buy **all popular patterns of Depression and elegant glass dinnerware.** All pieces must be in mint condition, without chips or cracks, a foggy appearance, or substantial scratching. Favored patterns include: Adam, American Sweetheart, Anniversary (pink only), Bubble, Cameo, Cherry Blossom, Christmas Candy (teal only), Dogwood, Doric, Doric & Pansy, Floral (Poinsettia), Holiday, Homespun, Iris & Herringbone, Lace Edge, Mayfair, Miss America, Moonstone, Parrot, Princess, Pyramid, Royal Lace, Swirl (ultramarine only), Tea Room, Waterford (pink), Fostoria American (unusual pieces), Fostoria June, Fostoria Versailles, Cambridge Caprice, Cambridge Rosepoint, Heisey Orchid, and Heisey Rose.

Larry D. Cook
P.O. Box 211
Walnut, IA 51577

	We Pay
Adam, footed iced tea, pink	40.00
American Sweetheart, cream soup bowl, monax	70.00
Cameo, footed juice tumbler, green	35.00
Cherry Blossom, dinner plate, pink	14.00
Christmas Candy, soup bowl, teal	20.00
Dogwood, pitcher, pink w/decoration, 80-oz	100.00
Floral, lemonade pitcher, pink	150.00
Homespun, cup & saucer, pink	9.00
Lace Edge, sherbet, pink	50.00
Mayfair, goblet, blue, 7¼"	125.00
Mayfair, dinner plate, pink	32.50
Miss America, water goblet, pink	30.00
Moderntone, juice tumbler, cobalt blue, 5-oz	25.00
Moroccan Amethyst, salad plate, 7¼"	5.00
Princess, flat iced tea tumbler, green	20.00
Royal Lace, berry bowl, cobalt blue	17.50
Waterford, goblet, pink	50.00
Other patterns, pieces & colors	40%-75% of book values

Collector wanting to buy **Cherry Blossom, Fire-King restaurant ware, Rose Cameo, and Royal Lace patterns** — all pieces. Buying only mint glass without defects; no reproductions. **Will pay prices listed in latest edition of appropriate Florence references.** Actual UPS and insurance costs reimbursed. Call first, after 7 pm weekdays.

Richard O. Thomas
242 Shelton Shop Rd.
Stafford, VA 22554
703-659-7161

As a child I was attracted to the rainbows of colored glass when visiting antique shops with my mother. I began my first collection at age twelve and now have my own business specializing in Depression era glassware that I enjoy equally as well. Below is a list of patterns and colors I am currently buying which command as much as 60% of book value, depending on present demand. I would also be interested in purchasing other Depression patterns and kitchenware at up to 50% of book value. Parts (lids and bottoms) for Depression butter dishes, cookie jars, and candy dishes are also needed in all patterns. Glassware purchased must be free of chips and cracks. Signs of wear should be minimal on items such as dinner plates. Examples of patterns wanted include:

American Sweetheart, pink & monax
Mayfair, pink & blue
Sandwich, Hocking, clear
Iris, clear
Princess, pink
Dogwood, pink
Parrot, green
Cameo, green & yellow
Moderntone, blue
Sharon, pink

Pamela Wiggins
6025 Sunnycrest St.
Houston, TX 77087
713-649-6603

Wanted: **Beaded Block (clear blocks) and Frosted Block (stippled blocks) patterns by Imperial Glass Company and Lenox pattern by Imperial** (made from about 1927 through 1981). Most pieces are unmarked. We have clients for a wide variety of pieces in many shapes and colors in both patterns. Be aware that most price guides on Depression glass erroneously lump both Beaded Block and Frosted Block patterns together and refer to both of them as Beaded Block. Neither pattern has pieces that were produced in all colors or all shapes. Contrary to popular opinion, an item marked 'Made in USA,' does not have increased value, nor does an item produced in crystal have less value than colored items. Scarcity is the only determinate of value. A collector's club for aficionados of both Beaded Block and Frosted Block is being formed. We welcome inquiries. Please see our listing here for specific wants as well as other areas of interest.

ARIANA
Judith C. and Richard F. Tritschler
11 Colonial Terrace
Pompton Plains, NJ 07444
201-835-2063 (NJ) or 717-296-6708 (PA)

We pay 10% over prices listed in 1994-95 price guides for the following pieces in both patterns:

Square plates in all shades of blue & carnival/iridescent
Covered butter dishes, round, in all colors
Bowls, 9", in all colors

Depression Era Glassware

Syrup pitchers in all colors
All pieces produced in amber opalescent, red, & baby pink (not the common salmony hue)
All pieces with metal handles & inserts
Covered candy boxes resembling apples (a pushed-down version of the covered pear candy box)
Bowls with 5½" top edge diameter, without handles
Plates, round, in all colors & sizes except crystal, marigold carnival/iridescent, & clambroth carnival/iridescent
Berry/jelly/creme soup bowls, green, with two handles
All pieces produced in amber or vaseline, except square plates
All square plates produced with opalescent edges
All pink jug/pitchers produced in blue or opalescent colors

We are paying 50% of current market/price guide values for:

Flow Blue
Lydia E Pinkham advertising & ephemera
Cambridge Rose Point
Fostoria Stardust
Gorham, Strasbourg & Medici sterling silver
Royal Doulton Cadence & Tiara china
Postcards from Walker Lake, Shohola, Shohola Glen, Shohola Falls, Parker's Glen, & Twin Lakes, Pennsylvania
Anything relating to hedgehogs
Prints, original artwork & postcards by May L Farini
All items relating to Feigenspan Brewery, Newark, NY & Tritschler & Tiesse Brewery, Clinton, IA

I am buying pink Depression-era glassware in the following patterns: **Adam, American Sweetheart, Florentine #1 and #2, Mayfair (Hocking), Princess, Royal Lace, and Sharon**. Also buying **elegant glassware in pink by Cambridge and Fostoria. Royal Lace** is also wanted in cobalt blue.

In **pink kitchenware**, I am looking for juice reamers, canisters, mixing bowls, refrigerator dishes, measuring cups and spice sets. All items should be in perfect condition. Photos and descriptions would be helpful when you reply.

Other wants include **children's tea sets made of glass or china**. I prefer older sets made before 1950 that are decorated with floral patterns, small children, Blue Willow, etc. Also looking for **children's spice and canister sets**. Thank you for responding.

Diane Genicola
25 E Adams Ave.
Pleasantville, NJ 08232
609-646-6140

We are buying **Depression glass for resale**. We buy most patterns and colors. All glass must be in perfect condition — free of chips, nicks, cracks, and scratches. We also buy **elegant glass** of the Depression era such as Heisey, Cambridge, Fostoria, Fenton, Imperial, Paden City, and Duncan & Miller. We also buy **glass kitchen items** such as reamers, canisters, mixing bowls, refrigerator dishes, butter and cheese dishes, measuring cups, spice shakers, rolling pins, cruets, etc. Please send a list of what you have for sale and your asking price. Pictures are also helpful. Mint condition glass only wanted, please! Other wants include but are not limited to the following:

Blue Willow
Coors
Franciscan
Hall
Marx Toy Trains
Royal China (Currier & Ives, Memory Lane)
Staffordshire (Liberty Blue)
Children's Dishes
Fiesta
Goebel Friar Tuck Monks
Marbles
Roseville
Stangl Birds
Reamers

The Glass Packrat
Pat and Bill Ogden
3050 Colorado Ave.
Grand Junction, CO 81504

I am interested in glassware in the patterns listed here:

Imperial Hunt Scene, by Cambridge, in all colors
Rose Point, by Cambridge
Wildflower, by Cambridge (I need 10-oz water tumblers & 5-oz juice tumblers)
Manhattan, in pink
Mayfair Open Rose, by Hocking in pink
Deerwood (Birch Tree), by US Glass Co
Black Forest
Candlewick, by Imperial (I need the sugar & creamer set)

Any item in these patterns is wanted. **I would pay 90% of book price and postage.** No items with chips or cracks please.

Kathy Chitty
14 Union St. S
Concord, NC 28025
704-786-4296

Dollhouse Furniture

I buy **plastic furniture manufactured from 1946 through the 1950s** made by companies such as Renwal, Marx, Ideal, Acme, Reliable, etc., in the scale of ¾" per foot. I buy only pieces that are in excellent condition: no warping, chips, cracks, or melted spots. Pieces need not be marked with manufacturer's name to be of interest. I reimburse postage for shipping.

Marian Schmuhl
7 Revolutionary Ridge Rd.
Bedford, MA 01730
617-275-2156

	We Pay
Acme, swing	10.00
Ideal, folding card table	15.00
Ideal, folding card table chair	15.00
Ideal, fireplace	15.00
Ideal, lawn mower	18.00
Ideal, entertainment center (TV, phonograph, radio)	15.00
Ideal, tilt-top pie-crust table, round	10.00
Plasco, TV, w/circular cardboard picture insert	12.00
Plasco, grandfather clock	10.00
Renwal, broom	40.00
Renwal, carpet sweeper	10.00
Renwal, highchair	15.00
Renwal, sliding board	8.00
Renwal, vacuum cleaner, w/bag	15.00
Renwal, wringer washing machine, w/agitator & lid	20.00

Dolls and Dollhouses

I'm a beginning **Annalee** doll collector, and even though I especially love the Christmas dolls, I'd like to hear about any you have for sale. There's very little published information on these dolls, so it's kind of a learn-as-you-collect type of hobby for me. They've been made since the 1950s, and most of them will have production dates on their tags. I prefer the older dolls but have bought several more current examples as well. There is a complete nativity set I'd love to find. Annalees are made of felt over posable wirework frames, and their faces are whimisical and hand painted with wonderful expressions. From what I see, values fluctuate from giveaway prices to pretty expensive. I've found enough to buy to keep me happy at reasonable prices, so I probably won't be interested in high-priced dolls unless they're very special. I'll try to give an idea of the values I've been paying, but would negotiate.

Sharon Huxford
1202 Seventh St.
Covington, IN 47932
Phone or FAX 317-793-2392

	We Pay
Small dolls, ca 1960s-80s, 7" to 8"	**25.00+**
Medium dolls, ca 1960s-80s, 12" to 18"	**45.00+**
Large dolls, ca 1960s-80s, 20" to 30"	**75.00+**
Christmas tree ornaments	**6.00+**

I am a Barbie collector who will pay top dollar for **Barbie dolls, her friends, clothes, and accessories**. I am particularly interested in items circa 1959 through 1972. I love Ponytails, Bubble Cuts, and American Girl Barbies. Please call me or write if you have any of these Barbie items. All calls and letters will be answered.

Aylene Krichinsky
7101 Pacific Ave.
Ft. Pierce, FL 34951
407-468-9148

I am interested in buying **Barbies, Kens, Skippers, Francies, and their clothes dated 1959 to 1966** — a single piece or an entire collection. Listed below are some of the things I am seeking. Top prices paid for rare and unusual items, such as gift sets, prototypes, and foreign issues of Barbie. Prices are currently at an all-time high, so now is the best time to pull those dolls out of the attic. The prices below are for excellent condition items and should be used only as a guide. For example, dolls with their original boxes increase these prices by 50%. Prices also increase according to the condition of the doll. Please send photos of your dolls so we can offer you a fair price.

Irene Davis
27036 Withams Rd.
Oak Hall, VA 23416
804-824-5524

	We Pay
#1 Ponytail Barbie	**1,500.00+**
#2 Ponytail Barbie	**800.00+**
#3 Ponytail Barbie	**300.00+**
1961-1963 Ponytail Barbie	**100.00**
Bubble Cut Barbie	**50.00+**
Skipper	**20.00**
Francie	**30.00+**
Ken, flocked hair	**50.00**
Barbie Gift Set	**100.00-1,000.00+**
Mod Fashions	**20.00+**
Barbie Cases	**10.00-20.00+**

I enjoy collecting **dolls, furniture and accessories dating from 1960 to 1965 and am especially interested in Barbie**. The dolls I am most interested in are the Ponytail, Swirl Ponytail, Bubble Cut, and American Girl Barbies. These came in black-and-white striped or solid red bathing suits with sunglasses, gold hoop earrings, and high heels on a black wire stand or a wire stand with a round plastic disk base. Many fashion clothes were produced. I am interested in clothing with the early Barbie logo label and the accessories that went with these fashions. Also manufactured at the same time was a line of **Suzy-Goose furniture** made by Mattel for Barbie. The line included a canopy bed and a small single-drawer chest, a vanity and stool, and a tall wardrobe.

The price I will pay very much depends on the rarity, age, and condition of the dolls and accessories. The values you find in price guides are for mint-in-box items, and very few little girls left their dolls in the box. Please, when you write to me let me know how much you want for your items.

Beth Summers
233 Darnell Rd.
Benton, KY 42025

Private collector will pay top dollar for **Barbie dolls, friend dolls, clothes, houses, store displays, accessories, and Barbie-related items.** I prefer items made before 1975. Also wanted are Barbie dolls from after 1975, but only those that are mint in box.

Denise Davidson
834 W Grand River Ave.
Williamston, MI 48895
517-723-4611

We pay top dollar for mint-in-the-box older dolls. **Barbie, Ginny, Play Pals, hard plastics, compositions, paper dolls, and bisque dolls** are wanted. We are also looking to buy **children's treadle sewing machines and Victrolas as well as common and rarer pieces of children's furniture** such as early sofas, baby grand pianos, popcorn machines, dressers, kitchen cabinets, stoves, etc. Prices could vary depending on condition.

Sandy Blair
Box 1409
Forney, TX 75126
214-564-1220 or 214-564-3486 (evenings)

Dolls	**We Pay**
#1 Barbie, mint in box	**2,000.00**
#2 Barbie, mint in box	**1,500.00**
Peter Play Pal, mint in box	**500.00**
Pattie Play Pal, mint in box	**300.00**
Bye-Bye Baby	**200.00**
GI Joe	**50.00**

Children's Things	**We Pay**
Treadle Sewing Machine	**500.00-2,500.00**
Victrola	**200.00-1,000.00**
Stove	**200.00+**
Popcorn Machine	**150.00+**
Baby Grand Piano	**150.00+**

Dolls and Dollhouses

I'm looking for **Barbie and her friends**. Any dolls including new ones (if they are mint in box) are wanted. Price depend on doll, age, condition, etc. I'm also interested in **Marilyn Monroe, Gone with the Wind dolls, Elvis, Star Trek, Star Wars, GI Joe, and the Dionne Quintuplets,** or any dolls similar to these. Please send SASE along with your asking price for a reply. Photographs are always helpful.

T.L. Rodrick
R.R. #2, Box 163
Sumner, IL 62466

I purchase **any and all types of modern dolls made by different manufacturers from the 1950s through the 1970s**. They can be made by Mattel, Ideal, Alexander Doll Co., Kenner, Hasbro, etc. Since modern dolls were mass produced, condition is everything! So I would only be interested in purchasing those dolls in near-mint to mint-in-the-box condition. Some Barbie and Friends dolls are acceptable in excellent condition. Please send your descriptions and prices to the address below. Thank you!

Mariam F. Donerian
42 Patsun Rd.
P.O. Box 133
Somersville, CT 06072-0133

Barbie and Friends	We Pay
#850 C 1959 #1 Barbie	**500.00+**
#850 C 1959 #2 Barbie	**500.00+**
#850 C 1960 #3 Barbie	**150.00+**
#850 C 1960 #4 Barbie	**75.00+**
#850 C 1961 #5 Barbie	**50.00+**
#850 C 1961-67 Bubble Cut Barbie	**35.00+**
#1070 C 1965 Bendable Leg American Girl Barbie	**75.00+**
#1150 C 1966 Color Magic Bendable Leg Barbie	**50.00+**
#1100 C 1967 Francie (Barbie's cousin), Black version	**100.00+**
Any Clothing, from 1959 to 1980, mint in package	**10.00+**

Other Dolls	We Pay
Ideal, Thumbelina, 1960s	**15.00+**
Ideal, Little Miss Revlon, 10"	**25.00+**
Ideal, Little Miss Revlon, 18" or 21" fashion doll, ea	**50.00+**
Ideal, Shirley Temple, vinyl, 1957, 15"	**75.00+**
Hasbro, Jem series, 1980s, 12", ea	**5.00+**

Kenner, Darci & Friends series, 1970s, 12", ea ....**10.00+**
Kenner, Strawberry Shortcake Berrykins series, 1980s, ea........................**10.00+**
Madame Alexander, Easter doll, 1968, 8" or 14", ea ....**100.00+**
Mattel, Marie Osmond modeling doll, 1970s, 30"......................................**25.00+**
Mattel, Chatty Cathy, talker, 1960...**35.00+**

I am interested in purchasing dolls in mint condition and especially mint-in-the-box **hard plastic dolls from the 1950s**. Examples would be Ginnys, Tonis, Sweet Sues, Effanbees, Madame Alexanders, 1950s Shirley Temples, etc. They must have their original clothing and be in excellent to mint condition.

I also purchase **Nancy Ann Storybook dolls of the 1930s through the early 1950s**. These also must be in excellent to mint condition and include their hats or hair ribbons. **I will pay 75% of book price**.

Jacquie Henry
Box 17
Walworth, NY 14568
315-986-1424

I collect and repair old dolls. Wanted are **antique infant and doll dresses, shoes, and bonnets as well as accessories to dress up old dolls, and various doll parts** (composition legs, arms, and heads) to use for repairs. These are for my personal collection as well as some resale. Please send a photo or detailed description and SASE. Ship items only with approval. Please also see my listing under Victorian Collectibles in this book.

Joyce Andresen
P.O. Box 1
Keystone, IA 52249

Pre-1964 dolls of all types are wanted. Send photo with markings and measurements. Do not send item without speaking to us first. We have over twenty years experience and are very proud of our knowledge and honest reputation. We also look for fine antique doll clothes, shoes, and accessories such as toys, teddy bears, etc. We do not do repairs for the public, but we do restore the dolls we buy — so don't let condition stop you from contacting us! Thanks!

Dempsey and Baxter
1009 E 38th St.
Erie, PA 16504

Wanting to buy **Sasha or Ginny dolls**. I will pay up to $100 for dolls designed by the late doll maker, Sasha Morganthaler, from Switzerland. I am also interested in purchasing Ginny dolls and will pay up to $50 each for these. Thank you.

Bonnie Joe Thomas
6221 N Albert Ln.
Glendale, WI 53217-4147
414-964-1108

I buy **unusual and rare dolls, especially hard plastic dolls from the 1950s and 1960s**. Preferred are Mary Hoyer and Madame Alexander dolls. Also of interest are Howdy Doody, Byelos, Black Americana, Shirley Temple, Schoenhut (also animals), bisque, Barbie (1958 through 1959), and GI Joe (1964). I am also interested in buying tagged doll clothing and accessories for these dolls. **I will pay 40% of book price for any of the dolls mentioned**. Any doll or doll clothing in as in condition is negotionable.

Millie Schick
Burholme Thrift Shoppe
7106 Rising Sun Ave.
Philadelphia, PA 19111
215-742-8877
(Mon., Wed., Fri. or Sat. 10 am to 3 pm; closed July and Aug.)

I am buying a variety of dolls made prior to 1972. All conditions considered. Wanted are dolls needing restoration, parts, wigs, and accessories. For my personal collection, I prefer good quality dolls in original clothing. When priced reasonably, I will take and restore basket-case dolls, more desirable dolls, and bears. Prices reflect dolls needing 'TLC' to excellent condition.

I am a nut for **Shirley Temple**! Wanted: all lists offering Shirley dolls and related items. As my hobby is restoration, I desire dolls to repair, especially 1930s composition dolls and dolls needing much care. Please see my listing for examples of prices paid.

Rebecca Chizzo
21 Whitetail Ln.
Sudbury, MA 01776
508-443-5948

Shirley Temple	**We Pay**
Mohair Wigs, ea	**12.00+**
Clothing, Shoes, or Purses, ea	**5.00+**
Vinyl Dolls (no cut hair, ea)	**20.00+**
Composition Dolls (needing restoration), 1930s, ea	**35.00+**

Other Dolls	**We Pay**
Barbies, prior to 1972, ea	**20.00+**
Boudoir Dolls (also clothing), ea	**15.00+**
Ginny (also other 1950s dolls), 8", ea	**20.00+**
8" Hard Plastic Doll Parts or Clothing, ea	**3.00+**
Kewpies, Cameo, vinyl & compo, ea	**15.00+**
Dolls w/Googly Eyes, ea	**25.00+**
Foreign or Unusual Trolls (no Asian made), ea	**15.00+**
All Other Doll Parts, ea	**2.00+**

I am interested in buying **Barbie, Ken, and Midge dolls from 1959 through the early 1960s**. They must be in good condition but not necessarily mint in the box. Also, I am looking for outfits for Barbie and Ken from the same years. Clothes should be in good condition. Also needed to complete outfits are miscellaneous pieces such as accessories or partial outfits. **Metal dollhouses from the 1950s made by Marx and Wolverine** are sought as well. These must be in good condition. Pieces of hard and soft plastic **doll furniture made by Marx, Renwal or Superior** are wanted to go with the dolls and dollhouses. Odd pieces of rooms are okay, as I need to complete rooms I have. I will pay fair prices for everything.

Susan Pitman
28 Swan
Beverly, MA 01915
508-927-2551

I am interested in **Raggedy Anns and related items**. Especially Belindys, Uncle Clem, Camels, Arthur Dog, Percy Policeman, Henney, etc. Early handmade Raggedys are considered on an individual basis. All prices given are for dolls in good to very-good condition. Prices vary greatly based on condition and sizes. Books and related items are priced on individual basis. For other wants see Pepsi-Cola in this book.

Gwen Daniel
18 Belleau Lake Ct.
O'Fallon, MO 63366
314-978-3190

	We Pay
Volland Ann, w/wooden heart	400.00+
Volland Andy	200.00+
Volland Belindy	400.00+
Mollie Ann	400.00+
Mollie Andy	400.00+
Mollie Baby	800.00+
Georgene Ann or Andy, w/black outline nose, ea	150.00+
Georgene Belindy	300.00+
Georgene Camel w/Wrinkled Knees	400.00+
Knickerbocker Ann, talker	50.00+
Knickerbocker Andy, talker	50.00+
Knickerbocker Belindy	200.00+
Knickerbocker Camel w/Wrinkled Knees	50.00+

I collect **Raggedy Ann and Andy dolls, related character dolls, and related miscellaneous items** such as books, toys, music boxes, etc. Due to the fact that values of cloth dolls is very dependent on their condition, it would be nearly impossible to list a buying price. I appreciate your time and giving consideration to my want listing.

Kim Avery
104 Longwood Rd.
St. Marys, GA 31558

Door Push Plates

I collect **advertising porcelain door push plates** that were used on entrance doors to grocery stores, drugstores, and any store in general that sold manufacturers' products. They were attached to screen doors where you normally reached out to push the door in or out. The push plate was colorful and advertised the company's product; it often carried the words 'push' or 'pull' as well. Size of the plates varied, but the average was 4x7". These were made of enameled steel (more commonly called porcelain). Some examples that exist are: Red Rose Tea, Tetley Tea, Salada Tea, Chesterfield Cigarettes, Dr. Caldwell's Pepsin Syrup, and Vick's.

I buy according to condition. Please send photocopy or photo with a description for a price quote. **I will pay $75 to $125** for nice additions to my collection. I pay the postage.

Betty Foley
P.O. Box 572
Adamstown, PA 19501-0572
717-484-4779

Egg Timers

I am interested in obtaining figural egg timers with or without glass sand tubes intact. German figurals might be stamped as such or have incised symbols. Those from Japan will also be appropriately marked. Timers are predominatly china, glazed bisque, or pottery. Others may be cast iron or carved wood. Condition of figurals should be very good to mint condition. Please, no damaging cracks, severe chips or noticeable repairs. Prices below reflect timers in excellent condition and with sand tube intact.

Jeannie Greenfield
310 Parker Rd.
Stoneboro, PA 16153

	We Pay
Chimney Sweep, w/ladder slung over shoulder, marked Germany	**30.00**
Black Chef, sitting, timer in right hand, marked Germany	**55.00**
Chimney Sweep, Goebel, dated 1972	**50.00**
Mammy, timer in right arm, Occupied Japan	**50.00**
Amish Boy & Girl, sitting on bench, cast iron, unmarked	**15.00**
Rooster, carved wood outline w/painted features, timer in hollowed-out neck, unmarked	**20.00**

EYE CUPS

I am looking for old eye cups in glass, china, or ceramic; weird shapes, sizes, or colors are wanted. Also looking for original boxes and bottles with eye cup stoppers or tops. Please send photos and prices or call.

Deborah and James Golden
3182 Twin Pine Rd.
Grayling, MI 49738
517-348-2610

FANS WITH ELECTRIC MOTORS

Collector/historian seeks **antique or unusual fans or motors**, especially early cast-iron models. Also looking for **catalogs, advertising or other related items**. Paying top dollar for items in mint condition but will also buy items in need of repair or restoration. Call 1-800-858-3267 with description for immediate cash offer. Description should include markings, nameplate information, dimensions, overall condition, blade diameter, and composition. Willing to pay finders fees. Other wants include **typewriters, cameras, microscopes, and telescopes**.

Michael Breedlove
15633 Cold Spring Ct.
Granger, IN 46530
800-858-3267

	We Pay
C&C Motors or Fans, ea	1,000.00
Claw-Footed Fans or Motors, ea	750.00
Eck Fans, ea	300.00
Edison Fans or Motors, ea	750.00
Emerson Fans, brass blade & cage, ea	150.00
Emerson Fans or Motors, on tripod base	500.00
GE Fan, serial number less than 20,000	500.00
GE Fan, serial number less than 200,000	250.00
Foreign Fans, ea	500.00
Holtzer Cabot Motors or Fans, ea	700.00

Lakebreeze Fans, ea **750.00**
Menominee Fans, brass blade & cage, ea **250.00**
Meston Fans, ea.......... **500.00**
Peerless or Colonial Fans, brass blade & cage, ea **200.00**
Toy Motors, ea.......... **100.00**
Trojan Fans, ea **300.00**
Toy Motors, ea.......... **100.00**
Water-Powered Fans, ea **500.00**
Any pre-1950 Fan, mint in box, ea.......... **150.00**
Pre-1900 Catalogs, ea **200.00**
Pre-1920 Catalogs, ea **100.00**

FAST FOOD COLLECTIBLES

We buy **older (prior to 1985) fast food items, especially McDonald's®.** We prefer mint in package (MIP/MIB) or mint condition. We do not buy bent, dented, chipped, stained, scratched, or loose toys in any condition of less that mint. We want most **old, odd, unique, regional, manager, owner-operator, and convention-type items**. If you have items in the above categories, please call, write or fax to:

Bill and Pat Poe
220 Dominica Cir. E
Niceville, FL 32578-4068
904-897-4163 or FAX 904-897-2606

We Pay

Playground Equipment, McDonald's® .... **25.00+**
Glasses, The Muppets Are Coming .... **10.00+**
Glasses, Hook EM Horns (Austin, TX area) .... **10.00+**
Statue, Ronald, 6-ft .... **100.00+**
Telephone, Ronald, sitting, Touch-Tone .... **50.00+**
Telephone, Ronald, standing, Touch-Tone .... **40.00+**
Speedy Items, old, ea.......... **5.00-100.00**
Book, The Story of Texas (Houston & Austin).......... **10.00+**
Map, The Story of Texas.......... **10.00+**
Toy, McDonald's® Garfield, plush in green McDonald uniform .... **20.00+**
Toys, Metrozoo (from south Florida) .... **10.00+**
Toys, 1990-91 McDonald's® Winnie the Pooh, plush, set.......... **15.00+**
Toys, 1988 McDonald's®) Matchbox, Super GT, all 16, ea .... **5.00+**

Toys, 1988 McDonald's® Doozers & Fraggle, w/offset wheels, ea ....**5.00+**
Toys, 1985 My Little Pony Charms & Transformers, ea ....**5.00+**
Toys, 1982 McDonaldland Express Food Containers, ea ....**5.00+**
Toys, 1982 McDonald's® Dukes of Hazzard Food Containers, ea ....**5.00+**
Boxes, McDonald's® Happy Meal, any prior to 1982, ea ....**1.00+**
Box, 1980 Dallas Cowboys Super Box ....**5.00+**
Box, 1977-78 Round Top Happy Meal, any ....**5.00+**
Baseball Cards, 1977 Milwaukee Brewers 'M,' set of 30 ....**10.00+**
Baseball Cards, 1990 Score McDonald's® ....**10.00+**
Baseball Cards, 1974 Padre's, w/round baseball container ....**25.00+**
Hard Bubble Displays, McDonaldland Express, Lego Little Travelers, Pop-oids, 1988-90 Mac Tonight, 1988 Matchbox Super GT, 1988 Sea World of Texas, 1988 Muppet Kids (test market), 1983-85 Ship Shape, 1986 Construct, 1988 Bambi, 1988 Sports Ball, or 1988 Turbo Macs, depending on condition ...**25.00-100.00+**

My friend Steve here is an advanced, serious **Big Boy** collector, and he is looking for any of the below items (or others) with the Big Boy logo on them — the older the better. Please call him if you have or know of any of these items for sale. He even wants the **Bob Big Boy** sign and doormat from the front of current restaurants that are closing.

Just remember, it must have the Big Boy logo (any variation), and the only thing he does *not* need are the vinyl banks and trading cards. The prices here are minimum buying prices and could be more depending on age, condition, etc. All replies confidential! If you have any of the items listed here, please call him, and he will make it worth your while. Thanks a lot.

Steve Soelberg
29126 Laro Dr.
Agoura Hills, CA 91301
818-889-9909

Big Boy **We Pay**

Ashtray, figural **300.00**
Bank, ceramic, brown or glazed, ea **350.00**
China, w/logo, ea ....**50.00+**
Comic Book, Big Boy #1 ....**200.00**
Counter Display, plaster, about 14" **1,000.00**
Counter Display, papier-mache, 18" **1,000.00**
Other Counter Displays, ea ....**25.00+**
Employee Awards & Trophies, ea ....**100.00+**
Employee Items, Promo Items, or Buttons, ea ....**25.00+**
Glass, 1988 Frisch's Evolution **100.00**

Hamburger Wrappers, early .... **50.00+**
Other Glassware Items, w/logo, ea .... **50.00+**
Lamp, ceramic figural w/shade **1,500.00**
Matchbook (up to 10 locations) .... **50.00+**
Menu, original only (1, 2, or 3 locations) **200.00**
Other Menus, early only, ea .... **100.00+**
Nodder/Bobbin' Head Dolls, ea **400.00**
Photos, Letters, or Newsletters, old only .... **25.00+**
Puzzles or Games, ea .... **35.00+**
Salt & Pepper Shakers, figurals, pr .... **200.00+**
Store Signs, porcelain, wood, etc, ea .... **100.00+**
Watches, ea .... **35.00+**

FEATHERCRAFT

Looking to add to my collection of **Mexican feathercraft**. These items were made in the 1940s possibly as souvenirs. At the present time, all that has been found available are bird pictures and trays. The pictures come in many different sizes and most of the framework is elaborately carved. Prices paid will vary with size, condition, and how unusual the item is. Also wanted is any information or such as where they were made, who made them, etc.

Aleta Wikert
272C Perry Hwy.
Harmony, PA 16037

FIESTA

Wanted: old Fiesta only — may be chipped but in pretty good shape. Send me a list of what you have.

Sandee Smith
111 S Van Buren
Pierre, SD 57501

FIGURINES AND FLOWER FROGS

Wanted: figurines **marked 'Designed by Erich Stauffer.'** These figurines depict children, nuns or angels. The child-like figures originally came with paper labels giving a title; these should be on the front of their bases. On the underside is always a number, identifying their series. Sometimes there are six different figures to a series. Therefore it is necessary to know exactly what activity each child is doing. Sometimes a figure will have 'Arnart Imports' and 'Hand Painted' on the base, while others may be marked with crossed arrows. Figures range from 4½" to 10" high; wall pockets were made too! An average retail price should be about $3 to $5 an inch high depending on the activity, props used, and condition.

Joan Oates
685 S Washington
Constantine, MI 49042
616-435-8353

I am interested in buying **animal figurines made by the Chic Pottery of Zanesville, Ohio**. This company also made figural planters and creamers. As information on this company is very scarce, I will describe the characteristics of the figures I have. Figures are hollow-molded white clay with only minimal painted details on white ground with a glossy glaze. Even with light detailing of only one to three colors and simplicity of form, each small figure has a distinct personality of its own. All my pieces are unmarked, however from research I know several marks were used. I am interested in hearing from anyone who has more information about this company and its products. Items wanted must be perfect with no chips or cracks. As there are so many unmarked figurines, please send a photo to help with identification along with SASE.

Linda Holycross
1202 Seventh St.
Covington, IN 47932

I am interested in **animal figurines, particularly horses, tropical fish, and greyhounds**. They can be made of china, glass, or pottery. Any size and any price range considered. Heisey and Imperial items are of special interest. Items must be perfect with no chips or repairs. Please send a good photograph of the item with price. **I will pay up to 90% of current book prices and shipping costs.**

Kathy Nascimbeni
609 Laundry St.
Kannapolis, NC 28083
704-933-5810

Girlie figurines in porcelain or chalkware are wanted: glamour girls, sexy ladies, naughties, bathing beauties. I pay between $20 and $500 (plus finder's fees) for pieces with sexy, naughty, risque, or glamour girl themes. The pieces may be figurals, mugs, flippers, ashtrays, nodders, etc. No crass or insulting pieces are desired. Examples are listed here:

Risque figurines of bathing beauties or glamour girls
Imaginative or whimsical representations of naughty women
Ashtrays with reclining bathing beauty whose legs 'nod' in the breeze
A figurine of a seemingly innocent lady — when flipped over, a more risque aspect is revealed

Quality of workmanship, fineness of detail, individual beauty, imagination, theme appeal, condition, and rarity are some of the factors I consider when pricing.

Dave
1101 Bay St., Apt. #1206
Toronto, Ontario
Canada M5S 2W8
1-800-801-8517

Wanted: **bisque and china bathing beauties and nudes**. These may be with or without wigs. No Japanese items wanted. Other wants include **dolls, other figurines, compacts, and compact purses**.

Lori Landgrebe
2331 E Main
Decatur, IL 62521
217-423-2254

	We Pay
Bathing Beauty, w/wig	**200.00+**
Compact/Purse Combination, before 1940	**200.00+**

Figurines and Flower Frogs

We have need of certain **DeGrazia figurines, plates, ornaments, and the Cocopah Girl figurine**, which was issued for the Hummel Club.

Dills Desert Place
1006 N Buena Vista Ave.
Farmington, NM 87401
595-325-0110

Wanted: **Brother Juniper figurines.** These are small male religious figures made by Publishers Syndicate Shatford Company in the 1950s. Each figurine has a little printed message. **I pay $20 and up**, depending on the figure.

Joy DeNagel
132 E Somerset Ave.
Tonawanda, NY 14150
716-836-3841 (best time 10 pm EST)

I am interested in purchasing **quality retired Pendelfin rabbit figurines and display pieces made prior to 1970.** Quality and condition are extremely important. Please send picture and/or description along with price desired. I will respond to all inquiries.

George Sparacio
P.O. Box 791
Malaga, NJ 08328
609-694-4167

I buy **American and European-made figural nude flower frogs**. Many of these frogs depict a woman or women scantily clad or with a flowing drape behind them. These items were used to enhance floral bouquets and arrangements. They were made in various countries but predominately in Germany, Japan, and the United States. I am interested in purchasing frogs in colored glass by famous glasshouses such as Cambridge, Fenton, Steuben, and also those made of ceramic materials. They can be marked or unmarked. Of special interest are those depicting two women dancing or skating. I will happily reimburse you for all actual shipping and insurance charges. I do not purchase items that have been repaired, cracked, or chipped. Premiums paid for any marked pieces in glass or ceramic.

Linda Peris
261 Bonnie Brae
Elmhurst, IL 60126
708-782-5369

Flower Frog Nudes	**We Pay**
Ceramic, under 4", ea	**20.00+**
Ceramic, 4" to 6", ea	**30.00+**
Ceramic, 6" or larger, ea	**40.00+**
Cambridge, ea	**75% of book value**
Fenton, ea	**75% of book value**
Fostoria, ea	**75% of book value**
Heisey, ea	**75% of book value**
New Martinsville, ea	**75% of book value**
Steuben	**75% of book value**

FIRE-KING

We buy **all unusual Fire-King dinnerware, kitchen and novelty items made by Anchor-Hocking from 1938 through 1940**. We buy all colors including jadite, azur-ite, turquoise, blue, pink, gray, and several decal patterns such as Blue Mosaic, Game Bird, and Honeysuckle. We like all kitchenware, especially jadite, black dot, Kitchen-Aide, and hand-painted items. We do not buy white with gold trim pieces or scratched, faded, chipped, or otherwise defective pieces. We pay for all shipping and insurance on items we purchase. Please include a large SASE with all correspondence.

April and Larry Tvorak
HCR #34, Box 25B
Warren Center, PA 18851
717-395-3775

	We Pay
Ball Pitcher, bull's eye, jadite	**200.00+**
Batter Bowl, turquoise blue, w/handle	**85.00+**
Bowl, turquoise blue w/basket weave	**12.00+**
Bowl, jadite w/raised wheat	**12.00**
Bowl, soup; restaurant jadite	**18.00**
Custard Cup, jadite	**12.00**
Demitasse Cup & Saucer, jadite	**25.00**
Gravy Boat, white	**10.00**

Fire-King

Juice-Saver Pie Plate, jadite	**85.00+**
Plate, jadite w/raised wheat	**15.00**
Splash-Proof Bowl, w/decal	**10.00+**
Novelty Football, amber, 2-pc	**25.00+**
Any Salt & Pepper Shakers, w/good lids, pr	**14.00+**
Fire-King Casserole Cookbook, 1944	**15.00+**

We specialize in **all Fire-King**. We do not buy any white or white with gold lines. We only buy pieces that are not chipped, cracked, or faded. So take a look in your cabinets, and I'm sure you'll find some Fire-King. If you want to make some money, give us a call. We are known for treating our customers as fair as we can and giving them the best deal we can.

Two of a Kind
115 E Main St.
Delphi, IN 46923
317-563-6479 or 317-742-1412

Jadite	**We Pay**
Ashtray	**5.00-10.00**
Bowl, Teardrop (Swedish Modern), 4-pc set	**50.00**
Bowl, Colonial Rim; 3-pc set	**20.00**
Bowl, Restaurant Ware, flanged	**10.00+**
Cigarette Box, w/rose-topped lid	**12.00+**
Cup & Saucer Set, demitasse; Jane Ray	**20.00**
Cup & Saucer Set, demitasse; other than Jane Ray	**10.00**
Gravy Boat	**20.00+**
Grease Jar	**10.00**
Pie Plate, juice saver	**30.00+**
Pitcher, ball style	**75.00+**
Any Sheaf of Wheat Piece, ea	**5.00+**

Turquoise	**We Pay**
Batter Bowl	**75.00+**
Bowl, Splash Proof, 4-qt	**15.00**
Soup Bowl	**7.00**

Miscellaneous Fire-King	**We Pay**
Bowl, mixing; Stripe, 3-pc set	**20.00+**
Bowl, mixing; Kitchen-Aide, 4-pc set	**45.00+**
Butter Dish, not clear bottom	**5.00+**

Grease Jar, Kitchen-Aide....................17.00
Grease Jar, Stripe....................13.00+
Grease Jar Lid....................3.00
Tulip Lid, screw-on type....................2.00
Measuring Cup, 50th-Anniversary....................5.00
Measuring Cup, sapphire blue, no spout....................50.00
Nipple Cover, sapphire blue....................50.00
Plate, Alice, w/red or blue trim, ea....................15.00
Salt & Pepper Shakers, pr....................14.00

I am looking for the following pieces of jadite. I am looking for pieces in mint or near-mint condition. I will not accept anything chipped, cracked, or badly scratched. The bottom is usually marked Fire-King Oven Ware or Fire-King Oven Ware Made in USA. I pay all shipping charges.

Jadite pieces wanted include:

Milk Pitcher, 20-oz, plain
Jane Ray Demitasse Cups & Saucers
Butter Dish, jadite bottom with clear lid
Swedish Modern Teardrop Mixing Bowls, in 8¾", 6¾" & 6¼" sizes
Mixing Bowls, ribbed similar to Jane Ray cups, in 4¾", 5⅜", 6", 7½", & 9" sizes
Lids, for ribbed bowls, clear with ribbing, in 4¾", 5⅜",& 6" sizes

I do not know what these items are going for, but I am willing to pay any reasonable price for them.

Wendy Seamons
614 N Main
Lewiston, UT 84320
801-258-2852

FISHING

I buy **old fishing lures and other related items** such as nets, creels, reels, decoys, dealer catalogs, honor badges, and empty lure boxes. Prices depend on age, condition, and rarity. Top prices paid for new in the box lures. The following are examples of prices paid for wooden glass-eyed lures.

Dave Hoover
1023 Skyview Dr.
New Albany, IN 47150
812-945-3614

	We Pay
Creek Chub Catalog, 1938	95.00
Creek Chub Sucker	200.00
Creek Chub Gar	200.00
Creek Chub Dinger	30.00
Creek Chub Beetle	65.00
Creek Chub Ding Bat	15.00
Creek Chub Weed Bug	125.00
Heddon Underwater Minnow, 5-hook	85.00
Heddon Musky Surfusser	250.00
Heddon Dummy Double	400.00
Heddon Pumpkinseed	50.00
Heddon Zarragossa	115.00
Heddon Black Sucker	750.00
Heddon Manitau Minnow	650.00
Millers Reversible	1,500.00

We buy **unusual and original fishing lures, reels, tackle boxes, old fishing lures with glass eyes and good paint, and 5000c Ambassador reels with four screws**. Other wants include cookie jars, McCoy and Shawnee pottery, and all varieties of glassware (especially from the 1930s and 1940s). All glassware must be in good condition — no cracks, chips, etc. We reimburse actual UPS and insurance charges.

Jim Kirkpatrick
Rt. 1, Box 22
Mineola, TX 75773
903-569-6518

	We Pay
Reels	5.00+
Wooden Lures	5.00+
Shawnee	5.00+

McCoy ....5.00+
Cookie Jars..7.50+
Glassware ....3.00+

As an old-time collector, I will pay the following prices for **quality tackle in excellent condition**. The listings are mostly Heddon but I will also buy most other manufacturers' items. Sorry — no plastic or repaints wanted.

Harold Ruth
Rt. 1, Box 38
Paton, IA 50217
515-968-4544

Heddon **We Pay**

Black Sucker..800.00
Bottlenose Tadpolly 275.00
Moonlight Radiant 2,000.00
Sharkmouth Minnow...300.00
Wood River Runt...25.00
Yowser 75.00
400 Killer 300.00
700 Muskolunge Minnow, 5-hook 400.00
740 Wood Punkinseeds, ea..50.00+
800 or 900 Swimming Minnow, ea 250.00
4-15 Reel..900.00
Whitehouse Angler Reel 50.00
Wood Reel or Lure Boxes ....75.00+

Other Companies **We Pay**

Winchester Reels, ea ....50.00+
BF Meek #3...700.00
Meek Milam #2, brass 1,200.00
Meek Milan #2, silver 900.00
Winchester Lure, 5-hook 250.00
Tackle Catalogs, pre-1940, ea 10.00-100.00

FLAGS

'Not an old rag, but a flag, and we'll buy it!' We actively pursue **old original historical flags and related items** — having purchased over 1,000 examples over the past three decades. We buy old military flags, naval battle ensigns, obsolete national, and maritime merchant ship flags. Tell us the size, construction (printed, appliqued, machine or hand embroidered), the flag's material (silk, wool, cotton), and fully describe or sketch the flag, or even better, send us a photo of your available flag. Prices for your flag will vary greatly based on the flag's age, condition, country of origin, and any available documented background information on the flag. We are also seeking old flag-associated items and parts but *not* modern or new commercial examples. If you are in doubt as to what you have, based on our long-time and extensive experience with flags, we also can provide a flag identification service.

The Colours
c/o Ben K. Weed
P.O. Box 4643
Stockton, CA 95204

	We Pay
American Flags, old	**35.00+**
Battle Streamers	**15.00+**
Battle Pole Rings (engraved)	**20.00+**
Cords & Tassels	**25.00+**
Flag Books	**10.00+**
Flag Cover Bags (military issue only)	**10.00+**
Flag Stands, metal, old & unusual only	**10.00+**
Flag Identification Services, per item	**35.00**
Fragment Flag Pieces (w/documentation)	**20.00+**
Guidons (swallow-tailed w/numbers & PQMD tag)	**15.00+**
Military Unit Flags (depot-made only)	**75.00+**
Military Flags & Pennants, worldwide	**35.00+**
Navy Basic Training Books	**3.00**
Navy Flags (Navy Yard-made & dated)	**10.00+**
Parade Programs, 1991 Desert Storm Victory NY/DC	**5.00+**
Photos, clear flat display views of flags	**10.00+**
Photos, troop w/clear view of unit flag	**10.00+**
Photos, parade w/clear view of old flag	**3.00+**
Plates of Flags (from old dictionaries, etc.)	**5.00+**
Prints (Old Glory or flags in combat)	**15.00+**
Pole Tops (eagles, spears, national emblems)	**10.00+**
Referrals (to others w/flags, if purchased	**10% finder's fee**
Rare Examples of the Above	**1,000.00+**

FRATERNAL ORGANIZATIONS

Masonic and Shriners items wanted: jewelry, coins, tokens, books, paper items, memorabilia — anything Masonic for my collection. Some trade items are available. **Tokens medals, coins, and other small collectibles** considered.

David Smies
Box 522
Manhattan, KS 66052
913-776-1433

FURNITURE

I am looking for specific pieces of 19th-century furniture. Let me hear from you.

Mary Wilson
P.O. Box 20233
Houston, TX 77225
713-938-6849 (pager) or 713-661-4656 (home/office)

We Pay

Period Signed Hitchcock Chairs, set of 4 or 6, black or brown, would consider odd chairs that work together if a set is not available, per chair....**up to 200.00**
Corner Cabinet, 19th-century only, can be rustic ....**up to 800.00**
Shaving Stand, w/attached mirror, 19th-century only ....**up to 400.00**

GAMBLING

I'm a major buyer and importer of **antique casino chips and plaques** from the world over, with a particular interest in casino chips (jetons) and plaques from France, Belgium, and Italy. I also collect mother-of-pearl and ivory poker chips from the USA and abroad. Some of my favorite gambling collectibles are the clay poker chips from the illegal clubs of the 1920s and 1930s. I'm also very interested in **gambling supply catalogs**, because many of the older catalogs show the actual chips and other gambling material that were used in actual casinos and clubs. This is very valuable information for a collector of gambling material. I have listed below some of the pieces I need to help complete my collection. I find the best way for you to describe what you have available is to take a Xerox copy of the piece and list its color and your asking price. Thank you for your time.

John Benedict
P.O. Drawer 1423
Loxahatchee, FL 33470
Phone or FAX 407-798-2520

We Pay

Casino de Vichy 100,000 Plaque .... **200.00+**
Casino de Vichy 1,000,000 Plaque .... **250.00+**
Casino Aix-les-Bains 100,000 Plaque .... **200.00+**
Casino Plombiers-les-Bains Placque, any denomination .... **75.00+**
Casino de Monte-Carlo Plaque (of superior quality), Day's #11a or #12d, ea .... **100.00+**
Casino de Monte-Carlo Plaque (of superior quality), Day's #13a or #13b, ea .... **125.00+**
Casino de Monte-Carlo Plaque (of superior quality), Day's #15a .... **150.00+**
Casino de la Mediterranee 100,000 Plaque .... **125.00+**
Casino de la Mediterranee 500,000 Plaque .... **150.00+**
Atlantic City Casino Plaque, any denomination (must be authentic), ea **200.00+**
Casino Plaque, any over 1,000,000 denomination .... **250.00+**
Full Box of 100 Poker Chips, marked Floridian Casino 1 or Floridian Casino 10, ea **1,000.00**
Full Box of 100 Poker Chips, marked Floridian Casino 100 .... **1,500.00**
Mother-of-Pearl Poker Chips or Plaques, w/lettering & denominations, ea ... **30.00+**
Ivory Poker Chips, w/lettering & denominations, ea .... **25.00+**
Posters, European casinos, lg, ea **300.00**

Complete Series of Casino Chips & Plaques — **We Pay**

Casino de Monte-Carlo .... **1,000.00+**
Casino Tucuman .... **100.00+**
Casino Challes-les-Eaux .... **300.00+**
Casino Evian-les-Bains .... **500.00+**
Las Vegas, Sands Casino .... **1,500.00+**
Las Vegas, any other casino .... **500.00+**

Casino Suppy Catalog — **We Pay**

Casino de Monte-Carlo .... **1,000.00+**
Casino Tucuman .... **100.00+**

Casino Challes-les-Eaux....................300.00+
Casino Evian-les-Bains....................500.00+

GLASS KNIVES

I am a friendly and enthusiastic collector of glass knives, and a member of the National Glass Knife Collector Club. There are a few glass knives that I don't yet have, and these are hard to find, but I will pay top prices for them. (I already have lots of glass knives with the common patterns of 3 stars, 3 pinwheels, or daisy-like flowers.) A rubbing, xerographic copy, or photo is much appreciated. Size and color are important because some glass knives are common in some sizes and colors and rare in others. Some of the hardest to find are in crystal, for example the Westmoreland Thumbguard with ribbed handle. Small nicks on the blade are acceptable, particularly if the knife is very rare. Please write. The following prices are approximate, and other glass knives are also wanted.

Adrienne Esco
4448 Ironwood Ave.
Seal Beach, CA 90740
310-430-6479

We Pay

Forest Green or Amber Grid (Aer-Flo), ea....................**200.00**
Crystal Thumbguard, w/ribbed handle....................**150.00**
Pink, plain handle, 8" to 8½" only....................**150.00**
Crystal Mini Thumbguard, 6" to 6½" only....................**125.00**
Pink ESP or BK....................**150.00**
Crystal Dagger, w/intact hand-painted decor....................**80.00**
Box Only, for Candlewick knife....................**5.00**

GLASSWARE OTHER THAN DEPRESSION GLASS

Wanting to buy the **Dewdrop pattern made by the Jeannette Glass Company from 1953-1956**. This pattern was made in crystal only. Dewdrop has alternating rows of smooth glass with rows of tiny-sized beads of glass so it almost has a striped effect. The prices below are listed in *Collectible Glassware of the '40s, '50s & '60s* by Florence, published by Collector Books. I will consider other pieces of Dewdrop.

Deedra Moore
Box 223
Ermine, KY 41815

	We Pay
Pitcher	**25.00**
Plate	**10.00**
Punch Bowl & Base	**24.00**
Snack Plate	**4.00**
Tumbler	**10.00**

I am interested in purchasing **Durand art glass**. I am also actively seeking original Durand sales catalogs as well as other Durand advertising or information. Condition is very important as cracked or chipped art glass has not much more than decorative value. Please send photo, description, and price along your phone number, or call and describe. Durand art glass was a division of Vineland Flint Glass Works in Vineland, New Jersey. This division was geared toward the manufacture of fine hand-blown art glass in the style of Tiffany and Steuben. Production began in 1924 and continued until 1931. Early Durand was unmarked. Later pieces were generally signed Durand or have Durand in script written across a large letter V.

Edward J. Meschi
129 Pinyard Rd.
Monroeville, NJ 08343
609-358-7293 or FAX 609-358-7293

I am a private collector looking for the pieces listed below. I will only purchase pieces in good condition. The glassware I am looking for was **made by Anchor Hocking during the '60s and '70s**. It is called **Early American Prescut**. There are several pieces in the line that do not have its notable star on them. They are the candelabra and the three-piece rectangular ashtray set.

Donna Smoots
P.O. Box 11507
Pueblo, CO 81001
719-543-4343

We Pay

Ashtray Set, rectangular, 6⅜x4" **8.00**
Ashtray, round, 5⅜" **4.00**
Ashtray, 4" (originally sold in set of 4) **3.00**
Bowl, paneled, 11¾" **20.00**
Bowl, serving; 9" **8.00**
Bowl, round, 7¼" **7.00**
Bowl, round, 4¼" **3.00**
Bowl, dessert; 5⅝" **5.00**
Cake Plate, w/base, 13½" **15.00**
Candy Jar, w/lid, 7¼" **7.50**
Candy Jar, w/lid, 5¼" **6.00**
Candelabrum, 7x5⅝", ea **15.00**
Cigarette Box, jeweled w/lid, 4¾" **8.00**
Coaster Set, 6-pc, per coaster **1.00**
Deviled Egg Tray, 11¾" sq **15.00**
Entertainment Set, 21-pc (13" serving tray, 10¾" serving bowl, 8-qt punch bowl, 8 cups & hangers, black plastic salad spoon & fork) **57.00**
Glass, juice; 5-oz **3.00**
Glass, water; 10-oz **4.00**
Glass, iced tea; 15-oz **5.00**
Flower Basket & Block, 6x4½" **7.00**
Hostess Tray, rectangular, 12x6½" **6.00**
Lamp Base, kerosene, lg **100.00**
Lazy Susan Set, 9-pc(tray, bowl, 6 relish dishes & brass swivel) **25.00**
Pitcher, 60-oz **15.00**
Pitcher, sq, 40-oz **6.00**
Relish Tray, 3 compartment, 12x6½" **5.00**
Relish Tray, 5 compartment, 13½" **10.00**
Snack Tray, 11" **4.00**
Snack Tray, 4 compartment, 11" **10.00**
Snack Set, 8-pc (4 10" plates & 4 cups) **5.00**
Water Set, 7-pc (60-oz pitcher & 6 10-oz glasses) **39.00**
Iced Tea Set, 7-pc (60-oz pitcher & 6 15-oz glasses) **45.00**

Complementary Table Serving Sets (in box) **We Pay**

Breakfast Set, 15-pc (6 juice glasses, 18-oz pitcher, sugar, creamer, salt & pepper shakers, w/12-oz syrup server) **45.00**
Table Server Set, 11-pc (butter dish, sugar, creamer, salt & pepper shakers, & 2

cruets w/stoppers)..**22.50**
Table Server Set, 7-pc (butter dish, sugar, creamer, salt & pepper shakers)....**15.00**
Sugar & Creamer Set, 4-pc (tray, sugar w/lid & creamer)...........................**12.00**

I am a serious collector of **iridescent stretch glass**. I am interested in all sizes, shapes, and colors — regardless of which company produced the item. I am particularly interested in pieces in ice blue, tangerine, red, black, ivory (custard), wisteria (purple), and teal. Please send a complete description of the piece or pieces you have for sale along with a photo, if possible, and your asking price. I am especially interested in the items listed below.

Also wanted are **Van Borough crystal stemware, tumblers, and accessory pieces made by Royal Doulton**.

Cal Hackeman
8865 Olde Mill Run
Manassas, VA 22110
703-368-6982

Stretch Glass	**We Pay**
Cake Stand, any color	**25.00-40.00**
Candlesticks, pink, tall, pr	**75.00-100.00**
Candlesticks, tangerine, tall, pr	**100.00-200.00**
Candlesticks, dolphin, short or tall, pr	**25.00-150.00**
Candlesticks, any other color, tall, pr	**25.00-100.00**
Punch Cup, any color	**20.00-35.00**
Tea Cup & Saucer Set, any color	**20.00-40.00**
Toothpick Holder, any color	**35.00-75.00**
Vase, dolphin handles, fan form	**25.00-100.00**
Other Vases, Compotes, Bowls, Plates, Trays, Sugars, Creamers, or any type Shakers	**Write**

Victorian colored glassware was very popular in the late 1800s and that is when sugar shakers, syrup pitchers, and cruets were often made in colored glass with opalescent swirls and other fancy designs. Patterns and designs are numerous and base colors range from cranberry to clear and blue to black. Original lids are important but I will still buy if parts are missing. I will also buy loose lids for sugars and syrups. Beware of reproductions as Fenton and other glass companies reproduced these items. Send photo and description. **Patterns wanted include**:

- Coin Spot
- Mt Washington
- Daisy & Fern
- Spanish Lace

Spatter
Any Opalescent Design
Swirl
Plus Hundreds of Others

Jeff Bradfield
90 Main St.
Dayton, VA 22821
703-879-9961

I am buying **crystal that is known as cut to clear, cased, or cut overlay**. It is actually glassware with one or more overlying colors through which a design has been cut. I am especially interested in acquiring colored stemware from the brillant period (1890s) with deep cuttings and good colors. I am not interested in that which is currently being imported from overseas.

Paula Atwell Whitmore
401 College Pl., #14
Norfolk, VA 23510
804-627-1869

	We Pay
Bowl	**40.00+**
Candlesticks	**25.00+**
Hock Wine Goblet	**25.00**
Sherry Wine Goblet	**20.00**
Cordial Goblet	**15.00**

GOAT-RELATED ITEMS

I buy moderately-priced pre-1950 goat-related items such as books or booklets on goats, Billy Whiskers series books, figurines, carvings, and photos (goats with carts, packs on ships, etc.). Send description of item and condition. If the item is a figurine or carving send a photo also. Prices paid depend on condition and whether or not I already have a similar item.

Linda Toivainen
R.R. 1, Box 128 Middle Rd.
Waterboro, ME 04087

	We Pay
Books or Booklets, ea	1.00-5.00
Billy Whiskers Series Books, ea	2.00-10.00
Photos, pre-1950, ea	1.00-5.00

GOLF COLLECTIBLES

I am buying golf memorabilia. Listed here are some of the items I want:

Wood & Steel-Shafted Clubs
Youth-sized Wooden-Shafted Clubs
Books & Bookends
Autographed Score Cards
Tournament Programs
Contestant Badges & Equipment (must be documented)
Photographs
Flyers, Prints, Paintings & Other Art
Old Catalogs
Early Magazines
Golf Records
Films
Stereoscoptic Cards
Pipe Racks & Stands
Ashtrays & Lighters
Pen Desk Sets & Inkwells
Doorstops, with golf club, golf ball logos, or golf motifs
Statues, of bronze, silver, china, etc.
Children's Toys & Games (early)
Golf Balls & Bald Molds
Tees, with maker's name
Golf Bag Stands, early, with half bag attached to lower half of stand
Putter Practice Stands
Golf Advertising, Posters, & Broadsides
Walking Sticks & Canes
China & Pottery Items, by Gerz, Lenox, Winton, O'Hara, Doulton, Copeland, Wedgewood, etc

Richard Regan
293 Winter St., #5
Hanover, MA 02339
617-826-3537

	We Pay
Common Wood-Shafted Clubs, 1910-1937, ea	**5.00-1,500.00+**
Spliced Woods, pre-1905, ea	**100.00-1,500.00+**
Odd Clubs, pre-1920, ea	**75.00-1,500.00+**
Golf Balls, pre-1904, ea	**5.00- 1,000.00+**
Golf Books, 1st printings, 1920-1970, ea	**5.00-100.00**
Golf Books, 1st printings, pre-1920, ea	**10.00-500.00+**
MacGregor Woods: M85, M75, 693 or Penna WW, ea	**75.00-500.00+**
Putter's Ring 1A, B66, Scottsdale IMG, IMG5, IMG6, ea	**50.00-500.00+**

I buy **wood-shafted golf clubs from years prior to 1930 and also old golf items** such as tees, balls, etc. I do not buy steel-shafted clubs or clubs with coated shafts. A magnet can be used to determine if the shafts are coated steel or wood as the coated shafts sometimes resemble wood shafts.

Arthur H. Vanderbeek
15 Pearl St.
Rouses Point, NY 12979
518-297-6146

	We Pay
Driver	**12.00+**
Iron	**10.00+**
Putter	**12.00+**
Ball, old only	**5.00+**
Tees, in boxes or bags	**10.00+**
Miscellaneous Items, ea	**10.00+**

GRANITEWARE

I am always looking for **quality swirl graniteware in all colors** (blue, cobalt blue, green, brown, and red). Also wanted are **unusual gray pieces or common gray pieces with original paper or stamped labels**. Listed are just a few pieces I want with prices I pay for items in excellent condition. Please call or send a photo.

Daryl
P.O. Box 2621
Cedar Ripids, IA 52403
319-365-3857

Swirl Colors	We Pay
Butter Churn, green	**up to 1,000.00**
Butter Churn, blue	**up to 850.00**
Cream Can, colors other than old red, ea	**up to 250.00+**
Cream Can, old red	**up to 1,000.00+**
Sugar Bowl, colors other than old red, ea	**up to 400.00**
Coffeepot, old red	**up to 750.00+**
Muffin Pan, all colors, ea	**up to 400.00+**
Measurer, all colors, ea	**up to 400.00+**
Water Pitcher, all colors, ea	**up to 250.00+**
Funnel, colors other than old red, ea	**250.00+**
Funnel, old red	**up to 500.00**

Gray	We Pay
Biscuit Cutter	**up to 300.00**
Match Safe	**up to 200.00**
Butter Churn, floor model	**up to 1,000.00**
Comb Case	**up to 250.00+**
Shaker Set	**up to 250.00+**
Castor Set	**up to 1,000.00+**

GRAPETTE

If an items says Grapette, Orangette, Lymette, Lemonette, or Cherryette, we are interested. We buy mint to near-mint condition items and will pay fair prices for items that interest us. Condition is very important, so please describe any flaws when you write. If possible, a photo of the item is very helpful along with your price. As avid collectors of Grapette memorabilia, we buy:

- Advertising Signs
- Clock
- Bottle Openers
- Store Displays
- Extra Bank Lids
- Thermometers
- Coolers
- Calendars
- Bottle Carriers
- Cardboard Signs
- Grapette Cat & Elephant Banks
- Unused Pop Bottle Caps
- Stadium Cushions
- Many Other Items Wanted

Dee and Connie Mondey
P.O. Box 272
Haslet, TX 76052-0272
817-439-4807

HAGEN-RENAKER

I buy all Hagen-Renaker figurines. I especially want extra-large animals which are about 2" to 12" in size. But I will buy collections of the smaller pieces as well (sizes range from ¼" to 2"). Hagen-Renaker also did a line of Disney pieces in both large and small sizes, and I'm looking for these as well. Condition is not important but items in less than mint condition will lower the price I'm willing to pay. (I will even buy some pieces with missing parts.) I will reimburse all postage and insurance charges.

Catherine Chipkewich
12080 San Jose
Redford, MI 48239-2559
313-937-0203

	We Pay
Cat, Siamese, 6" to 7"	**20.00+**
Cat, Siamese, 2"	**3.00**
Cow, Jersey, standing, 7" to 8"	**30.00+**
Deer, recumbent, 4"	**15.00+**
Deer, fawn, standing, 2" to 4"	**10.00+**
Dog, Collie, standing, 6"	**25.00+**
Dog, Dachsie, standing, 5x11"	**35.00+**
Elephant, walking, 8" to 10"	**40.00+**
Foal, bucking w/nose touching ground, 4" to 5"	**25.00+**
Giraffe, standing, 8" to 10"	**30.00+**
Horse, running, 2"	**10.00+**
Horse, Golden Drafter, 7" to 8"	**50.00+**
Pixie, sitting, crawling, etc; 2" to 4", ea	**15.00+**
Woodpecker, w/wire legs, 2" to 3"	**3.00**
Zebra, standing, 6" to 7"	**30.00+**

HALL CHINA

We buy **all Hall teapots, all china coffeepots, lids, infusers, all decaled teapots and coffeepots, hand-painted and musical items (must be complete), plus other Hall items**. These were made between 1920 and 1960. We don't buy new stuff, cracked, or chipped items. Prices listed are examples. Condition will dictate actual price as will rarity of some items. You will be reimbursed for shipping and insurance. Write us first for best price. All letters answered.

Harold G. Davis
P.O. Box 74
Galloway, OH 43119

Teapots	We Pay
Auto	350.00
Aladdin	30.00
Albany	35.00
Air Flow	35.00
Baltimore	30.00
Basket	75.00
Basketball	350.00
Bird Cage	350.00
Boston	20.00
Cleveland	40.00
Doughnut	250.00
Football	350.00
French	25.00
Globe	45.00
Hollywood	35.00
Hook Cover	25.00
Illinois	85.00
Indiana	85.00
Kansas	150.00
Los Angeles	30.00
Melody	100.00
Nautilus	100.00
New York	25.00
Ohio	80.00
Parade	30.00
Philadelphia	30.00
Rhythm	80.00
Saf-Handle	80.00
Sani-Grid	40.00
Star	40.00

Streamline **40.00**
Surfside **80.00**
Windshield **35.00**

Decaled Pots **We Pay**

Blue Willow **100.00**
Cactus **100.00**
Blue Blossom **125.00**
Blue Garden **125.00**
Blue Blossom Drip Coffee **200.00**

I collect **old Hall teapots** and do have quite a few, but like all collectors, I'm always looking for one I don't have. There is no way to list the numerous teapots I would like to purchase. A purchase depends on the amount of gold, age of the teapot, its condition, shape and color, plus your asking price.

Barbara Craft
2021 Lincoln
Emporia, KS 66801

HALLMARK COLLECTIBLES

New collector is interested in Hallmark Christmas ornaments, mint in box or no box. I would prefer 'cute' plastic types — animals, children, angels, and Santas — but would consider satin and glass balls. I would especially like to buy 'Baby's First Chirstmas 1981 (boy),' 'Baby's First Christmas 1984 (girl),' 'Frosty Friends,' 'Muppets,' or outer space-related ornaments. Send description of ornament(s), year made (if known), and asking price.

Karen Geary
5178 U.S. Hwy. 60 W
Paducah, KY 42001

HALLOWEEN

We want to buy **all types of old Halloween items from the 1880s through the 1950s**! We especially like German papier-mache candy holders, such as witches, black cats, pumpkin characters, and vegetable people. We also want papier-mache Halloween lanterns (cat heads, pumpkins, etc.) with tissue paper faces, as well as celluloid Halloween toys. Other items we want are:

Toys, hard plastic, from the 1940s through 1950s
Noisemakers, tin with wood handle & Halloween scenes
Clickers, tin with Halloween themes
Early Composition Pumpkin People
Dennison Catalogs (Halloween decorations)
Halloween Postcards, pre-1920
Jack Pumkinhead Material From *Wizard of Oz* Stories
Any Other Unusual Old Halloween Items

Sample prices are listed below. We answer all letters. See other wants listed under Christmas in this book.

Bob and Diane Kubicki
R.R. #1
W Milton, OH 45383
513-698-3650

We Pay

Book, *Jack Pumpkinhead of Oz*, old version .... **30.00+**
Candy Container, composition vegetable man, 8" .... **100.00+**
Candy Container, composition black cat, removable head, glass eyes, 4" ... **65.00+**
Candy Container, composition black cat in dress, removable head, marked German **225.00**
Candy Container, papier-mache witch, German .... **175.00+**
Clicker, tin w/Halloween theme .... **2.00+**
Lantern, papier-mache black cat w/paper face .... **45.00+**
Lantern, pumpkin head w/tissue face, 6" .... **45.00+**
Lantern, German papier-mache pumpkin, 4" .... **65.00+**
Noisemaker, tin w/Halloween theme & wood handle .... **7.00+**
Noisemaker, ratchet-type w/composition pumpkin man .... **75.00+**
Postcard, vegetable people, dated 1911 .... **5.00+**
Pumpkin, composition, w/vegetable People, German, lg .... **285.00+**
Pumpkin Man in Top Hat, composition, 4" .... **45.00+**
Tambourine, German paper & wood pumpkin face .... **55.00+**
Toy, clown on wheels, hard orange plastic .... **12.00+**
Toy, witch on motorcycle, hard plastic .... **25.00+**
Toy, black cat on pumpkin, celluloid, 3" .... **55.00+**

Toy, pumpkin car w/witch & black cat, 4" long .... **100.00+**
Trade Catalog, Dennison's (Halloween decorations), 1920s .... **12.00+**

HEAD VASES

I will buy any head vase that you have to sell – ladies, men, children, or animals! These vases must be a head form with a hole in the top for flowers, etc. Price paid will depend on condition and style of head. Please send picture if available or detailed description. I will buy one or thousands! Especially lady heads!

Jean Griswold
701 Valley Brooks Rd.
Decantur, GA 30033
404-299-6606

HEISEY

We buy **all kinds of Heisey glass** as long as it is in mint condition — no chips or cracks and very little signs of wear. We particularly are interested in Heisey colors and pay book price for Alexandrite (lavender).

Susan Correa
12636 Shirley St.
Omaha, NE 68144
402-333-7425

We Pay

Alexandrite, nut cup .... **book value**
Alexandrite, other Empress Alexandrite pieces, ea .... **book value**
Flamingo (pink), all pieces, ea .... **50% of book value**
Sahara (pale yellow), Empress w/Chintz or Formal Chintz, ea... **90% of book value**
Sahara, all others, ea .... **50% of book value**
Marigold, all pieces, ea .... **75% of book value**
Tangerine, all pieces, ea .... **85% of book value**
Cobalt, all pieces, ea .... **90% of book value**

Zircon, all pieces, ea .... **70% of book value**
Other Types of Elegant Glass .... **Call or Write**

Collector wanting to buy Heisey **Plantation pattern (all pieces)**. Pieces in other Heisey patterns will be considered, but Plantation is highest priority. Immediate wants are listed below; only buying mint glass without defects. I will pay prices listed in latest edition of appropriate Florence references. Actual UPS and insurance costs reimbursed. Call first, after 7 pm weekdays.

Richard O. Thomas
242 Shelton Shop Rd.
Stafford, VA 22554
703-659-7161

Heisey Plantation **We Pay**

Underplate (for punch bowl), 18" .... **book value**
Blown Sherbert/Sundae Dish .... **book value**

HOLLY HOBBIE

We buy **Holly Hobbie figurines, porcelain dolls, and adult dinnerware only**. All of these items should be marked with either Holly Hobbie, H. Hobbie, or H.H. Most of them have the year and the name of the item. For example, Holly Hobbie-MCMLXXIV is on the bottom of the Keepsake series; some will have a tag on them. Also they are more valuable if they have their original boxes. We don't buy crazed, chipped, cracked, or mended items. We reimburse actual UPS and insurance charges.

Ted and Helen McCale
1006 Ruby Ave.
Butler, MO 64730-2500

We Pay

Figurine, A Mother Is Love, girl w/rag doll, 1976 .... **100.00**
Figurine, A Merry Touch, girl & boy putting packages on sled, 1986 .... **75.00**
Figurine, A Mother's Love, Love Is a Sweet Bouquet, lady w/baby, 1984 . **60.00**
Figurine, Anniversary, Beautiful Dreamer, dancing girl, musical, 1983 .... **40.00**
Figurine, Birthday, for ages 7, 8, 9, 10, 11, 12, 13, or 16, 1983, ea ... **15.00-25.00**

Figurine, Blue Girl, kitten w/standing girl holding toy, 5⅜"........................**25.00**
Figurine, Christmas Greetings, girl & boy at mailbox, 1983........................**70.00**
Figurine, Christmas Magic, girl & boy on rocking horse, 1987.................**150.00**
Figurine, Mother's Remembrance, girl w/2 lambs, 1974..........................**100.00**
Figurine, Hobbie Horse B 003, girl & boy atop rocking horse, miniature...**15.00**
Figurine, Love, girl w/rag doll, pewter miniature, 1977...........................**40.00**
Figurine, Love Is a Dance of Joy, dancing boy & girl, 1984........................**55.00**
Figurine, Months of Joy series, January, March, October, November, or December, 1983 or 1984, ea..**30.00**
Figurine, girl w/2 lambs (untitled), 1977..**100.00**
Figurine, Mother's Stitch a Bond of Love, mother & daughter sewing quilt, 1978..**80.00**
Figurine, My Favorite Flavor, girl & boy w/ice cream truck, 1985...........**100.00**
Figurine, My Favorite Things, Holly Hobbie, musical, 1982........................**75.00**
Figurine, O Christmas Tree, girl & boy decorating tree, 1988..................**100.00**
Figurine, Partridge & Pear Tree, Christmas 1981, pewter miniature..........**40.00**
Figurine, Ready for Santa, girl & boy in front of fireplace, 1989.............**100.00**
Figurine, Waiting for Santa, girl & boy waiting for Santa, 1984.................**60.00**
Plate, A Mother's Love, woman putting on a child's rain gear, 1979.........**20.00**
Plate, Christmas Greetings, girl & boy at mailbox, 1983, 8"........................**20.00**
Plate, Happy Hearts, Love Starts in Happy Hearts, girl & boy w/hearts, 1983, 8"...**20.00**
Plate, Joyful Love, Love Is a Dance of Joy, dancing boy & girl, 1984..........**25.00**
Plate, Love Collection, Gift of Love, girl pinning flower on boy, 1979, 8".**20.00**
Plate, Mother's Sweet Love, woman & child w/cookie jar, 1980...............**20.00**
Plate, The Recital, girl at piano & boy w/violin, 1983, 8"..........................**45.00**
Plate, Sharing Merry Times, girl & boy putting packages on sled, 1986....**20.00**

HOMER LAUGHLIN

We are interested in locating **embossed Oven-Serve with or without decals**. We collect all colors and will buy only those made by Homer Laughlin Company (HLC) in very good to excellent condition. We are also attempting to locate further information with regard to the embossed Oven-Serve line. Our only available reference is Huxford's *The Collector's Encyclopedia of Fiesta.* We will pay 60-70% of book value; higher prices paid for unusual pieces.

Also wanted are dinnerware pieces in the following Homer Laughlin Company shapes: Kwaker, Century, Nautilus, Eggshell, Georgian, and Theme. Decals may vary; however, we are particularly interested in HLC #W530 as shown on page 22 of *The Collector's Encyclopedia of Homer Laughlin* by Joanne Jasper. Pieces must be in good-plus to excellent condition. We are willing to pay 50% of book value, more for rarer pieces.

A. and J. Solomon
P.O. Box 23
Ebensburg, PA 15931
814-269-3038 or 814-344-8580 (leave message)

HULL POTTERY

We buy Hull in the **House 'n Garden** line. This heavy oven-proof dinnerware was manufactured in Mirror Brown and trimmed with white/ivory foam dip. Contact us if you have any of the dinnerware pieces or the many accessory items produced in Crookville, Ohio. We will discuss the condition and price of each piece and will reimburse UPS and insurance charges. If agreeable, we will buy, trade, or sell. Also of interest is any piece with a rooster or the Gingerbread series. Some specific items wanted include:

Canister Set, round, #556-#559
Carafe, 2-cup size, w/lid, #505
Serving Dish, oval, #574
Corn Server Set, #573
Continental Mug, #571
Spaghetti Platter, oval, #582
Corky Piggy Bank, large, #197
Salad Server, rectangular, #583
Snack Tray, oval, #554
Fish Platter, #596
Stein, jumbo, #572

Mr. and Mrs. C.D. Tyrie
130 E Young
Princeton, KY 42445
502-365-5263

ILLUSTRATOR ART

I am an avid Maxfield Parrish collector interested in prints, books, magazines, ads, and calendars. Please send a detailed description and a photo of your Parrish items along with your asking price. I will respond immediately to all offers.

Lisa Stroup
P.O. Box 3009
Paducah, KY 42002-3009

INSULATORS

Wanted: quality glass insulators and company trade catalogs. These were used in electrical and communication lines.

Mike Bruner
6980 Walnut Lake Rd.
W Bloomfield, MI 48323

	We Pay
Barclay Patent	25.00
Brookfield Beehive, purple	20.00
California Electrical Works, aqua	60.00
Canadian Diamond Pony, teal	20.00
Chicago, aqua, teardrop	80.00
Dominion 42, cornflower	55.00
EC & M, aqua	18.00
EC & M, green	35.00
Fred M Locke, cobalt	100.00
Harloe's Patent, aqua	85.00
Hemingray, cobalt	35.00
HG Company, amber	10.00
HG Company, cobalt, smooth base	60.00
Liquid, aqua	180.00
Pennyquick, deep green	35.00
Seilers Patent, aqua	150.00
Western Union (WU), cobalt	35.00

JEWELED-BRASS ITEMS

These jewel-encrusted beauties adorned posh dressing tables and boudoirs of 1900 through the 1940s. Richly **colored, faceted glass jewels and cabochon imitation stones embellish brass and plated brass (gold-tone) items** such as dresser trays, boxes, frames, vases, perfumes, powder containers, dishes, hand mirrors, vanity sets, lamps, etc. Delicate filigree work, ornate embossing, faux pearls, or enameling adorn pieces. Items wanted have fine quality jewels secured by a rim of metal; no glued-on stones, please. Also seeking **antique purses with ornate jeweled frames** and small, very fancy brass purses which are jewel-encrusted, hinged, with metal tassel and chain.

The variety of jeweled-brass items manufactured is extensive. Pieces may have glass, ceramic, or marble components. Colored glass insert dishes usually have intaglio designs. Items may be footed. Trays often have a fine lace doily under glass. Perfume bottles may be entirely brass with jewel ornamentation or of colored glass with applied jeweled filigree. Markings include: Czechoslovakia, Austria, France, N.Y., Empire Art Gold, Apollo, Silvercraft, or it may be found unmarked. I prefer items that are heavily jewel-encrusted with elaborate brasswork. Also buying **Czechoslovakian jeweled brass and glass jewelry**.

Victorian Touch
Valerie Roberts
P.O. Box 4
Micanopy, FL 32667
904-466-4022

We Pay

Boudoir Lamp, stick type, heavily jeweled & embossed, French silk shade pr **180.00**
Box, hinged lid w/faceted jewels & stones, footed, 3x5" **75.00**
Dress Clip, heavy openwork, pink & purple jewels, 3" **38.00**
Dresser Cotton Jar, cranberry cut-to-clear, jeweled foot & cap, pearls **110.00**
Dresser Dish, handled jeweled holder, blue glass dish etched w/fairy & cherub **85.00**
Dresser Tray, ribbon designed handles, lace doily, jeweled, 12" dia **95.00**
Necklace, purple glass beads & brass, jeweled & enameled medallion, Czechoslovakia **70.00**
Perfume, pink cut glass, applied filigree w/enameling, jewels, 6" **125.00**
Perfume Atomizer, heavy embossing w/metal flowers & jewels, 8" **85.00**
Pin Tray, jeweled stand, hanging jeweled dish w/intaglio design **65.00**
Picture Frame, 24 lg colored jewels, bow crest, Empire Art, 15" oval **135.00**
Powder Jar, opaque glass, lid w/jewels, stones, pearls, gargoyles **80.00**
Purse, tapestry w/figural design, jewels & stones on frame of foliate openwork, chain **175.00**
Purse, teardrop shape, ornate jewels, pearls & enameling, jeweled metal tassel, compartments & compact, marked Trinity Plate, 2½x4" **185.00**
Salt, 3 tiered intaglio dishes on jeweled stand, footed **85.00**
Vase, embossed, jeweled w/pearls, amber glass insert **65.00**

JEWELRY

For those of us who love wearing and owning vintage costume jewelry, it is a real thrill to have the opportunity to buy new pieces. As a collector/dealer of **all types of costume jewelry**, I am currently buying quality items in good condition (plating not worn, enamel not chipped, pin-back closures and clasps in working order, etc.). I am looking for all types of signed items, unsigned sets (necklace, bracelet, earrings, or brooch in combination of two or more), colorful brooches, and early plastic items such as bangle bracelets and figural pins in the shape of people and animals. I am also interested in purchasing other ladies' items such as **compacts, beaded or mesh bags, make-up items, and virtually anything decorated with rhinestones**. Lots of broken jewelry or pieces missing stones are also desired to use for repairs.

Pamela Wiggins
6025 Sunnycrest St.
Houston, TX 77087
713-649-6603

	We Pay
Designer Items (Haskell, Eisenberg, Hollycraft, etc), ea	**up to 100.00**
Other Signed Items (Coro, Lisner, BSK), ea	**up to 50.00**
Unsigned Sets	**up to 50.00**
Colorful Unsigned Brooches, ea	**up to 30.00**
Early Plastic Pieces, ea	**up to 50.00**
Compacts, ea	**up to 25.00**
Beaded or Mesh Bags, ea	**up to 50.00**
Make-Up Items, ea	**up to 10.00**

I am on a quest to find the earrings that I remember playing dress-up with when I was a tot. Now that I've been to a few flea markets, I know they were made by **Hollycraft** and I have inadvertantly become the owner of several pieces of quite diverse Hollycraft —but still haven't found my mother's beautiful multicolored earrings. If you've got any Hollycraft (it doesn't have to be the multicolored stuff, either!) let me know!

Ruth J. Katz
2109 Broadway Ste. 10-54
New York, NY 10023
212-870-1471

I am collecting **all kinds of cameos** but especially am looking for shell or stone pieces made before 1940. The older the item and the more unusual the better. Scenic pieces are also desired.

Please send photo along with your address, phone number, and your asking price. Please note any wear or damage and describe materials if possible. Also give me any provenance (history) if known. My general pricing structure is as follows and depends on age, condition, and scarcity. I will send you a deposit of 10% of your asking price if your photo looks promising. If after inspection I decide not to purchase your items, I will return them at my expense and forfeit my deposit. I am also soliciting information from collectors and dealers on cameos for research project.

Dorothy Hodges
148 W Ave. L
Calimesa, CA 92320
909-795-3170

Cameos	**We Pay**
Costume Glass or Plastic, ea	**5.00-10.00**
Gold-Filled Shell or Stone, ea	**15.00-35.00**
Gold Shell or Stone, ea	**50.00-100.00**
Sterling, Shell or Stone, ea	**25.00-35.00**
Unusual Material, rare & old	**Call or Write**

I am an active buyer of **vintage costume jewelry** and am purchasing by the piece, a boxful, or an entire estate! The jewelry I am seeking is from the Victorian era up to the 1950s and 1960s. I especially like jewelry from the 1930s and 1940s, but you need not be familiar with exact age. Pieces can be signed or unsigned. I like large pins, clips, and bracelets, but I am interested in any old jewelry. I pay very fair market prices if condition is good, but I also buy jewelry that needs stones and pin-backs. I also buy quantities of loose rhinestones, old parts and pieces by the bag or warehouses full! A picture or photocopy of items along with price wanted can help you attain a quick sale, or you can call and describe items.

The Curiosity Shop
Lynell Schwartz
P.O. Box 964
Cheshire, CT 06410
203-271-0643

	We Pay
Bakelite Pins or Bracelets, carved, wide, good color	**75.00+**
Bakelite Geometric Bangles, dots, zigzags, stripes, etc	**150.00+**
Bakelite Figural Pins	**75.00+**
Haskell Necklaces, w/pearls	**75.00+**

Haskell Earrings .... **25.00+**
Haskell Pins .... **50.00+**
Schiaparelli .... **75.00+**
Trifari Clips or Pins, 4" or larger .... **150.00+**
Trifari Pins, crown shaped .... **75.00+**
Trifari Gold-Tone Pieces .... **10.00+**
HAR Genies .... **Call or Write**
Unsigned Pins, Bracelets, Necklaces, Clips, Etc .... **Call or Write**
Box Lots or Estate Settlements .... **Call or Write**
Compacts, figural or unusual .... **75.00+**
Purses, mesh, beaded or needlepoint .... **100.00+**
Handbag Frames .... **25.00+**

I collect **rhinestone jewelry**, especially large pins, clips and brooches that have colored stones. I like jewelry that looks like people, faces, butterflies, crowns, bugs, bows, flowers, birds, etc. Large animal pins that have a clear body (usually found marked Trifari) and plastic (Bakelite) pieces and wide colorful bracelets are of special interest. I like fancy colorful rhinestone necklaces and jewelry sets. **Jewelry made between 1920 through 1960** is preferred, but I will also buy newer pieces if they are large or colorful. I prefer jewelry that is signed or marked in some way, but I will buy unsigned jewelry. I pay fair market prices for jewelry I like. As a collector, I often pay more than dealers.

Ronald Fitch
315 Market St.
Suite 2G
Portsmouth, OH 45662
614-353-6879

We Pay

Boucher (Marcel, MB) .... **up to 250.00**
Coro, Staret, or Napier .... **up to 500.00**
Eisenberg (or marked w/script E) .... **up to 600.00**
Chanel, or Chenel .... **up to 600.00**
Christian Dior (Grosse) .... **up to 350.00**
Ciner, or Har .... **up to 325.00**
Hattie Carnegie (HC) .... **up to 300.00**
Hobe, or Rebajes .... **up to 500.00**
Hollycraft, or De Lillo (Wm de Lillo) .... **up to 350.00**
Joseff-Hollywood .... **up to 300.00**
Kenneth Jay Lane (KJL) .... **up to 250.00**
Leo Glass, or Stanley Hagler .... **up to 500.00**
Mager Bros (Tomag, Mager) .... **up to 400.00**
Miriam Haskell .... **up to 300.00**

Nettie Rosenstein .... **up to 750.00**
Schiaparelli, or Reja .... **up to 400.00**
Schreiner .... **up to 350.00**
Trifari (or KTF or TKF) .... **up to 750.00**
Yves St Laurent (YSL), or Monet .... **up to 400.00**

I buy **quality costume jewelry from the 1800s through the 1950s**. I'm especially looking for animal pins, bracelets, and rings in rhinestones, sterling, gold filling, plating, etc. — the more unusual the better. I like tremblers and other movable jewelry and figurals. They must be in excellent condition. I also buy the **small blown-glass animals** sold in five-and-dime stores during the 1940s and 1950s.

Celie's Pretty Things
2942 Lynda Ln.
Columbus, GA 31906
706-561-3953

We Pay

Animal Pins **5.00-35.00**
Animal Bracelets or Rings **10.00-40.00**
Signed Jewelry (not animal) **5.00-50.00**
Unsigned Jewelry (not animal) **5.00-35.00**
Tremblers or Movable Jewelry .... **20.00+**
Glass Animals, sm **3.00-5.00**
Glass Animals, lg **4.00-7.00**

We buy **all types of jewelry from the 1800s to the present**. Our main focus is designer costume jewelry, but we also buy sterling and gold jewelry. I pay top dealer prices. We have been doing mail order for eight years and have a showroom located in Reseda. Please write and let us know what you have.

Patsy Comer's Antiques & Jewelry
7249 Reseda Blvd.
Reseda, CA 91335
818-345-1631

We are interested in buying your **costume or estate jewelry**. Our interest range from plastic to gold items. Rhinestones in colorful, clean, clear stones are wanted in whimsical designs such as animals, bugs, crosses, etc. Signed sets with good quality hand-set stones are wanted as well as plastic or Bakelite whimsical brooches, Black items, hand-carved or polka-dot bracelets, unsigned sets, etc. Victorian sterling or Deco-styled items are preferred. We especially want pieces marked Taxco with amethyst quartz settings or pieces by Jensen and Unger. Other Victorian items of gold with garnets, diamonds, pearls, etc., or with Deco influence in white gold filigree and diamonds are desirable. Also wanted are retro-period pieces in rose gold, rubies, and diamonds.

As you can see we 'play' with almost any kind of jewelry. We have been dealing for many years through the mail. Feel free to call or write.

Nancy and Julie Beall
1043 Greta St.
El Cajon, CA 92021
619-588-1488

I buy **class rings and some other rings if they have a karat mark** (10K, 12K, 14K, etc.) or if they are stamped sterling. While I like rings, I sometimes buy other jewelry. Items may be worn or broken as I can recycle these to make or repair other jewelry. Please write, describing what you have to sell, enclosing a photo or photocopy, and SASE for a prompt and fair offer. Or ship 'First Class-Insured' for offer by return mail. Always include your name and address.

Clifton A. Mather
P.O. Box 299
Otter Rock, OR 97369

	We Pay
Men's Class Ring, 10K	**15.00**
Women's Class Ring, 10K	**7.00**
Sterling Ring, per oz	**2.00**

Wanted: **Mexican silver** in large pins such as flowers, birds, animals, masks, or free-forms. The same forms are wanted in bracelets and necklaces — the larger the better. Pieces were made of solid silver and may be jeweled with amethyst, turquoise, jade, or colored glass. Other examples may have enameled work. I collect **sterling Mexican items** such as boxes, belts, flatware, etc., as long as they are pretty or interesting. I buy one piece or a collection. Send photo or Xerox and description of any writing found on the item. Pieces vary in style and size making it impossible to quote prices without seeing them. Indicate the price you expect, and we will try to agree. Please enclose SASE if you want a reply.

Jewell Evans
4215 Cork Ln.
Bakersfield, CA 93309
805-833-3776

I buy **old jewelry, especially Victorian**. I like mourning lockets and rings, hair jewelry, bangle bracelets, and anything unusual. I also like costume jewelry by Miriam Haskell, Hattie Carnegie, Eisenberg (not Eisenberg Ice), and Cartier. I'm only interested in unusual, good-quality pieces.

Millie Schick
Burholme Thrift Shoppe
7106 Rising Sun Ave.
Phil., PA 19111
215-742-8877 (Mon., Wed., Fri. or Sat. 10 am-3 pm; closed July & Aug.)

JOSEF ORIGINALS

We buy **Josef Originals made from 1945 to 1985**. This is the period when Muriel Joseph George designed all the figurines and animals. It is very important that each piece is examined for chips and breaks. Because of the way they were fired, the figurines can break and be glued back together so it is hard to tell if a piece is broken. We do not buy figures made by George Good or Applause who bought the company in 1985. All pieces are marked on the bottom with Josef Original in a stamped ink or incised mark and usually have an oval sticker that is black with gold or silver letters.

Jim and Kay Whitaker
Eclectic Antiques
P.O. Box 475, Dept. WB
Lynnwood, WA 98046
206-774-6910

	We Pay
Birth Month, common jewel, Japan	**8.00-10.00**
Birth Month, non-jewel, Japan	**10.00-12.00**
Birth Month, jewel, California	**13.00-16.00**
Birth Month, non-jewel, California	**11.00-14.00**
Figurine, International	**12.00-15.00**
Figurine, Birthday Girl, angel w/number	**10.00-15.00**
Figurine, miscellaneous, 3½" to 4½", ea	**12.00-15.00**
Figurine, miscellaneous, 5½" to 6½", ea	**20.00-25.00**
Figurine, miscellaneous, 7½" to 8½", ea	**30.00-35.00**
Figurine, miscellaneous, 9" to 10½", ea	**35.00-45.00**
Figurine, animals other than mice, depending on size, ea	**5.00-10.00**
Figurine, mice	**4.00-5.00**

KANSAS

For a short time from the late 1800s to around 1912, there were many glass and pottery plants in the area of southeast Kansas. Abundant natural gas (which began to run out by 1912) attracted two well-known fruit jar producers (Mason and Ball) to the Coffeyville area. Other glass plants (whose products are unknown today) also located there as well as several window-glass plants. A few of the products known to have been produced in the area are listed below. Also listed are sample miniature bricks which were put out by as many as a dozen or so different brick and tile plants.

Here, as everywhere else in the early days of the United States, a popular way for a merchant to advertise was to sell or give away a ceramic or glass souvenir featuring a view of a local park, a building, or a special event to visitors and local customers as well. Most of these plates, vases, jugs, etc., were made in Germany and England, as were view postcards and other items. Some souvenirs carried the message 'souvenir of (name of town, state).' We buy these as well as similar items with street names, buildings, etc. found on them. We also want postcards, calendars, or any advertising material.

Listed below are glass, pottery, souvenir, advertising, and related items we buy. We will buy other items and even some damaged pieces if contacted for prices. Please note that my hometown, Dearing, may also be spelled Deering.

Billy and Jeane Jones
P.O. Box 82
Dearing, KS 67340
316-948-6389

We Pay

Premium Glass Fruit Jar, Coffeyville, KS, pt or qt, ea **10.00**
Premium Glass Fruit Jar, Coffeyville, KS, half-gal, ea **12.00**
Premium Glass Fruit Jar, Coffeyville, KS, 1-gal, ea **35.00**
Premium (Plain) Fruit Jar, sizes as above, ea **8.00**
Premium 'Improved' Jar, ea **15.00**
Premium Lid w/'Coffeyville,' ea **3.00**
Premium Wire Clip, ea **4.00**
Premium Magazine Ads, Etc, ea **3.00**
Lace Edge Glass Plate, w/'Premium Jar,' Coffeyville, 7", ea **60.00**
Lace Edge Glass Plate, w/'Ball Jar,' Coffeyville, 7", ea **90.00**
Lace Edge Glass Plate, w/'Pioneer Glass,' Coffeyville, 7", ea **50.00**
Ball, The Mason, or Premium Wooden Boxes, Coffeyville, ea **75.00**
Coffeyville, Independence, Cherryvale, Buffalo, etc, Miniature Bricks, ea ... **15.00**
Any Tin or Cardboard Advertising Sign, Etc, marked as above .... **Write**
Ashtray, Dearing, marked Smelter, early 1900s, ea **20.00**
Stoneware Jug, bottom incised 'Made in Coffeyville,' brown .... **Write**
Stoneware Crock or Churn, bottom incised 'Made in Coffeyville,' brown **30.00**
Terraco O&H Coffeyville, KS; Pitcher, terra cotta, brown pottery **30.00**
Coffeyville Pottery & Clay Co (ie, Coffeyville Stoneware Co) Miniature Jug **40.00**
Coffeyville Pottery & Clay Co (ie, Coffeyville Stoneware Co) Crock, Churn or Jug, smaller than 3-gal, ea **30.00**
Coffeyville Pottery & Clay Co (ie, Coffeyville Stoneware Co) Crock, Churn or Jug, larger than 3-gal, ea **25.00**
Any Stoneware w/Sponge Decor, Advertising, marked as above, etc, ea .... **Write**
Magazine Ad, etc, relative to above **2.00**
Magazine Ad, Rea-Patterson Milling Co **2.00**
Advertising Signs (including Rea-Patterson), tin, cardboard, paper .... **Write**
Advertising Signs, Page Milk, Sweetheart Flour, Dearing, Millers Cash Stove, etc, ea **10.00**
Advertising Thermometer, Sweet & Pure or Sweetheart Flour (excellent condition only), ea .... **100.00+**
Picture or Postcard, any company listed, ea .... **Write**
Picture, Dearing, marked Smelter, ea **10.00**
View Postcard, Dearing, early 1900s, real photo, ea **15.00**
View Postcard, Coffeyville, Chanute, Independence, ea **3.00**
View Postcard, other southeast KS towns, ea .... **1.00+**
Calendar, Dearing, early 1890-1930, ea **15.00**
Calendar, Coffeyville, Chanute, or other southeast KS towns, ea .... **3.00+**
Calendar Plate, Dearing or Deering, early 1900s, ea **30.00**
Calendar Plate, Coffeyville, Independence, early 1900s, ea **20.00**
Calendar Plate, Caney, Wayside, early 1900s, ea **12.00**
Calendar Plate, Parsons, Oswego, Altamont, early 1900s, ea **12.00**
Plate, Dearing or Deering, china, scenic view, early 1900s, ea **20.00**
Plate, towns as listed above, china, scenic view, early 1900s, ea **10.00**
Plate, Dearing, marked White's Amusement Park, ea **25.00**
Bottle Cap, Carlton Hall, ca 1950s, ea .... **25¢**

Trade Tokens, Dearing, KS; Millers Cash Stove, etc, ea **25.00**
Hotel to Depot Tokens, metal or paper, Dearing, Coffeyville, etc, ea .... **Write**
Vase, Jug, etc, Dearing, china, scenic view, ea **15.00**
Vase, Jug, etc, other southwest KS cities, china, scenic view, ea **8.00**
Spoon, Dearing, sterling, ea **20.00**
Spoon, other southeast KS towns, sterling .... **Write**
Souvenir Item, Dearing, Heisey custard or other glass companies, ea **35.00**

KAY FINCH CERAMICS

We especially want animal and bird figures and prefer those on the pink clay with pastel decoration, though we would be interested in hearing about any you might have for sale. We don't collect any of the 'people' figures, except the small angels. This line of ceramics was made in California from the 1940s until 1963. Most pieces are signed.

Sharon Huxford
1202 Seventh St.
Covington, IN 47932
Phone or FAX 317-793-2392

We Pay

Figures, 3" to 4" .... **35.00+**
Figures, 5" to 6" .... **50.00+**
Figures, 7" to 9" .... **65.00+**
Figures, 12" .... **200.00+**
Larger Figures .... **Call**
Cookie Jar, dog or cat .... **Call**

KENTUCKY DERBY GLASSES

I buy Derby glasses made prior to 1974. Glasses must have bright colors and have no chips, cracks, flaws, or fading. I'll split postage and shipping costs. Prices for glasses dating before 1952 will be negotiable. Other wants include: **Van Briggle, McCoy with floral designs, Nippon, Coca-Cola, cigarette memorabilia, Evening in Paris items, older McDonald's® items, chil-**

dren's books in mint condition from before the 1950s, and books authored by Janice Holt Giles, Jesse Stuart, or Robert Penn Warren.

Betty Hornback
707 Sunrise Ln.
Elizabethtown, KY 42701
502-765-2441

Derby Year	We Pay
1953	**45.00**
1954	**45.00**
1955	**40.00**
1956	**60.00**
1957	**45.00**
1958, both styles, ea	**70.00**
1959	**30.00**
1960	**30.00**
1961	**40.00**
1962	**20.00**
1963	**22.00**
1964	**Do Not Buy**
1965	**20.00**
1966	**20.00**
1967	**20.00**
1968	**15.00**
1969	**Do Not Buy**
1970	**20.00**
1971	**15.00**
1972	**15.00**
1973	**15.00**
1974	**6.00**
Any Unofficial Derby Glass, ea	**5.00**

KNIVES

I buy **Bowie knives of any type and design up to 1920**. I prefer knives with stag, ivory, or mother-of-pearl handles but will buy all types. I am especially interested in Bowie knives with engraved or presentation blades. I am interested in knives in very good to excellent condition, but I will purchase knives in lesser condition if they are rare.

There are hundreds of varieties of Bowie knives. I am very interested in knives by these makers:

Samuel Bell
John Chevalier
Tiffany
Will & Fink
Schively
Alfred Hunter
Mark & Rees

It is helpful if you can send a photo or drawing of the knife you wish to sell. I will answer all letters. These are only a few examples of prices I will pay. I have been buying edged weapons for over 25 years; contact me for the best price.

David Hartline
P.O. Box 775
Worthington, OH 43085

Bowie Knives	**We Pay**
American, stag handle, 10" blade	**200.00+**
American, by Alfred Hunter, 10" blade	**500.00+**
American, marked California Knife	**500.00+**
California Gambler's Dirk, maker marked	**550.00+**
Confederate, knuckle bow type	**600.00**
English, marked IXL, 8" blade	**175.00+**
English, w/Bowie horse head pommel	**300.00+**
English, by George Woestenholm, stag grips	**200.00+**
English, maker marked, mother-of-pearl handles	**500.00+**

LACE AND NEEDLEWORK ITEMS

We buy — or find buyers for — a wide range of lace and linens, both collector's quality and wearable, usable, decorator's lace, and linens. No two pieces of antique lace are ever alike. If you provide a photocopy (a Xerox made with a dark background is better than a photograph, because it provides better detail) we can identify your lace for you and give you an approximate value.

Elizabeth M. Kurella
The Lace Merchant
P.O. Box 222
Plainwell, MI 49080
616-685-9792

Lace and Needlework Items

We Pay

Chantilly, shawls or veils, handmade, ea **100.00-300.00**
Chantilly, shawls or veils, machine, ea **50.00-100.00**
Irish Crochet, collars w/lots of raised work, ea **50.00-75.00**
Point de Gaze, shawls or veils, handmade, ea **200.00-500.00**
Point de Gaze, collars or edgings, ea **50.00-100.00**

We are interested in buying antique ecru lace and are looking for truly exceptional quality items. We buy **antique lace clothing from the 1920s and earlier** — exquisite lace gowns, dresses, jackets, coats, and blouses; ecru lace wedding veils; wax flower head pieces; antique lace and silk wedding shoes; ecru lace fans and parasols; collars; collarettes; headdresses and cuffs; lace doll and children's clothing. Also wanted are exquisite ecru lace bed and pillow covers; lace curtain panels; lace tablecloths; lace yardage, trims, appliques and scraps; metallic (gilt) thread lace garments; doilies; and trimmings.

Pieces may have elaborate embroidery, fringing, cutwork, pulled or drawn threadwork, or may incorporate figural designs. Lace can be extremely fine and delicate or of a thick, heavy texture. Articles must be in excellent or easily mendable condition. Age stains are often inevitable; stained items should be priced accordingly. *Please do not launder articles.* We do not buy black lace. Appreciate offers of reasonably priced box lots of lace for repair work. Please send photo and price.

We are also interested in purchasing **old needlepoint and Aubusson-style tapestry work** with figural and floral designs in muted colors, particularly larger pieces which may have been removed from old French settees. I prefer romantic figures, cherubs, flower and leaf designs, pastoral scenes, birds, and floral needlework incorporating glass beads. I would also like to purchase **antique handbags of tapestry, petitpoint and needlework** with these same motifs. Also interested in **furniture covered in needlework and fancy upholstery fringes and trimmings**. I do not wish to buy the newer machine-made Belgium tapestries (often faded), or items with religious, Oriental, or patriotic themes. A photograph along with price would be most appreciated.

Victorian Touch
Valerie Roberts
P.O. Box 4
Micanopy, FL 32667
904-466-4022

We Pay

Ecru Lace Gibson Girl Dress, 1890s **195.00**

Ecru Lace Jacket, heavy lace w/net lace inserts....................................... **220.00**
Wedding Gown, 1890s, silk lining, w/lace veil & lace silk shoes............ **255.00**
Lace Blouse, delicate w/elaborate design **125.00**
Ecru Lace Coat, ankle length, heavy Venetian needle lace **350.00**
Lace Bed Cover, pieced lace w/embroidery, knotted fringe **155.00**
Lace Baby Bonnet.. **25.00**

LAMPS, LANTERNS, AND LIGHTING FIXTURES

We buy select old lamps. We collect **unusual early oil lamps and the later electric Deco-type figural lamps**. Quality, condition, and rarity are important to us. The oil lamps with glass bowl and metal figural stems are fairly common, and it is the **all-glass lamps with figural stems** that we seek. We have written the books and collector manual-price guides for Aladdin kerosene and Aladdin electric lamps so we can help you identify and value them. We will buy certain ones needed for our collection. The lamps must be complete and in excellent working condition to bring the best prices. Write for free information on our books and annual antique lamp show and sale. Please describe your lamp (kind of glass, color, frost, etc.); photographs are very helpful.

J.W. 'Bill' and Treva Courter
3935 Kelley Rd.
Kevil, KY 42053
Phone or FAX 502-488-2116

We Pay

Lamp, clear glass w/lady figure (usually frosted)............................... **1,000.00+**
Lamp, clear or black glass w/figural lady's bust..................................... **200.00+**
Lamp, clear glass figural owl, swan, etc, ea .... **up to 1,000.00**
Lamp, three-face Warrior, etc, ea .... **400.00+**
Lamp, any unusual glass... **Call or Write**
Lamp, mechanical types such as Hitchcock or Mays, complete, ea .... **250.00+**
Shades, colored glass, 7" dia, ea.. **100.00+**
Aladdin, clear glass, electric, w/lady figures (more in color)....... **200.00-500.00**
Aladdin, student style.. **Wanted**
Aladdin, Model 1, 2, 3 or 4, kerosene, ea .... **200.00+**
Aladdin, parlor style.. **500.00+**
Aladdin Shade, green cased glass .... **250.00+**

Aladdin Whip-O-Lite Shade (more if pleated) .... **75.00+**
Aladdin Lamp Catalogues, Brochures, Posters .... **Wanted**

Brass and cast-iron floor lamps in clean condition that are older than circa 1940 are sought. They may be marble, plastic, porcelain, glass, or have other trims. I like **bridge lamps with arms** that hang to one side holding a glass shade. **Art Deco, Art Nouveau, Mission, torchieres and fancy-type lamps** are the most desired. I will also buy glass or glass and metal shades of various types, and metal parts of lamps including bases, arms, socket covers, shade holders, finials, and trims. I will also consider **metal table lamps, chandeliers, and their parts**. Lamps from the 1940s and 1950s having a large center socket and usually with three surrounding candle sockets are not wanted. Send height and weight measurements, descriptions, photo, and any other information such as manufacturer. Do not send lamps or shades without prior agreement. I will answer all offers. Do not call collect. Most prices will be determined by evaluation.

Janet Hume
11000 S Bryant
Oklahoma City, OK 73160
405-794-7493

We Pay

Lamps, weighing less than 8 lbs .... **10.00+**
Lamps, weighing over 8 lbs .... **15.00+**
Deco or Nouveau Lamp .... **20.00+**
Mission Style Lamp .... **30.00+**
Glass Shade .... **5.00+**
Glass & Metal Shade .... **10.00+**
Torchiere Shade .... **10.00+**

I want to buy **old fireman, bicycle, barn, ship, and railroad lanterns**. I prefer brass, copper or nickel, and silver- and gold-plated lanterns. Any tin railroad or lantern marked D.D. Miller, Steam Gauge & Lantern, F. Mayrose & Co., J.H. Kelly, or C.T. Ham Co. is wanted as are any lantern catalogs; advertisements; or green, amber, or blue globes.

Bobby G. Yocum
1875 Ft. Wayne St.
Oroville, CA 95966
916-532-0986

	We Pay
Nail City No 140 Regal, w/blue or green globe	**50.00-300.00**
SG&L Co No 0	**25.00-200.00**
SG&L Co No 2, tubular	**25.00-200.00**
SG&L Co Vesta Railroad	**50.00-300.00**
SG&L Co No 1	**25.00-200.00**
SG&L Co No 2	**25.00-200.00**
SG&L Co No 4	**25.00-200.00**
SG&L Co No 5, conductor's	**25.00-200.00**
Adlake the Queen	**50.00-300.00**
Adlake the Pullman	**50.00-300.00**
Dietz Mill, tubular	**25.00-200.00**
Dietz King Fire	**50.00-300.00**
Dietz No 6 Vesta	**50.00-300.00**
Dietz No 76	**25.00-200.00**
Dietz No 3	**25.00-200.00**
Dietz No 8	**25.00-200.00**
Dietz No 39	**25.00-200.00**
Armspear No 4	**25.00-200.00**

I am a collector of **miner's candlesticks, sometimes called sticking tommys, and oil wick lamps**. I will buy these lighting devices. Please send picture and description along with desired price.

Bob Claybrook
68701 D St.
Cathedral City, CA 92234
619-324-7872

LAW ENFORCEMENT COLLECTIBLES

We are buyers of **quality antique law enforcement badges and related items** including reward posters, law enforcement-related documents, handcuffs, leg irons, photos of lawmen and outlaws, presentation nightsticks, and weapons belonging to lawmen or outlaws. We are also interested in **items related to the gangsters of the 1920s through 1930s** such as Pretty Boy Floyd, Bonnie and Clyde, The Barker Gang, and John Dillinger.

Antiques of Law and Order
H.A. Tony Perrin and J. Larry Croom
3877 Hwy. 88 W
Mena, AK 71953
501-394-2863

	We Pay
Badge, regular	35.00+
Badge, solid gold (10K through 14K)	250.00+
Badge, sterling	75.00+
Photo	25.00+
Cuffs	25.00+
Irons	25.00+
Nightstick, presentation	50.00+
Reward Poster	20.00+
Documents, ea	10.00+

LEFTON

I am interested in purchasing Lefton china manufactured in the 1940s through 1960s. Please send photo or description of piece (or pieces) together with information about the fired-on mark (or paper label) with identification number (or numbers). The item must be in mint condition with no chips, cracks, or repairs. I have a lot of interest in dinnerware. Please write for information about my book, *Collector's Encyclopedia of Lefton China*, published by Collector Books of Paducah, Kentucky.

Lefton China Collectibles
1101 Polk St.
Bedford, IA 50833

LICENSE PLATE ATTACHMENTS

I collect **cast-aluminum license plate attachments also known as crests, piggybacks, and add-ons**. These attachments were made of heavy sand-cast aluminum. The purpose of these crests were largely promotional. They were sold for about fifty-nine cents in all tourist meccas. Florida must have been like heaven for the traveling salesman who wrote orders for these crests. It seems every city and beach in Florida had a crest boasting its name and slogan. Examples would be: 'Miami Beach,' 'Land of Sunshine,' or 'World's Playground.' They all seemed to have adornments flanking both sides of the name — for instance, 'Florida' with a palm tree on one side and a sailfish on the other.

I have sufficient 'Miami,' 'Miami Beach,' and 'Florida.' I want attachments from other Florida cities, towns, and beaches, as well as cities and towns from other states. **I am paying $30 to $50** depending on rarity and condition. I will also consider broken ones if repairable. Please contact me for prices.

Edward Foley
P.O. Box 572
Adamstown, PA 19501-0572
717-848-4779

LICENSE PLATES AND LICENSE PLATE KEY CHAINS

We buy **B.F. Goodrich painted brass license plate key chain tags** made for years up to and including 1940. **Early porcelain auto license plates** in excellent condition from all states and cities are wanted as well.

Jim Crilly
8261 141st St. N
Seminole, FL 34646-2835
813-393-7295

B.F. Goodrich Key Chain License, 1940	We Pay
Arizona	**50.00**
Arkansas	**50.00**
Louisiana	**50.00**
Mississippi	**50.00**
Nevada	**50.00**
New Mexico	**50.00**
South Carolina	**50.00**
Vermont	**50.00**

License Plates and License Plate Key Chains

Porcelain Auto License Tags	We Pay
Alabama, 1912 through 1915, ea	**up to 400.00**
Arkansas, 1911 through 1913, ea	**up to 400.00**
Colorado, 1913 or 1914, ea	**up to 300.00**
Delaware, 1909 or 1910, ea	**up to 400.00**
District of Columbia, 1912 through 1917, ea	**up to 300.00**
Kentucky, 1910 through 1913, ea	**up to 300.00**
New Mexico, 1920 through 1923, ea	**up to 200.00**

I collect **DAV (Disabled American Veteran) and B.F. Goodrich license plate key chain tags**. Key chain tags must be in good condition; pairs are preferred but singles will be accepted. **Will pay according to state and year but from $1 to $5 for most**. Collections are also purchased.

Virginia L. Young
15463 McNeil Rd.
Sterling, NY 13156
315-947-5840

LIGHTNING ROD BALLS

Lightning rod balls, hardware, weathervanes, and catalogs are wanted. Prices are for items in mint condition only.

Mike Bruner
6980 Walnut Lake Rd.
W Bloomfield, MI 48323

	We Pay
D&S, cobalt	**35.00**
Doorknob, orange	**110.00**
Electra, red	**45.00**
Flat Quilt, cobalt	**50.00**
Flat Quilt, gold mercury	**100.00**
Maher, red	**80.00**
National, silver mercury	**75.00**
Plain Round, blue	**25.00**

Plain Round, red 25.00
Plain Round, green....................35.00
Plain Round, orange....................90.00
Plain Round, yellow 120.00
Ribbed Horizontal, red....................80.00
Round Pleat, amber....................65.00
Round Pleat, green 35.00
Shinn System, amber 25.00
SLR Co, green 60.00
Swirl, cobalt 110.00

LITTLE GOLDEN BOOKS

I am interested in Little Golden Books from Western Publishing Co. in Racine, Wisconsin. I am particularly interested in Disney titles and those illustrated by Richard Scarry. Books should be in good condition with covers intact, no torn pages, and minimal marking. Prices vary depending on condition, age, edition, rarity, and title. Please send a description of your title(s) and asking price. Be sure to include copyright date and edition.

Terri Stalions
105B Calvert Dr.
Paducah, KY 42003

LOG CABINS

We buy all unusual miniature log cabins in glass, tin, cast iron, wood, or any other permanent material. Common items are purchased if priced lower. We want **any pre-1950 item that depicts a log cabin**. We will purchase newer items that are unusual or priced right including stamps, coins, and pictures. We want all books relating to log cabins including those on construction, lore, history, and trivia. We purchase postcards depicting log cabins or other log structures. Condition is a very important factor, especially regarding Towne Log Cabin Syrup containers. We do *not* buy post-1950 Log Cabin Syrup bottles or tins.

James F. Taylor
515 Sixth St.
Rapid City, SD 57701
605-341-3224

	We Pay
Towne Log Cabin Tins, pre-1927, ea	100.00+
Towne Log Cabin Spoons, common, ea	12.00
Bank, figural cast-iron log cabin	40.00+
Book, *The Log Cabin in America*	15.00
Books, relating to log cabins, old, ea	20.00+
Books, relating to log cabins, after 1980, ea	30% of cover price
Cookie Jar, log cabin shape, pre-1950	50.00+
Old Handmade Log Cabins, ea	50.00+
Post-1950 Handmade Log Cabins, ea	20.00+
Postcards, w/pictures of log cabins, ea	2.00+
Pre-1900 Items, ea	40.00+

LOCKS

I would like to purchase **any unusual padlock (with or without keys)**. I am looking for combination padlocks, cast-iron padlocks with animals or mystical symbols, fancy railroad locks with intertwined letters, unusual shapes, or any locks with names on them such as Keen Kutter or Winchester. I will pay a premium for locks that have trick openings or require multiple movements to open. Condition of the lock will determine the ultimate price. Normal wear and tear is understandable.

Don Friedman
660 W Grand, Apt. 4E
Chicago, IL 60610
312-226-4741

Lock Marked:	We Pay
Adams Express Company, Penna Div	700.00
Apex 1909 Seattle	350.00
B & OS WRY	400.00
Canton Lock Co, combination lock	1,000.00
Dan Patch	125.00
Katz, combination lock	150.00
Keen Kutter, shaped, w/railroad names on back, ea	150.00+
Union Pacific System-The Overland Route	450.00
MOPAC RY, Women Toilet Lock	300.00
MOPAC RY, Men Toilet Lock	400.00
Panama California Exposition	550.00
Winchester, combination lock	200.00
1904 World's Fair, St Louis, MO	300.00

Other Locks	**We Pay**
Cast Iron, hunchback shape	**1,100.00**
Cast Iron, mailbox shape	**250.00**
Cast Iron, vase shape	**1,000.00**

LONGWY

I am a private collector of all pieces of this cloisonne-type porcelain which was produced in the north of France near the Luxembourg-Belgian border. I am most interested in acquiring large pieces which are decorated in the bold Art Deco colors of turquoise, yellow, green, orange, and white. The pieces should be marked and in good condition with no chips or cracks.

Paula Atwell Whitmore
401 College Pl., #14
Norfolk, VA 23510

	We Pay
Bowl, 11"	**100.00**
Candlesticks, 8½", pr	**50.00**
Charger, 14"	**400.00**
Pin Dish, 3"	**25.00**
Plant Stand	**500.00**
Tile, 8" sq	**150.00**
Vase, 15"	**200.00**

LUNCH BOXES AND THERMOSES

I am collecting and would like to purchase children's lunch boxes and thermoses. My favorites are from 1950 to the 1990s. I am mainly interested in metal and vinyl lunch boxes and their matching thermoses, however there are some of the plastics that I would like to own. Below is a listing of many that I would like to buy and approximate prices that I would pay for them in excellent condition. Price may be lower for lesser condition. Hundreds more are wanted than those listed here; thermoses are needed also. Photos would be helpful to judge condition. Please send SASE when inquiries are sent. Thank you for your consideration.

Terri's Toys & Nostalgia
Terri Ivers
1104 Shirlee Ave.
Ponca City, OK 74601
405-762-8697 or 405-762-5174

	We Pay
Action Jackston Lunch Box	**up to 100.00+**
All American Lunch Box	**up to 100.00+**
Americana Lunch Box	**up to 100.00+**
Annie Oakley Lunch Box	**up to 100.00+**
Banana Splits Lunch Box	**up to 100.00+**
Barbie Lunch Box, Ponytail	**up to 100.00+**
Beany & Cecil Lunch Box	**up to 100.00+**
Beatles Lunch Box	**up to 100.00+**
Boating Lunch Box	**up to 100.00+**
Boy on Rocket Lunch Box	**up to 100.00+**
Bobby Soxer Lunch Box, vinyl	up to 100.00+
Boston Bruins Lunch Box	**up to 100.00+**
Boy on Rocket Lunch Box	**up to 100.00+**
Bullwinkle Lunch Box	**up to 100.00+**
Captain Astro Lunch Box	**up to 100.00+**
Captain Kangaroo Lunch Box	**up to 100.00+**
Carnival Lunch Box	**up to 100.00+**
Cartoon Zoo Lunch Box	**up to 100.00+**
Casey Jones Lunch Box, metal w/dome top	**175.00**
Casey Jones Lunch Box, train	**up to 100.00+**
Casey Jones Thermos	**75.00**
Casper Lunch Box	**up to 100.00+**
Children Lunch Box	**up to 100.00+**
Col Ed McCauley Lunch Box	**up to 100.00+**
Dateline Lunch Box, blue or pink vinyl, ea	**up to 100.00+**
Deputy Dawg Lunch Box, vinyl	**up to 100.00+**
Dr Seuss Lunch Box, vinyl	**up to 100.00+**
Dream Boat Lunch Box, vinyl	**up to 100.00+**
Dudley Do-Right Lunch Box	**up to 100.00+**
Dutch Cottage Lunch Box, dome top	**up to 100.00+**
Fess Parker Lunch Box, vinyl	**up to 100.00+**
Firehouse Lunch Box, dome top	**up to 100.00+**
Flag-O-Rama Lunch Box	**up to 100.00+**
Frontier Days Lunch Box	**up to 100.00+**
Gene Autry Lunch Box	**up to 100.00+**
Great Wild West Lunch Box	**up to 100.00+**
Green Hornet Lunch Box	**up to 100.00+**
Gunsmoke Lunch Box, w/double LL's in Marshall	**up to 100.00+**
Hogan's Heroes Lunch Box	**up to 100.00+**

Hometown Airport Lunch Box .... **up to 100.00+**
Hopalong Cassidy Lunch Box .... **up to 100.00+**
Howdy Doody Lunch Box .... **up to 100.00+**
It's About Time Lunch Box .... **up to 100.00+**
Jetsons Lunch Box, dome top, 1963 .... **275.00**
Jetsons Thermos, 1963 .... **75.00**
Junior Nurse Lunch Box .... **up to 100.00+**
Knight in Armor Lunch Box .... **up to 100.00+**
Liddle Kiddles Lunch Box .... **up to 100.00+**
Linus the Lion Hearted Lunch Box .... **up to 100.00+**
Lost in Space Lunch Box, dome top, 1966 .... **130.00**
Lunch 'N' Munch Lunch Box .... **up to 100.00+**
Mickey Mouse & Donald Duck Lunch Box, metal .... **up to 100.00+**
Mod Floral Lunch Box .... **up to 100.00+**
Monkees Lunch Box .... **up to 100.00+**
NHL Lunch Box .... **up to 100.00+**
Our Friends Lunch Box .... **up to 100.00+**
Pathfinder Lunch Box .... **up to 100.00+**
Popeye Lunch Box, 1962 .... **up to 100.00+**
Popeye Lunch Box, Japan, black background, 1982 .... **100.00**
Porky's Lunch Wagon Lunch Box, dome top .... **up to 100.00+**
Psychedelic Lunch Box, dome top .... **up to 100.00+**
Rifleman Lunch Box .... **up to 100.00+**
Ringling Brothers Lunch Box .... **up to 100.00+**
Roscoe Lunch Box, 1990 .... **50.00**
Roy Rogers Lunch Box, vinyl .... **up to 100.00+**
Sandwich Lunch Box **40.00**
School Days (Mickey Mouse) Lunch Box .... **up to 100.00+**
Soupy Sales Lunch Box .... **up to 100.00+**
Smokey the Bear Lunch Box .... **up to 100.00+**
Smurfs Lunch Box, metal **30.00**
Snack Shack Lunch Box, vinyl .... **up to 100.00+**
Star Trek Lunch Box, dome top **300.00**
Star Trek Thermos **125.00**
Supercar Lunch Box .... **up to 100.00+**
Tinker Bell Lunch Box .... **up to 100.00+**
Tom Corbett Lunch Box, full lithograph .... **up to 100.00+**
Toppie the Elephant Lunch Box **500.00**
Toppie the Elephant Thermos **200.00**
Underdog Lunch Box, metal or vinyl **200.00**
Underdog Thermos **100.00**
Volkswagon Bus Lunch Box, metal w/dome top **150.00**
Yosemite Sam Lunch Box .... **up to 100.00+**
Hundreds More Wanted .... **Call or Write**

MAGAZINES

Wanted: **circa pre-1950 movie magazines**, such as *Film Fun, Hollywood, Modern Screen, Motion Picture, Movieland, Movie Story, Photoplay, Picture Play, Screen Guide, Screenland, Screen Romances*, etc. I'm also interested in magazines with **Ginger Rogers on the cover**, whether it be *Liberty, Life, Look,* or *Time*. Magazines need to be in good condition. I pay shipping.

Tom Morris
P.O. Box 8307
Medford, OR 97504
503-779-3164

I buy **humor magazines published by college students** (not the magazine *College Humor*). I am also interested in **posters, anthologies, histories, or ephemera related to college humor magazines**. I am interested in all years up to the present. See below listing which reflects average prices paid.

Other wants include **Wizard of Oz, W.W. Denslow (book, magazine, and poster illustrator), college literary societies, and Soviet political and satirical posters**. See also Character Collectibles in this book for my listing on **Dr. Seuss**.

Michael Gessel
P.O. Box 748
Arlington, VA 22216
703-532-4261

	We Pay
Annapolis Log	4.00
Boston Bean Pot	4.00
Brown Jug	5.00
California Josh	10.00
California Pelican	6.00
Columbia Jester	6.00
Cornell Widow	6.00
Dartmouth Jack-O'-Lantern	6.00
Harvard Lampoon	6.00
Michigan Gargoyle	5.00
MIT Voo Doo	5.00
NYU Mercury	4.00
Ohio State Sundial	6.00
Ohio Green Goat	5.00
Penn State Froth	4.00

Pennsylvania Punch Bowl **6.00**
Princeton Tiger **6.00**
Stanford Chaparral **6.00**
Temple Owl **4.00**
Virginia Reel **4.00**
West Point Pointer **5.00**
Williams Purple Cow **5.00**
Yale Quip **10.00**
Yale Record **6.00**

MAGIC

I eagerly seek **magic memorabilia of all types**, particularly paper relics of magic's 'golden age' (1890 through 1920). Prices paid will depend on scarcity, historical significance, content, and condition of the item. It is almost impossible to list suggested prices here without seeing a particular item. So call or write, and we can talk specifics. Depending on the item, I might go below or above the ranges listed here. A free swap list is also available to other magic collectors.

Ken Trombly
1825 K St., NW
Ste. 901
Washington DC 20006
FAX 202-457-0343

We Pay

Vintage Posters, ea .... **40.00+**
Houdini Posters, ea .... **500.00+**
Other Houdini Items, ea .... **5.00-500.00+**
Children's Magic Sets, ea **25.00-125.00**
Magic Books, ea **5.00-500.00**
Scrapbooks of Magicians, ea .... **20.00+**
Photos & Articles Dealing w/Magic, ea .... **5.00+**
Prints or Engravings of Magicians, ea .... **10.00+**
Magic-Themed Premium Items, ea .... **5.00+**
Magicians' Sheet Music .... **10.00+**
Pin-Back Buttons, ea .... **10.00+**
Other Items Wanted .... **FAX or Write**

MAJOLICA

I am interested in purchasing 19th-through early 20th-century **Majolica pitchers with floral designs**. I would ask that the pitchers be in good to above average condition. I would be happy to reimburse actual UPS and insurance charges and am willing to pay current book value.

Laura L. Walker
3907 N Blvd.
Tampa, FL 33603
813-229-6332

MAPS AND ATLASES

We pay the following prices for all material we can use. 20th-century oil company maps, official state, and provincial highway maps that fold as well as similar materials are wanted. AAA maps, travel brochures, tourist maps, National Geographic Supplements, and similar items are sought also. Prices for antique maps vary and are based on their date, location, size, maker, etc. Top prices are paid for all atlases and other books containing maps. As long as contents are sound, the condition of the covers and bindings is not critical. Buying prices range between $1,000 and up for early to mid-19th century and about $25 for items from the late 19th century. Please call or send on approval for our offer. You are welcome to ship anything mentioned on approval at our expense for a cash offer by return mail. Kindly pack items securely and mail 'UPS Special 4th Class/Book Rate.'

Charles R. Neuschafer
New World Maps, Inc.
1123 S. Broadway
Lantana, FL 33462-4522
407-586-8723

20th-Century Folding Maps	**We Pay**
1980 to present, ea	**25¢**
1970-1979, ea	**50¢**

1960-1969, ea ....75¢
1950-1959, ea 1.00
1940-1949, ea 2.00
1930-1939, ea 3.00
1920-1929, ea 6.00
1910-1919, ea 10.00

AAA, Travel Brochures, Etc. **We Pay**

1930-1939, ea 2.00
1920-1929, ea 3.00
1910-1919, ea 5.00
1900-1909, ea 10.00

MARBLES

I am primarily a collector wanting **marbles from the 1800s through the 1930s**. Boxes, bags and unusual marbles are very desirable. I'll buy some or all of your collection, whichever you prefer. Call or write for offers on other items not listed here. I will pay more if marbles have mica or lobes.

D.J.M. Marbles Just For Fun
P.O. Box 18924
Fairfield, OH 45018
513-829-5656

We Pay

Swirl, up to 1" 1.00-50.00
Swirl, 1⅛" to 2"..25.00-100.00
Onionskin, up to 1"..5.00-50.00
Onionskin, 1⅛" to 2" 50.00-300.00
Lutz, up to ⅞" 50.00-300.00
Lutz, 1" to 1½" 300.00-800.00
Lutz, over 1½"..Call

I need your help to find old **marbles from the 1850s to the 1940s**. I will consider any and all marbles. Please let me know if you have any marbles or questions. Good, clear photos are very helpful. Please call, write, or send information to:

Anthony Niccoli
823 E 25th Ave.
N Kansas City, MO 64116
816-471-1370

	We Pay
MF Christensen, bricks, slags, etc, ea	**5.00+**
Christensen Agate, flames or multicolored swirls, ea	**5.00+**
Akro Agate, oxbloods, corkscrews or sparklers, ea	**5.00+**
Peltier Co, multicolored rainbows, comics, etc, ea	**5.00+**
Miscellaneous Machine-Made Marbles, ea	**1.00+**
Peewees, ½" or smaller, ea	**1.00+**
Hand-Made Swirls, divided, solid or ribbon cores, ea	**5.00+**
Hand-Made Lutz, banded, opaque or onionskin, ea	**50.00+**
Hand-Made Sulphides, colored, painted, etc, ea	**50.00+**
Hand-Painted Chinas, flowers, scenic, pinwheels, etc, ea	**10.00+**
Clambroths, Onionskins, or Agates, ea	**10.00-100.00**
Cyclones, Guineas, or Superman Marbles, ea	**75.00-200.00**

Collector **paying current book price for pre-1940, glass, mint-condition marbles**. Sulphides, cat's eyes, clearies, Chinese checker (game), or clay marbles are *not* wanted. Needed are swirls of all types, clambroth, Indians, tri-colored, mica, flames, corkscrews, handmade and machine-made marbles, etc. No ordinary marbles wanted. If you're unsure, ship marbles with *no chips, dings, or nicks* and I'll make an honest offer. Please include your phone number. Thank you!

Yvonne Marie Holmberg
7229 Pine Island Dr., NE
Comstock Park, MI 49321-9534
616-784-1715

I am a private collector of **antique marbles**. I am most interested in handmade marbles which can usually be identified by one or two pontil marks (these appear as rough spots). Machine-made marbles made up to the 1930s may also be of interest. I'm also interested in old pottery, mineral, and decorated china marbles. I am especially searching for sulphides which are usually clear (sometimes colored) glass marbles that contain silvery figures of animals, birds, people, or objects.

A picture of your marbles would be most helpful, along with a written description. The price I will pay depends on a number of factors including size, rarity, and condition — I prefer mint to near mint. No cat's eyes, game marbles (solid color like Chinese checker marbles), or post-1930s marbles will be considered. If you wish to ship your marbles on approval, postage and insurance will be at your expense. If, however, I purchase your marbles I will reimburse you.

Daria Canino
HC 73 Box 991
Locust Grove, VA 22508
703-972-1525

We are interested in purchasing **hand-made marbles** and in particular the following types: Lutz, Indians, large swirls, and opaques — the bigger the better! Only marbles in near-mint to mint condition are of interest. Also we are seeking specimens of comic and advertising marbles such as Tom Mix and Cotes Master Loaf. Prices will vary depending on size and condition of marbles.

Dr. Bradley Bastow
950 Blue Star Hwy.
S Haven, MI 49090
616-637-1388

We buy **marbles and marble-related items**. This includes individual marbles, original boxes, tournament trophies and medals, toys, games, and literature. We can use **anything related to marbles, the game of marbles, and the history of marbles**.

Stanley and Bob Block
P.O. Box 51
Trumbull, CT 06611
203-261-0057

MATCH HOLDERS AND MATCH SAFES

I am an advanced collector interested in purchasing **quality pocket match**

safes. I collect all categories with emphasis on figural, enameled, fancy, and unusual pocket match safes. I am interested in one item or an entire collection. I am also seeking **any related printed material** including catalogs, advertisements, patents, etc., **produced prior to 1915**. I respond to all inquiries. Listed below are a few of the items I am interested in buying.

George Sparacio
P.O. Box 791
Malaga, NJ 08328
609-694-4167

	We Pay
Agate Types, ea	**75.00+**
Baden Powell, figural	**225.00+**
Billiken, figural, sterling	**350.00+**
Chamberlain, portrait	**200.00+**
Cigar, figural, enamel band	**450.00+**
Daniel Boone, figural, brass	**175.00+**
Domino, figural, vulcanite	**50.00+**
Enameled, ea	**125.00+**
Fire or Firemen Motif, ea	**125.00+**
Figural, most types, ea	**125.00+**
Niello, on silver, Russian	**150.00+**
Oriental, figural type, brass, ea	**175.00+**
Pig, figural as running, brass	**155.00+**
Portrait of Famous Person	**150.00+**
President Grant, portrait	**275.00+**
Sentry House, enameled sterling	**600.00+**
Stanhope Peep-Eye, any type, ea	**100.00+**

I am buying **all types of table match holders with advertising**. I am *not* interested in tin kitchen match or box holders that hang on the wall, nor in pocket match safes or holders with the exception of those shown below. I want match holders that hold loose matches and have a striking surface as well as those that hold match boxes or matchbooks. They may be made of ceramic, glass, metal, Bakelite, or wood.

Mike Schwimmer
325 E Blodgett
Lake Bluff, IL 60044-2112
708-295-1901

We Pay

Match Striker, ceramic **20.00-75.00**
Match Striker, other than ceramic **20.00-50.00**
Match Box or Matchbook Holder, ceramic **20.00-75.00**
Match Box or Matchbook Holder, other than ceramic **20.00-40.00**
Match Holder, tin wall type, with cigar or cigar store advertising, ...**20.00-50.00**
Match Safe, Match Box or Matchbook Holder, pocket type, with cigar or cigar store advertising **15.00-45.00**

NAUTICAL MEMORABILIA

We buy **any nautical pieces** — small or large and in between! We are interested in everything from ashtrays to anchors. We will reimburse for actual shipping costs. If you send a photo along with description and price, we will return your photo.

R. Ouellette
3510 Stanton Rd.
Oxford, MI 48371

NORTH DAKOTA COLLECTIBLES

We live in a small rural community in southwest North Dakota and are interested in buying **items originating in North Dakota, South Dakota, and Montana prior to the 1950s**. Wanted are souvenir items with town names (especially North Dakota towns of Bowman, Rhame, Marmarth, Scranton, Reeder, Amidon, Haley, and Griffin).

Items of most interest with these names are souvenir glassware items in red, green, blue or white; advertising mirrors; and crocks. No alcohol or tobacco promotional items wanted please. We also buy **Dakota Territory memorabilia, small artifacts or cavalry items, books by North Dakota or regional authors, pottery by Messer (see Pottery in this book), and old salt and pepper collections.**

We pay from $10 to $100 for most items with no cracks or chips. Please send a photo or a detailed description. We will try to pay your asking price, or we will make you an offer.

North Dakota Collectibles

Stan and Carrie Soderstrom
003-3rd St. SW
Rt. 2, Box 300
Bowman, ND 58623

We Pay

Advertising Mirrors .... **8.00+**
Cavalry Items .... **5.00+**
Dakota Territory Memorabilia .... **5.00+**
Messer Pottery .... **20.00+**
Salt & Pepper Sets .... **5.00+**
Souvenir Glass, clear or colored .... **10.00+**

NUTCRACKERS

I buy **nut bowls, nut picks and nutcrackers** that are toy soldiers, German made, brass, mechanical, etc. We buy all unusual nutcracker collections.

Pape's Pecan Co.
P.O. Box 1281
Seguin, TX 78155
210-379-7442

We Pay

Nut Bowls, ea **3.00-100.00**
Nut Picks, silver, ea **3.00-50.00**
Knife Picks, ea .... **3.00-50.00+**
Nutcracker, toy soldier, German **30.00-150.00**
Nutcracker, woodcarver **20.00-80.00**
Nutcracker, brass .... **20.00+**
Nutcracker, mechanical .... **20.00+**
Nutcracker, Betel nut **20.00-200.00**

OUTBOARD BOAT MOTORS

I collect toy metal outboard boat motors. These may be electric, tin windup, steam powered or gas powered. Most of these motors were made in Japan in the 1940s through the 1960s by KO. I will pay 10% extra if you have the original box and instructions and also offered is a 10% finders fee. Wooden boats and old tin windup toys are also wanted.

Richard Gronowski
140 N Garfield Ave.
Traverse City, MI 49686
616-491-2111

We Pay

Black Mercury, 100 HP **100.00**
Evinrudes, 40 HP or 75 HP, ea **75.00**
Gales, 35 HP or 60 HP, ea **75.00**
Johnsons, 40 HP or 75 HP, ea **75.00**
Oliver, 35 HP **100.00**
Mercury, 60 HP, 70 HP or 80 HP, ea **75.00**
Other Johnsons, Mercurys, Evinrudes, Scotts, Gales, ea **50.00**
Gas Powered Sea-Fury or Wen-Macs, ea **50.00**
Twin-Cylinders, any of the above makes, ea **125.00**
Steam-Powered: Polly-Wog, Snapper, Allyson, Pittman, Dolphin Boiler, Attwood Steam Craft, ea **150.00**
Generic Brands: Langcraft, Pheasant, Sprite, Famus, Super, Lafayette, Sea-Dart, Frog, Orkin, Wolf, Triumph, Mermaid, Tornado, Hurricane, etc, ea **25.00-35.00**
Wood Boats or Tin Windups .... **Call or Write**

PAPER MONEY

Collector/dealer since 1965 of all **paper money and related items of the US and Confederate States of America** wants to buy all state notes from the 1700s until the 1860s. Old bank checks and bonds are also wanted. Material we buy should be in nice condition; damaged or badly worn material has little value. Prices paid are subject to inspection. All materials sent are paid for within forty-eight hours or returned. We pay postage one way.

William J. Skelton
Highland Coin and Jewelry
P.O. Box 55448
Birmingham, AL 35255
205-939-3166, extension 3

	We Pay
Bank Checks, pre-1900, w/Reserve stamps & vignettes, ea	**10¢-1.00**
Macerated Money Items (made of old money ground up at the US Treasury in Washington, DC, in early 1900s)	**25.00-50.00**
CSA $500 Bill	**50.00+**
CSA $100 Bill	**10.00+**
CSA $50 Bill	**10.00+**
CSA $20 Bill	**5.00+**
CSA $10 Bill	**5.00+**
CSA $5 Bill	**5.00+**
CSA $2 Bill	**6.00+**
CSA $1 Bill	**6.00+**
CSA 50¢ Bill	**3.00+**

US Currency, Large-Sized Type, Through 1923	**We Pay**
$1 Note	**10.00+**
$2 Note	**15.00+**
$5 Note	**10.00+**
$10 Note	**15.00+**
$20 Note	**25.00+**
$50 Note	**60.00+**
$100 Note	**120.00+**

We have over twenty years experience with **coins, paper money and exonumia**. We are knowledgeable and reputable. Do not send your items until you speak with us. Send photocopies of your items, as this will help to determine condition. Condition is a prime factor in determining value. Whether it be Confederate, broken banks, fractional currency, large size, etc., we are interested. No foreign paper money from this century wanted.

Dempsey and Baxter
1009 E 38th St.
Erie, PA 16504

PAPERWEIGHTS

I am buying **figural advertising paperweights that are miniatures of what they advertise or are made out of the material that they advertise**. All paperweights must have the product name or manufacturer's name on them.

Don Friedman
660 W Grand, Apt. 4E
Chicago, IL 60610
312-226-4741

	We Pay
Perry Superstile, NY (turnstile)	**100.00**
Ireland & Matthews Mfg Co, Detroit (brass cuspidor)	**35.00**
Coleman Lamp Co, Wichita, KS (Coleman lamp)	**60.00**
Lyon Bumper Metal Stamping Co, Long Island, NY (automobile bumper)	**75.00**
CT Ham Mfg Co (lantern)	**75.00**
Mueller (fire hydrant)	**30.00**
Canada Cycle & Motor Co, Toronto (bicycles, skates or accessories)	**75.00**
TA Cummings Foundry Co (manhole cover)	**40.00**

I am interested in buying **antique glass paperweights**. I would like to buy the early type of weights that are round, domed, or mushroom shaped. Some of these weights may have facets cut on the surface. The subjects within the paperweights may be people, animals, fruit, butterflies, birds, flowers, or millefiori which are arrangements of slices of canes of glass which resemble tiny flowers. The weights I am interested in are often small, from 2" to 3½" in diameter. The base of the paperweight should be ground smooth or cut in a star pattern — no frosted bases please, also no advertising weights.

Please feel free to write with a description of your paperweight(s). Dimensions are helpful as are pictures and any history you may know. Condition is important; however, some scratches or small chips are inevitable on paperweights of this age. Please include your asking price with your correspondence.

Daria Canino
HC 73 Box 991
Locust Grove, VA 22508
703-972-1525

Paperweights

Collector desires antique (pre-1900s) glass paperweights: French, American, English, and Bohemian. Millefiori, flowers, and fruit designs are preferred. Also desire modern, artist-signed paperweights such as Stankard, Ysart, and Kaziun as well as modern Baccarat, St. Louis, and Perthshire limited edition paperweights. **Pre-1966** *Paperweight Collector Association (PCA) Bulletins* **and other books desired.**

Private collector buying one paperweight or entire collections. On older paperweights, surface wear and minor chips to the base are not a problem. Please write or call first with description or photo together with your asking price.

Andrew Dohan
49 E Lancaster Ave.
Frazer, PA 19355
610-647-3310

We buy **antique French paperweights by Baccarat, Clichy, and St. Louis**. Prices depend on type and company. Also wanted are paperweights by US maker **Charles Kaziun** (deceased). **We are paying from $200 to $3,000** depending on the individual paperweight.

Stanley A. Block
P.O. Box 51
Trumbull, CT 06611
203-261-0057

PATTERN GLASS

I am buying early American flint and non-flint pressed glassware. Some items of particular interest are listed below.

Calvin L. Hackeman
8865 Olde Mill Run
Manassas, VA 22110
703-368-6982

Balder	**We Pay**
Salt & Pepper Shakers, pr	**45.00+**
Sugar Bowl, w/lid	**20.00+**

Toothpick	20.00+
Water Pitcher	25.00+

Dakota (Corn & Berry)	We Pay
Cruet	45.00+
Salt & Pepper Shakers, pr	45.00+
Spooner	30.00+
Sugar Bowl, w/lid	40.00+
Water Pitcher	50.00+

Hawaiian Lei (non-flint) by Higbee	We Pay
Banana Stand	50.00+
Bread Tray	25.00+
Candlesticks, pr	75.00+
Castor Set	100.00+
Champagne Glass	35.00+
Compote, octagonal	40.00+
Compote, square	50.00+
Compote, round, w/lid	30.00+
Cruet	45.00+
Cup & Saucer Set	20.00+
Goblets, except cordials, ea	30.00+
Honey Dish, square, w/lid	30.00
Ice Cream Set	100.00+
Mug	25.00+
Plate, square	20.00+
Platter	35.00+
Punch Bowl	85.00+
Punch Cup	25.00+
Sugar Lid	15.00+
Syrup	75.00+
Water Pitcher	50.00+
Any Piece in Color or Carnival	Call

New Hampshire (Bent Buckle)	We Pay
Bisquit Jar, w/lid	60.00+
Carafe	45.00+
Celery Vase	25.00+
Compote, lg	35.00+
Custard Cup	10.00+
Lemon Cup	10.00+
Milk Pitcher	60.00+
Plate	10.00+
Spooner	15.00+
Sugar Bowl, w/lid	20.00+

Water Pitcher, bulbous, ¾-gal .... 70.00+
Water Tumbler .... 15.00+
Wine, flared .... 20.00+
Any Piece w/Ruby Stain .... 25.00-200.00+

New Jersey **We Pay**

Butter Dish, on high standard .... 50.00+
Cake Stand .... 40.00+
Compote, w/lid .... 40.00+
Plate, dinner; 8" .... 10.00+
Salt & Pepper Shakers, pr .... 25.00+
Syrup .... 70.00+
Water Bottle .... 40.00+
Water Goblet .... 25.00+
Wine Goblet .... 30.00+
Water Tray .... 30.00+
Water Tumbler .... 25.00+

Teepee **We Pay**

Stemware, other than champagnes .... 10.00-20.00+
Wine Decanter/Carafe .... 35.00+
Water Pitcher .... 45.00+

Virginia (Galloway) **We Pay**

Basket .... 60.00+
Bowl, rectangular .... 20.00+
Celery Vase .... 40.00+
Compote, w/lid .... 50.00-90.00+
Champagne Glass .... 40.00+
Cracker Jar 100.00
Egg Cup .... 20.00+
Jelly Dish, w/handles .... 15.00+
Lemonades, ea .... 20.00+
Mug .... 20.00+
Pickle Castor .... 50.00+
Pitchers, other than medium tankard, ea .... 40.00-60.00+
Plate .... 15.00-25.00+
Rose Bowl .... 20.00+
Salt Dip .... 15.00+
Salt & Pepper Shakers, pr .... 25.00+
Sugar Shaker .... 25.00+
Waste Bowl .... 20.00+
Water Bottle .... 25.00+
Water Goblet .... 45.00+
Water Tray .... 50.00+

Punch Cups (pressed glass)	We Pay
Big Diamond	25.00+
California (Beaded Grape)	20.00+
Connecticut	20.00+
Dakota, etched or plain	20.00+
Florida Herringbone	20.00+
Florida Palm	15.00+
Illinois	20.00+
Lion's Leg	25.00+
Louisiana	25.00+
Maine	15.00+
Maryland	15.00+
Mississippi (Magnolia)	25.00+
Missouri	20.00+
Nebraska (Bismark)	15.00+
Nevada	15.00+
New Jersey	25.00+
Ohio	20.00+
Oregon (Beaded Loop)	20.00+
Tennessee	20.00+
Texas	15.00+
Utah (Twinkle Star)	15.00+
Vermont, any color	20.00+
Late Washington	15.00+
Early Washington	25.00+
Wyoming (England)	20.00+

Other Patterns	We Pay
Carolina Water Tumblers, ea	15.00+
Illinois Candlestick, ea	25.00+
Loop & Petal Compote/Vase, canary, flint	200.00+
Other Colored Flint Pieces (candlesticks to salts), ea	20.00-250.00+

PENCIL SHARPENERS

I am looking for **pocket pencil sharpeners made of pot metal or Bakelite plastic**. I am especially seeking figural and comic character sharpeners. They can be marked US, Occupied Japan, Japan, Germany, or Bavaria. Paint and decals must be in good to mint condition.

Phil Helley
629 Indiana Ave.
Wisconsin Dells, WI 53965
608-254-8658

	We Pay
Airplane, Bakelite	**29.00**
Armored Car, metal on rubber wheels, w/whistle, Japan	**60.00**
Charlie McCarthy, Bakelite	**36.00**
Cinderella, decal on Bakelite, round	**27.00**
Donald Duck, Bakelite	**40.00**
Dog, metal, German	**40.00**
Drummer Musician, metal, German	**30.00**
Indian Chief, metal, Occupied Japan	**45.00**
Magnifying Glass w/3 Kittens, metal, German	**55.00**
Mickey Mouse, Bakelite	**50.00**
New York World's Fair, Bakelite	**35.00**
Nude Boy w/Silver Cap, metal, German	**40.00**
Popeye, decal on Bakelite, rectangular	**32.00**
Scottie Dog, Bakelite	**16.00**
Tank, Keep 'Em Rolling, Bakelite	**30.00**

PEPSI-COLA

I am interested in **anything from Pepsi-Cola and prefer older things** to reproductions. Small items as well as large ones are wanted. Please include photograph, if possible, along with description, condition, year, and asking price. An old soda bottle rack and Tiffany-styled ceiling light with the Pepsi logo are two things I'm especially intersted in.

Della L. Maze
3219 Adams St.
Paducah, KY 42001

I want **old Pepsi-Cola items** — especially the unusual ones. I will pay 80% of the current book value for good condition items. Other wants include **chalk and bisque angels**; no plastic or new angels are wanted. Interesting or bulk collections of **buttons, old store manniquins from the 1940s and earlier, St. Louis World's Fair items, Wizard of Oz items, monkeys and teddy bears** round out my collecting interests.

Gwen Daniel
18 Belleau Lake Ct.
O'Fallon, MO 63366
314-978-3190

Pepsi-Cola	**We Pay**
Bottle Carrier, 6-bottle size, metal	**20.00**
Bottle Carrier, 6-bottle size, wood	**50.00**
Bottle Carrier, 6-bottle size, wood w/Pepsi bottle on side	**80.00**

Other Wants	**We Pay**
Angel, chalk (for church), lg	**300.00+**
Angel, for nativity	**5.00+**
Other Religious Items & Statues	**Call or Write**
Mannequin	**200.00+**

PHOENIX BIRD CHINA

Wanted: Phoenix Bird dinnerware, a blue and white china of the early 1900s. Made by many Japanese manufacutures, its pieces encompass nearly 500 forms — many coming in various sizes as well as shapes. Wanted are those **pieces in unique shapes other than the usual place settings seen today** (i.e., soap dish with cover, washbowl, castor set, cracker jar or cracker trough).

Joan Oates
685 S Washington
Constantine, MI 49042
616-435-8353

We are interested in purchasing **unusual Phoenix Bird china pieces**. This blue and white china was made by many different companies mainly in Japan and England. It closely resembles a pattern called Flying Turkey, but we are not interested in any similar pattern, only the actual Phoenix Bird pattern. Some of the items we would like to purchase are listed below, but this list is by no means inclusive:

Chocolate Pot	Chocolate Cups
Matchbox Holder	Salt Dips

Phoenix Bird China

Chamber Candlestick
Dresser Tray
Castor Set
Cracker Jar

If you have any unusual pieces (pieces other than plates, cups and saucers, etc.), please send us a description and a picture, if possible. We will pay fair market value for pieces in good condition.

Joseph S. and Margaret Quimby
701 White Marsh Rd.
Centreville, MD 21617

PHONOGRAPHS

We buy **Victrolas, crank and early electric phonographs, related phonograph items, and music boxes**. As an expert restorer and repairer of phonographs, I also buy parts and junk machines that can be salvaged. We have been collecting and restoring for many years. We always seek to provide quality workmanship and enjoy it immensely.

Brett and Cheryl Hurt
6000 Amber Oaks Ave.
Bakersfield, CA 93306
805-872-6269

	We Pay
Advertising, phonograph or music related	5.00+
Music Box, Regina	1,500.00+
Music Box, Symphonion	1,000.00+
Needle Tin, Victor, 1,000 count	50.00
Needle Tin, Columbia, 500 count	35.00
Vogue Picture Record	35.00
Children's Record Guild of America	3.00
Edison Concert Cylinder Machine	1,500.00
Edison Opera Cylinder Machine	2,000.00
Victor Outside Horn Machine	500.00+
Columbia Outside Horn Machine	300.00+
Edison Concert Cylinder Record	25.00+
Edison Cylinder Record	1.00+

I'm looking for **table-model wind-up phonographs with or without horns and also any parts**. I also collect **phonograph-related items** such as advertising, record dusters, needle tins, cabinet keys, needle cutters, etc.

Hart Wesemann
600 N 800 W
W Bountiful, UT 84087
801-298-3499

PHOTOGRAPHICA

I am interested in purchasing **all types of photos, daguerreotypes, ambrotypes, tintypes, CDVs, cabinet cards, albumen prints, etc.** I prefer photos of the 1840 to 1920 period. Condition is important but is not the only criteria I use to purchase old photos. I will buy photos of all sizes with or without cases. I pay higher prices for more unusual scenes and subjects. I am also interested in purchasing old photo cases. Prices listed are only a guide, and actual price could be more or less, depending on subject and condition of the image. It is helpful if you can send a Xerox copy of the photo for sale. I will answer all letters. I have been buying photos for over 25 years; no one will pay more than me.

David L. Hartline
P.O. Box 775
Worthington, OH 43085

	We Pay
Daguerreotype, soldier	**100.00+**
Daguerreotype, outdoor town scene	**150.00+**
Daguerreotype, identified famous person	**500.00+**
Ambrotype, soldier w/weapons	**125.00+**
Ambrotype, famous person	**200.00+**
Ambrotype, California gold miner	**500.00+**
Tintype, Civil War soldier	**60.00+**
Tintype, soldier on horseback	**100.00+**
CDV, soldier w/sword	**50.00+**
CDV, President Lincoln by Brady	**100.00+**
Cabinet Card, Western lawman w/badge	**100.00**
Cabinet Card, Indian War soldier	**50.00+**
Cabinet Card, Annie Oakley	**150.00+**
Cabinet Card, Geronimo	**100.00+**

Photographica

Stereoscopic View, actual photo of Indians.......................................**25.00**
Albumen, soldier on horseback, 8x10" **50.00**
Albumen, Black soldiers.......................................**85.00**

We purchase **all types of photo-related items**. We are in the market for cameras, lenses, tripods, toys, figurines — anything that relates to photography. Prices will vary due to the condition and working order of the items. Describe make, model, condition, and/or give a brief description. Also wanted are **items relating to Kodak, AGFA, Konica, Nikon, Canon, and Hasselbland**.

Items wanted include:

- Advertising Items
- Ashtrays
- Belt Buckles
- Cameras (all types)
- Candy & Gum
- Cigarette Lighters
- Clocks
- Coasters
- Compacts and Vanities
- Containers
- Dart or Pellet Shooters
- Dishes or Tableware
- Jewelry
- Key Chains
- Lights
- Lenses
- Masks
- Music Boxes
- Ornamental Items
- Pencil Sharpeners
- Photographs
- Planters
- Puzzles
- Radios
- Salt & Pepper Shakers
- Stationery Items
- Statues & Figurines
- Soap
- Vehicles
- Viewing Devices

Harry E. Forsythe
3914 Beach Blvd.
Jacksonville, FL 32207

I buy **antique photo albums from the 1900s**. I like the more ornate ones the best. Also they must have **all photos intact**. Special interest include celluloid albums, albums with stands, and albums with music boxes. Price depends on condition. I'm also selling.

Dawn Persky
10070 SW 17 Ct.
Davie, FL 33324
305-424-5826

We are buying **hand-colored photographic works by Eugene Delcroix (New Orleans, 1891-1967)**. These black and white photographs were hand colored and framed by the artist and sold as souvenirs to tourists of the New Orleans area. Scenes include photographs of the French Quarter, rural landscapes, New Orleans area cemeteries plus many others. We are buying undamaged, signed work in original frames only. We also reimburse shipping costs.

Hugh Jones
835 Bourbon St.
New Orleans, LA 70116-3154
504-561-8498

	We Pay
Photograph, 4½x6½"	20.00+
Enlargement, about 10x12"	50.00+

I buy **daguerreotype images, portraits, occupationals, screet scenes, erotica, postmortems and military subjects in any condition**. These can be in leather or Union cases. Empty cases, mats and frames in quanity are also wanted.

Stereo daguerreotypes and Mascher cased images are particularly sought after. **Unusual viewers and all flat-mount stereo images** purchased. Collections or single pieces are wanted. Send photocopies in first instance or telephone if you wish to send on consignment. Postage or UPS charges reimbursed if consignment is requested. Other **interesting or unusual 19th-century photographic images considered**. Prices are for items in good condition. Fair or poor condition items considered at discounted prices.

Anthony Davis
P.O. Box 8935
Universal City, CA 91608
818-762-3540 or FAX 818-762-2503

	We Pay
Stereo Daguerreotype, still life	200.00+
Stereo Daguerreotype, portrait	300.00+
Stereo Daguerreotype, well-known personality	500.00+
Stereo Daguerreotype, nudes, ea	1,500.00+
Mascher Cased Stereo Daguerreotype, portrait	400.00+
Mascher Cased Stereo Daguerreotype, well-known personality	600.00+
Mascher Cased Stereo Daguerreotype, nudes, ea	1,800.00+
Daguerreotype, adult portrait, sixth or ninth plate, ea	30.00+

Daguerreotype, adult portrait, quarter or half plate, ea .... **100.00+**
Daguerreotype, child's portrait, sixth or ninth plate, ea .... **50.00+**
Daguerreotype, child's portrait, quarter or half plate, ea .... **150.00+**
Daguerreotype, well-known personality, sixth or ninth plate, ea .... **100.00+**
Daguerreotype, well-known personality, quarter or half plate, ea .... **250.00+**
Daguerreotype, exterior scene, quarter or sixth plate, ea .... **500.00+**
Daguerreotype, exterior scene, full or half plate, ea .... **2,000.00+**
Daguerreotype, erotica, ea .... **1,250.00+**

I buy **any photograph taken prior to 1910 except portraits**. I buy daguerreotypes, ambrotypes, tintypes, and paper — occupational, outdoor, pornographic, and sports scenes. I reimburse actual UPS and insurance charges. If you have anything unusual please write.

Don Williams
150 E Lakeview Ave.
Columbus, OH 43202-1217

I will buy **photographs of the Pacific Northwest including Montana**. Real photo postcards and stereoptican slides are wanted and must be signed. Send information and your price.

Carol Northrop
1016 8th St.
Edmonds, WA 98020
206-776-7519

I am interested in **any darkroom-related item with the Eastman Kodak name**. Beakers and other glass items are particularly wanted. I would pay top prices for perfect pieces. Please send a good photograph of the item with your price.

Kathy Nascimbeni
609 Laundry St.
Kannapolis, NC 28083
704-933-5810

PIE BIRDS

I am interested in purchasing older **pie birds or pie funnels,** (especially desired are those with advertising or pottery marks) — one or a collection. Prices will depend on condition, age, and rarity. I do answer all letters. Please enclose a good written description of the pie bird and/or a simple sketch. It is difficult to construct a want list, because I do not know all the ones that were produced, especially if foreign made. Thank you.

Lillian Cole
14 Harmony School Rd.
Flemington, NJ 08822-2606
908-782-3198

	We Pay
Apple, Cherry, or Peach Pie Funnel, ea	**40.00**
Eaton Improved Pie Funnel (Canadian Store)	**60.00**
Pie Boy, young boy w/hands cupped around mouth	**60.00**
Dopey Pie Funnel (price depends on contition)	**100.00+**

PIN-UP ART

I buy **old pin-up prints, calendars and other items** by artists such as Rolf Armstrong, Gil Elvgren, Alberto Vargas, George Petty, Earl MacPherson, Earl Moran, Al Buell, Zoe Mozert, Joyce Ballantyne, Billy De Vorss, and others. I do *not* buy photographic pin-up art. I buy any quantity from one item to large quantities. Condition is important. Prices listed below are for items in mint condtion. But I also buy some items in less than mint condition. Please call or write with detailed information, or if you have items in excellent to mint condition, send approval package, if you would like (or samples of your items if you have a large quantity). If I pay your price or if you accept my offer, I'll send a cashier's check immediately. If I don't buy, I'll return your package by insured UPS or priority mail at my expense. Please see my listing under Prints in this book.

Joan Jenkins
45 Brown's Ln.
Old Lyme, CT 06371
203-434-1852

	We Pay
Vargas *Comme Ci Comme Ca* Playing Cards, complete set	**90.00+**
Vargas Esquire Calendar	**35.00+**
Earl MacPherson 'Sketchpad' Calendar	**25.00+**
Earl MacPherson *Fun Hunting* Book	**60.00+**
Zoe Mazert Calendar, w/nude, lg	**50.00+**
Gil Elvgren Script Signature Pin-up Print	**10.00+**
Earl Moran Calendar, 12-page	**25.00+**
Rolf Armstrong *Radiant Youth* Calendar, lg	**75.00+**
Billy De Vorss Pin-up Print	**5.00+**

PLANTERS AND WALL POCKETS

Figural head wall pockets, Oriental people, and panda bear planters wanted by collector. I collect Oriental children (and people) planters and head wall pockets. I have a lot of different Royal Copley and Shawnee pieces. I pay anywhere from $1 to $22. I'm really interested in finding the panda bear planters that are marked Japan and are usually found seated on tree stumps, etc. I'm very fond of the Oriental shelf-sitter planters. Most pieces I buy are in near-perfect condition but don't necessarily have to be. I will pay to have items mailed to me. Some of the items I am interested in finding are listed below.

Rose Mary Hislope
202 Rear Howard Dr.
Wentzville, MO 63385

	We Pay
Panda & Cradle Planter, Shawnee USA 2031	**up to 20.00**
Oriental Boy w/Bamboo Side Planter, Royal Copley, 7½"	**up to 20.00**
Oriental Girl Wall Pocket, green dress, hat & big flowers in hair, gold trim, no mark, 5½"	**up to 22.00**

PLAYER PIANO ROLLS AND ROLLS FOR COIN-OPERATED PIANOS

Buying **standard player piano rolls and 10-tune nickelodeon (coin-operated) piano rolls of popular music only** — no foreign or classical needed.

Rolls need not be perfect just in average playable condition with no major tears or serious edge damage.

Standard player rolls (88-note rolls) are in boxes roughly 2" square. Older player rolls (65-note) have pin-ends and larger holes than standard 88-note rolls with ½" longer boxes. Nickelodeon rolls are in boxes roughly 5" to 6" square. Typical manufacturers of these 10-tune nickelodeon piano rolls are: Capitol, Columbia, Clark, Utomatic, and United States Music. Special wants include nickelodeon rolls (10- or 15-tune coin-operated piano rolls) made by the Capitol Roll Company of Chicago, Illinois.

As a guide, I will pay:

$5 to $10 for any standard player piano roll I can use. **Nothing in a red or brown box is wanted**.
$5 to $10 for any 65-note, pin-end player piano roll I can use.
$25 to $350 for any 10-tune coin-operated roll I can use.

Ed Sprankle
1768 Leimert Blvd.
Oakland, CA 94602-1930

Standard Player Piano Rolls	**We Pay**
Kansas City Stomp, Vocalstyle 50486	**500.00**
The Pearls, Vocalstyle 50488	**500.00**
New Orleans Blues, Vocalstyle 50508	**500.00**
Mamanita Blues, Vocalstyle 50478	**500.00**

POLITICAL

Political buttons of all kinds, new and old, are collectible, but the most desirable are the celluloid-coated pin-backs (cellos) produced between the 1890s and the 1920s. Many of these are attractively and colorfully designed, which enhances their value as historical artifacts. Most but not all buttons since then have been produced by lithography directly on metal discs (lithos).

Collectors generally favor presidential buttons — especially picture pins from 1960 or earlier. Jugates featuring presidential and vice-presidential candidates' photos are especially desirable, but there are numerous other specialities within the hobby, including state and local, third party, and cause items.

Value depends on scarcity, historical significance, design, and condition — buttons with cracks, gouges, deep scratches, and/or rust-colored stains (foxing) are not collectible. Reproductions exist, and many are marked as such, but some expertise is often needed to distinguish real from fake.

Political

Although my speciality is state and local buttons from 1925 or earlier, I will purchase other quality items in nice condition. Send me a photcopy of whatever you have (do not send the items themselves), and I will either make an offer or give an informal appraisal. I will respond promptly to any and all inquiries (include a reply postcard) whether about one button or a thousand. Prices below are for picture pins.

Michael Engel
29 Groveland St.
Easthampton, MA 01027
413-527-8733

Presidentials, 1896-1960	**We Pay**
Alton Parker, James Cox, John W Davis	**25.00+**
T Roosevelt, Wilson, Hoover, Truman	**10.00+**
Bryan, McKinley, CE Hughes	**5.00+**
Taft, Harding, Coolidge, Smith, Willkie, Landon, FDR or JFK, lg, ea	**10.00+**
Taft, Harding, Coolidge, Smith, Willkie, Landon, FDR or JFK, sm, ea	**up to 10.00+**
Jugates	**up to 100.00+**

Other Categories	**We Pay**
Socialist, Communist, or Prohibition Candidates, ea	**10.00+**
Eugene V Debs	**75.00+**
State & Local, before 1925	**up to 10.00**
Women's Suffrage	**10.00+**
Civil Rights or Vietnam	**up to 10.00**

The country's leading collector and scholar of **Richard M. Nixon memorabilia** will buy your Nixon collectibles. He will buy any item from the categories listed below. A photocopy or photograph of the items offered is requested for proper identification and his offer. An SASE will insure his response. He does not collect paper items, e.g. newspapers or posters. He does collect Nixon pin-back buttons, jewelry, novelty/3-D items, anti-Nixon and Watergate, postcards, first day covers, *Time* magazines with Nixon's picture on the cover, and campaign literature. Appraisal of your Nixon items is *free* with photocopy or photograph and SASE.

Eldon J. Almquist
975 Maunawili Cir.
Kailua, HI 96734-4620

Nixon Memorabilia **We Pay**

Campaign Ribbon....................**10.00+**
Toys, Games, Puzzles, or Novelty Items, ea....................**20.00+**
Glassware, any kind....................**15.00+**
Textiles, anything related....................**10.00+**
Books, about Nixon or Watergate, ea....................**5.00+**
Autographs, on any medium (authentic only), ea....................**100.00+**
Jewelry, any kind....................**5.00+**
Campaign Postcards, Brochures, or First Day Covers, ea....................**5.00+**
Inaugural Medals, Coins, Tokens, or Silver Art Bars, ea....................**10.00+**
Nixon White House Gift Items, or Souvenirs, ea....................**10.00+**
Nixon or Agnew Wristwatches, Pocket Watches, or Clocks, ea....................**25.00+**

Pin-Back Buttons **We Pay**

Eisenhower-Nixon Campaign, w/photo....................**10.00+**
Eisenhower-Nixon Campaign, words only....................**5.00+**
Nixon-Lodge Campaign, w/photo....................**10.00+**
Nixon-Lodge Campaign, words only....................**5.00+**
Nixon-Agnew Campaign....................**5.00+**
Any Other Nixon....................**5.00-100.00+**
Anti-Nixon or Watergate....................**10.00+**

POSTCARDS

I am a collector of **baseball postcards**. I am interested in any player, team, comic, etc., related to baseball. Condition must be very good to excellent. I also collect **any other baseball memorabilia**. You may send cards to me on approval with your price for my offer. A special want: anything Al Simmons! Other wants include **autographs, movie memorabilia, sterling silver, and table-model cigarette lighters**.

Bill Simmons
315 SW 77th Ave.
N Lauderdale, FL 33068-1220
305-726-3381

We Pay

Pre-1900 Photo, pro-team, ea....................**up to 100.00**
Post-1900 Photo, pro-team, ea....................**up to 50.00**

Non-Pro Team Photo, ea .... **up to 25.00**
Pre-1900 Photo, pro-player, ea... **up to 100.00**
Post-1900 Photo, pro-player, ea .... **up to 50.00**
Non-Pro Player Photo, ea .... **up to 25.00**
Comic, ea .... **up to 10.00**

I would like to buy postcards **featuring C.T. Streamline Bathing Beauties**. Cards are marked on the reverse 'Genuine Gurteich,' and 'C.T. Streamline Bathing Beauties, series of 10 cards.' **I will pay up to $5 each for very good unused cards** and less for used cards. Approvals appreciated.

Jerold M. Bennett
4510 Tallulah
San Antonio, TX 78218-3656
210-655-2108

Top dollar paid for **old postcards, photos, stereoscopic views, and pictorial souvenirs of Great Barrington, Massachusetts**. Other towns wanted include Housatonic, North Egremont, South Egremont, Alford, Sheffield, Glendale, Mt. Washington, Stockbridge, Monson, Enfield, Greenwich, Dana, and Prescott — all Massachusetts towns.

Gary Leveille
P.O. Box 562
Great Barrington, MA 01230

	We Pay
Postcard, Locust Inn	**8.00-12.00**
Postcard, showing fairgrounds	**3.00-12.00**
Postcard, real photo	**3.00-12.00**
Postcard, printed	**1.00-6.00**
Steroview	**3.00-12.00**
Photo	**5.00-20.00**

Wanted are **actual photos on postcards that show old beaches, fairgrounds, picnic groves, and Chautauqua grounds dating from 1850 through 1950** (the older, the better). Postcards are needed for the following states: Iowa (most wanted), Southern Minnesota, Eastern South Dakota, Eastern Nebraska, and Northern Missouri. I will consider any picture showing what I have listed here. Postcards wanted are for my own collection. Also of interest are **old county atlases and platbooks or any old county history book**.

Double Eagle Antiques
719 County T Rd.
Brayton, IA 50042
712-549-2410

We Pay

Beaches, 1850-1915, ea **1.00-10.00**
Beach, showing toboggan slide, 1850-1915, ea **4.00-10.00**
Beaches, 1915-1950, ea **1.00-5.00**
Fairgrounds, 1850-1930, ea **1.00-5.00**
Fairgrounds, shows horse racetrack, 1850-1930, ea **5.00-10.00**
Picnic Groves, 1850-1930, ea .... **1.00-10.00+**
Chautauqua Grounds, 1900-1930, ea **1.00-10.00**

POTTERY

The **Alamo Pottery of San Antonio** was in operation from 1944 to 1951. Alamo Pottery began as a producer of sanitary ware. Production of art pottery started in 1945 as a way to generate needed revenue. Alamo Pottery is cast vitreous porcelain glazed in solid colors. William H. Wallingford was the majority owner. Carlton Row was the plant manager from 1945 to 1951. The pottery usually had a shape number impressed on the bottom. Also stickers and ink stamps were used to mark the ware.

Thomas Turnquist
Box 256
Englewood, CO 80151

We Pay

Pitcher, #759, 7½" **60.00**
Pitcher, #760, 7½" **65.00**
Swan, #725, 5¼" **35.00**
Vase, #713, 7½" **25.00**
Vase, #722, 7¼" **30.00**

Vase, #902-5, 5" **20.00**
Vase, #903-5, 5" **30.00**

I am interested in buying **most art pottery, American and European**. Because of its design and decoration, price can vary a lot. But I will pay very well for the right piece, so check with me before you sell. Rookwood is a favorite with me, but I also want the following and others.

Bruce E. Thulin
P.O. Box 121
Ellsworth, ME 04605
207-667-5225

	We Pay
Brauchman	**50.00-150.00+**
Bretby	**50.00-150.00+**
CKAW	**100.00-500.00+**
Clarice Cliff	**100.00-800.00+**
Dalpayrat	**75.00-200.00+**
Dickens Ware	**100.00-300.00+**
Flame	**200.00-800.00+**
Flemington	**50.00-150.00+**
Gres Sylva	**50.00-200.00+**
Grueby	**300.00-3,000.00+**
Hampshire	**50.00-700.00+**
Harder	**50.00-200.00+**
Hunter	**50.00-300.00+**
LCT	**300.00-800.00+**
Marblehead	**50.00-1,000.00+**
Massier	**50.00-1,000.00+**
Moorcroft	**50.00-800.00+**
PRP	**50.00-800.00+**
Pierrefonds	**50.00-250.00+**
Pilkington	**50.00-200.00+**
Rookwood	**50.00-5,000.00+**
Scheier	**50.00-200.00+**
Sicard	**200.00-700.00+**
TH Deck	**300.00-1,000.00+**
Walrath	**300.00-600.00+**
WJW	**300.00-600.00+**

I am interested in buying **art pottery of any kind, but especially pieces made between 1870 and 1960**. Any large or small factory, one-man shop, marked and/or artist-signed pieces are wanted. Anything made in Ohio is preferred. Rookwood and Roseville are at the top of my list of artist-signed items wanted. Some pieces were not marked, and I will be glad to provide an explanation if interested as well as providing year of production for the following list of potteries. I will make offers. Please send a photo and/or explanation of marks, note flaws, repairs, etc., along with any questions with SASE.

Other wants include **marbles, paperweights, lead soldiers, and art glass of any kind — especially Galle Cameo**.

Frank Bernhard
2791 Fiesta Dr.
Venice, FL 34293

	We Pay
Cowan	**up to 100.00**
Hull	**up to 500.00**
McCoy	**up to 100.00**
Niloak	**up to 200.00**
Rookwood	**up to 5,000.00**
Roseville	**up to 500.00**
Van Briggle (need photo of bottom)	**up to 500.00**
Vernon Kilns	**up to 100.00**
Watt	**up to 100.00**
Weller	**up to 500.00**
Any American or Other Potter	**up to 500.00**

We **buy, sell, and collect American art pottery pieces**, especially Roseville, Hull, all wall pockets, McCoy, Weller, Watt, etc. We prefer pieces in mint condition but will consider pieces with insignificant chips, flecks, mold imperfections, and hairline cracks. We also buy unusual and/or collectible pieces for resale. Please call (collect calls will not be accepted) or mail lists with prices and conditions. Please include SASE. **We will pay 60% to 80% of book value depending on condition**.

Kelly Haskell
P.O. Box 213
Jacksonville, AL 36265

or

Barbara Johnson
P.O. Box 374
Jacksonville, AL 36265

or

The Shop
1344 Broadwell Mill Rd.
Jacksonville, AL 36265
205-435-4866

We live in a small rural town in southwest North Dakota and are interested in buying pottery made in North Dakota before 1965. Items may be marked **Dickota, Messer, Rosemeade, WPA (Ceramics Project, Works Project Administration) or UND (University of North Dakota, School of Mines)** and have paper stickers, incised, or ink-stamped marks.

Items wanted include shaker sets, figurines, sugar/creamer sets, vases, knickknacks, flowerpots, and miscellaneous pieces. Items must have no chips or cracks. Send a photo of your item or collection, if possible, along with a good description and your asking price.

Stan and Carrie Soderstrom
003-3rd St. SW
Rt. 2, Box 300
Bowman, ND 58623

	We Pay
Most Items, ea	**20.00-100.00**

We buy all damaged pottery — Rookwood, Roseville, Hull, Weller, and any other known marks. Send details of damage and price.

Marshall F. Brennan
217 Feathervale Dr.
Oroville, CA 95966

We restore pottery. That doesn't mean it is just glued together. We repair and paint to conceal the repair. This is not done in an attempt to deceive the buyer but to restore a work of art as closely as possible to its original condition rather than place it in the trash.

We buy damaged pottery in need of repairs such as chips, cracks, breaks, having missing pieces, etc. We specialize in Majolica, Roseville, Weller, Hull, Rookwood, Hall, McCoy, and other fine potteries.

The Finders Shoppe, Inc.
800-221-9177

We are wanting to buy **Roseville, Shawnee, Watt and Weller** pottery. We buy only pieces in excellent shape — no cracked, chipped or factory-defective pieces wanted. Items wanted include:

- Bowls
- Cookie Jars
- Figurals (birds, butterflies, animals)
- Jardiniers
- Planters
- Salt & Pepper Shakers
- Teapots
- Wall Pockets
- Candlesticks
- Creamers
- Lamps
- Pitchers
- Plates
- Sugar Bowls
- Vases

David W. Mayer
33 Mt. Vernon Pl.
Jamestown, NY 14701
716-487-0720

I am a collector interested in purchasing **Roseville, Weller, Rookwood, and Hull**. I want only pieces in mint condition — no cracks, chips, crazing or water mineral stains. I am intested in single pieces or a large collection. Please send description, photos, or call.

Fred L. Mitchell
835 Valencia
Walla Walla, WA 99362
509-529-4672

	We Pay
Hull (matte glaze only)	**40%-60% of retail**
Roseville	**50%-80% of retail**
Rookwood	**50%-70% of retail**
Weller	**50%-70% of retail**

I am a collector interested in buying any high-quality example of **Boch Freres or Keramis art pottery made in Belgium**. I am particularly interested in purchasing those pieces depicting animals or birds such as deer, antelopes, giraffes, penguins, and parrots. I am also interested in pieces with a strong Art Deco design.

I will generally pay book prices (*Schroeder's Antiques Price Guide*) for the higher-quality pieces and will answer all correspondence accompanied by a photo and asking price.

John T. Coates
324 Woodland Dr.
Stevens Point, WI 54481
715-341-6113

I am interested in buying several potteries:

- Sascha Brastoff
- Catalina Island
- Homer Laughlin Dinnerware
- Red Wing Dinnerware & Pottery
- Russel Wright Designs
- Brayton Laguna
- Kay Finch
- Metlox Dinnerware
- Stangl Dinnerware
- Vernon Kilns Dinnerware & Pottery

Please send description, price and condition of your items. Photographs are helpful and will be returned. I may be interested in other items not listed here. No phone calls, please. See also Vernon Kilns in this book. Thank you.

Ray Vlach, Jr.
5364 N Magnet Ave.
Chicago, IL 60630-1216

Dealer would like to buy (at dealer price) pieces of **Provencial Rose pattern by Poppytrail/Metlox**. I especially would like to find cereal and soup bowls as well as serving dishes. Also wanted are **Homestead and Red Rooster** lines by the same company.

Rebecca Hunt
Rocking Chair Mall
104 S Main
Lindsay, OK 73052
405-756-3941 (10 am to 6 pm)

We are buying pottery from the following list for resale. Please send a description of what you have for sale and your asking price. Pictures would also be helpful. All pieces must be in mint condition — free of all nicks, chips, cracks, bruises, glaze crazing, or any other damage.

Blue Willow	Coors
Currier & Ives by Royal China	Fiesta
Franciscan	Friar Tuck Monks by Goebel
Hall	Hull
Liberty Blue by Staffordshire	McCoy
Memory Lane by Royal China	Roseville
Shawnee	Van Briggle

The Glass Packrat
Pat and Bill Ogden
3050 Colorado Ave.
Grand Junction, CO 81504
303-434-7452 (6 pm to 10 pm, MST)

I am interested in purchasing **studio pottery by potters Jim and Nan McKinnell, Mark Zamantakis, and Jack Pharo**. The McKinnells have produced studio pots since the early 1950s. They have taught ceramics at several major universities. Mark Zamantakis has worked in clay for over forty years and is a top-level expert on wood-fired kilns. Jack Pharo taught ceramics at the Wichita Art Association from 1948 through 1973.

Tom Turnquist
Box 256
Englewood, CO 80151
303-988-0442

	We Pay
McKinnell Bowl, over 12" dia	**75.00**
McKinnell Vase, over 8"	**50.00**
McKinnell Vase, over 12"	**75.00**
Pharo Bottle, 5" to 8"	**30.00+**
Pharo Bowl, over 12" dia	**75.00**
Pharo Plate/Platter, 9" to 14" dia	**30.00+**
Pharo Vase, over 12"	**85.00**
Zamantakis Bowl, over 8" dia	**35.00**
Zamantakis Vase, over 8"	**40.00**

I buy **Tamac pottery made in Perry, Oklahoma**. Pieces include dinnerware, accessory, and floral pieces. All items are marked Tamac, Inc., Perry Okla. I pay premium prices for raspberry color, advertising, and unusual items. Mint-condition items only are wanted. UPS paid.

Carol Steichen
Rt. 1, Box 88A
Perry, OK 73077
405-336-5247

	We Pay
Bud Vase	15.00
Card Ashtray Set, ea piece	5.00
Casserole, w/lid	25.00
Chop Plate, 18"	17.50
Demitasse Cup & Saucer Set	15.00
Figurine, sm bird	15.00
Juice Glass	5.00
Pitcher, 2-qt	15.00
Pitcher, 4-qt	17.50
Teapot, w/lid	30.00
Spoon Holder	7.50
Wine Decanter, w/stopper	30.00
Wine Goblet	7.50

We buy **W.J. Gordy pottery** that was purchased by passing tourists during the last fifty years from his shop near Cartersville, Georgia. Some of the earlier pieces are marked GA Art Pottery. We only want pieces that are not chipped or cracked.

Rudy Ferguson
Resaca Mall Antiques
3050 Hwy. 41 N
Resaca, GA 30735-0517
706-629-0035

	We Pay
Bowl	15.00
Churn	45.00
Cup	8.00
Pitcher	25.00
Vase	15.00-25.00

American art pottery wanted: Teco (this is one of my favorites). Look for geometric and organic-shaped vases with square or built-in handles, buttresses, or reticulations. Sculptural leaves and plant forms were often used. Mostly matte glazes (a moss or mint green) were used, but pieces are also found in browns, yellows, grays and other assorted matte colors and may be highlighted with black/gray gun metal. Teco also made a fine micro-crystalline high glaze that looks like glitter in the light. Lamps, wall pockets, and tiles were also made.

Also wanted are Weller matte ware pieces. Some vases may have raised figures (frogs, lizards, snakes, nudes, people, insects, etc.) or may be of strong geometric design. The glaze is similar to that of Van Briggle in rose, pink, blue, gray, yellow, brown, and matte green. Colors may sometimes be mixed on the same piece, often with a veining effect or gun metal. Items may be signed Weller in small block print or hand inscribed. Other Weller lines wanted include Comet, Stellar, Cretone, Sicardo, Souevo (large Indian-styled vases), Blue Louwelsa, Marengo, etc.

We also buy **Mission oak and hammered copper lamps and vases**. See our listing under Art Deco in this book. Below is a partial listing of pottery wanted.

Arequipa	Chelsea Keramic
Clewell	Clifton
Grueby	Dedham
Paul Revere	Natzler
Newcomb College	Ohr
Robertson	Robineau
Rookwood	Roseville
SEG (Saturday Evening Girls)	Tiffany
UND (University of North Dakota)	Volkmar
Walley	Walrich
Walrath	Wheatley

Gary Struncius
P.O. Box 1374
Lakewood, NJ 08701
201-364-7580 or 800-272-2529

I love **items made in the 1940s and '50s** and am interested in bowls, lamps, and figurines such as animals, birds, Disney or comic characters, and funny little items. Signed items preferred. Pricing is open and depends on the item and its condition. A photo will help determine price.

C.E. Nolte
2979 S 15 Pl.
Milwaukee, WI 53215

	We Pay
Sascha Brastoff	**15.00-30.00**
Kay Finch	**15.00-40.00**
Hedi Schoop	**15.00-40.00**
Brad Keeler	**15.00-30.00**
Other American Potteries	**15.00-25.00**

PRECIOUS MOMENTS

Enesco's Precious Moments collectibles are becoming increasingly popular with collectors. Enesco first began production about 1978 of these figurines, bells, dolls, plates, and ornaments featuring children in various activities in soft pastel colors.

I am interesting in finding **figurines and dolls (no vinyl ones wanted)** to add to my collection. Especially wanted are original pieces, retired items, membership club pieces, and those with musical mechanisms. Figurines must be in mint condition with no chips, cracks, or repairs, with original box and papers. Please send a photo for identification, if possible, and describe marks on the base. Include your SASE for my reply. Listed below is only a very small sampling of figurines available. Please tell me about your items.

Patty Durnell
703 Tilton Rd.
Danville, IL 61832
217-443-4201

	We Pay
Angel & Girl at Heaven's Gate, 'No Tears Past the Gate,' 1986	**15.00**
Baby Boy, w/dog & stocking, 'The Greatest Gift Is a Friend,' 1986	**12.50**
Boy Banjo Player, 'Happiness Is the Lord,' 1984	**12.50**
Clown on Ball, 'Lord Keep Me on the Ball,' 1985	**12.50**
Commemorative Edition 5th Anniversary, 'God Bless Our Years Together,' 1984	**20.00**
Clown, w/dog & hoop, 'The Lord Will Carry You Through,' 1985	**15.00**

PREMIUMS

I am interested in buying **all premiums from the 1930s to 1950s** including radio, cereal, movie, and comic book promotions. In my opinion, they represent the golden years of the giveaway. As a child it was with great anticipation that I waited for approximately one month to receive the package in the mail. Upon opening it, I always had a great feeling of pleasure at seeing the enclosed treasure. This opinion may differ from others who now relate that they were often disappointed upon viewing the enclosed item. Perhaps as a child I had more imagination than they did. Some items listed below such as the Flash Gordon pin-back were obtained from movie theatres, but all items fall into the premium category, which by definition is a prize or reward for purchasing something. I am also interested in directions, paperwork, and mailers. Sample prices are for near-mint condition items. Lesser condition pieces acceptable at lower prices.

Ed Pragler
Box 284W
Wharton, NJ 07885
201-875-8293

	We Pay
Buck Rogers Propeller Ray Ring	1,200.00
Captain Battle Pin-Back, celluloid	500.00
Captain Marvel Statue	1,500.00
Captain Midnight Flight Commander Badge	1,000.00
Flash Pin-Back, lithographed	500.00
Flash Gordon Movie Pin-Back, celluloid	500.00
Green Lama Membership Kit, complete	400.00
Junior Justice Society Membership Kit, complete	500.00
Operator 5 Ring, enameled, solid band	3,000.00
Orphan Annie Altascope Ring	3,000.00
Orphan Annie Initial Ring	1,000.00
Orphan Annie Magnifying Ring	1,200.00
Sergeant Preston Ten-in-One Trail Kit, complete	400.00
Spider Ring, enameled, solid band	3,000.00
Superman Statue	1,500.00
Superman Patch, round	1,000.00
Other Premiums, ea	10.00-10,000.00

PRAYER LADIES

The original name for these porcelain ladies was Mothers-in-the-Kitchen; they were manufactured by Enesco during the 1960s. They were made with pink, blue, and white with blue-trimmed dresses. Their white aprons have a prayer on them. Their eyes are closed, and their reddish-brown hair is swept up into a bun. We buy only mint or near-mint prayer ladies without any cracks or chips. Since these ladies damage easily, a small nick may be acceptable. We buy any prayer ladies and pay more for the blue or rarer pieces. We pay all shipping and insurance on items we purchase. Please include large SASE with all correspondence. Prices listed are for pink ladies only.

April and Larry Tvorak
HCR #34 Box 25B
Warren Center, PA 18851
717-395-3775

	We Pay
Bell	15.00+
Bud Vase	15.00
Crumb Sweeper	65.00
Egg Timer	35.00+
Instant Coffee Container	25.00
Planter	15.00
Photo Holder	25.00+
Spoon Rest, flat	25.00+
Sprinkler	75.00+
Stringholder	35.00+
Teapot, Creamer & Sugar Set	125.00+
Wall Plaque	35.00

PRINTS

Maxfield Parrish illustrations are wanted such as magazine covers, advertisements, calendars, prints, and more. Parrish was a very successful commercial artist from the late 1800s through 1966. I am interested in collecting examples of his illustrations — the more unusual the better. Listed here are some items sought. Send me your list of any available items.

Edison Mazada Playing Cards, complete in original box
Edison Mazada Calendars, small, complete with pad
Puzzles, old & new
Tape Measures
Printed Fabric (from the 1960s)
Brown & Bigelow Calendar Landscapes
Crane's Chocolates Boxes
Old King Cole Tobacco Packs, Tins & Cigar Boxes

Books, w/Parrish illustrations and bindings
Ink Blotters

Cracker Hill
P.O. Box 403
Waldo, FL 32694-0403

Actively seeking **Maxfield Parrish** prints, posters, calenders, original drawings, and oil paintings. Condition is very important. Many factors determine condition when talking about paper products. Things such as tears, stains, foxing, mildew, and fading greatly diminish true value. Send photo description, and phone number, or call with info. Maxfield Parrish was a well-known American illustrator, whose place is etched in art history. From early magazine illustrations, Mazda calendars, and Brown and Bigelow landscapes a portfolio of prints was published.

Edward J. Meschi
129 Pinyard Road
Monroeville, New Jersey 08343
609-358-7293 or FAX 609-358-7293

I buy **old art prints and calendars** by Maxfield Parrish, R. Atkinson Fox, W.M. Thompson, Philip R. Goodwin, Frank Stick, Bessie Pease Gutmann, Gene Pressler, Paul De Longpre, Thomas Moran, Chandler, Philip Boileau, Maud Humphrey, C.K. Van Nortwick, and others. I also buy 'Child and Bluebird' scenes, prints, and calendars by Zula Kenyon and Adelaide Hiebel. Indian maiden prints and calendars by any artist (may be unsigned) are wanted. Condition is important. Prices listed below are for items in near-mint to mint condition. I also buy some items in less than mint condition. Please call or write with detailed information, or if you have items in excellent to mint condition, send approval package, if you like (or samples if you have a large quantity), along with your price (or request my offer). If I pay your price or if you accept my offer, I'll send a cashier's check immediately. If I don't buy, I'll return your package by insured UPS or priority mail at my expense. See also Pinup Art in this book.

Joan Jenkins
45 Brown's Ln.
Old Lyme, CT 06371
203-434-1852

	We Pay
Maxfield Parrish, book, *Knave of Hearts*, hardbound	**400.00+**
R Atkinson Fox, items w/unusual subjects, ea	**25.00+**
Indian Maidens, prints or calendars, ea	**15.00+**
Philip R. Goodwin, hunting prints, lg, ea	**35.00+**
Gene Pressler, Hawaiian girl prints, ea	**20.00+**
Paul De Longpre, floral prints, ea	**15.00+**
Bessie Pease Gutmann, uncommon prints, ea	**45.00+**
Philip Boileau, pretty lady prints, ea	**20.00+**
WM Thompson, prints & calendars, lg, ea	**25.00+**

I buy **Louis Icart etchings**. They have to be hand-signed originals in relatively good condition. They may be framed or unframed. I also buy **Maxfield Parrish** prints, calendars, books, and miscellaneous items. Again, only original art is wanted, framed or unframed. Prices vary according to condition and rarity of the item. I have been selling Maxfield Parrish prints for fifteen years and have advertised in numerous books and magazines. I have been selling Louis Icart for seven years. Send a stamped envelope or call. I will try to answer every inquiry.

Chris Daniels
135 E Shiloh Ave.
Santa Rosa, CA 95403
707-838-6083

Wanting to buy **Bessie Pease Gutmann prints or prints marked Bessie Collins Pease**. It is impossible to make a list because items are too numerous to mention here. Also of interest are **German children's dishes**.

Nancy Callis
Four Tami Ct.
Bloomington, IL 61701
309-837-0489

I want **Paul Jacoulet woodblock prints**. Any print or Christmas card produced by this artist are wanted. I am **paying anywhere from $100 to $2,500**, depending on subject and condition.

Bob Block
P.O. Box 51
Trumbull, CT 06611
203-261-0057

PURSES

I am a leading buyer of **vintage beaded and mesh bags, handbag frames, needlework purses, and compacts** of the Victorian era through the 1940s. I especially like unusual and fancy purses with elaborate designs and pay good prices for them.

Enameled mesh bags should have either a bright floral design, birds, scenes, or celebrity faces. The design could be simple with jewels in the frame or the body of the bag. I also buy novelty designs such as those with a compact incorporated into the frame or the body of the bag. I buy purses with Mickey Mouse or The Three Little Pigs dangling from the frame. Beaded bags should have tiny glass beads with scenes of people, houses, castles, animals, mountains, rug motifs or unusual subjects. Bags with fancy glass jeweled or enameled frames are wanted. I also purchase bags with watches imbedded in the frames or the body of the bag and metal or early plastic dance purses that may have glass jewels or tassels. I need vintage purse frames with holes for sewing that are not silver, but have fancy enameling, glass jewels, or a pretty pattern.

I buy one item or a collection. If you think your bag is exquisite or one of a kind, I will probably be interested in buying it. For a good visual reference, consult my book, *The Best of Vintage Purses*, by Schiffer Publishing of Pennsylvania. I would buy any bag similar to those pictured in this book. Send photocopies or pictures with SASE and the price you are asking if possible. I also buy **glass beads, costume jewelry, compacts, ladies' accessories, vintage purse advertisements, and related trade catalogs**.

The Curiosity Shop
Lynel Schwartz
P.O. Box 964
Cheshire, CT 06410
203-271-0643

	We Pay
Vintage Purse Frame	35.00+
Mesh Bag, w/celebrity face	250.00+
Mesh Bag, w/scene	100.00+
Mesh Bag, w/compact	125.00+

Purses

Mesh Bag, w/glass jewels .... **100.00+**
Mesh or Beaded Bag, w/Disney character or World's Fair theme, ea..... **100.00+**
Bag w/Watch (as part of the bag) .... **100.00+**
Dance Purse .... **140.00+**

We buy **antique purses and handbags (1930s and earlier)** of exceptional quality and workmanship. Of special interest are purses with jeweled and very ornate frames. Colored, faceted glass jewels and imitation stones are bezel set onto filigreed purse frames usually having metal carrying chains. Purses may be beaded, petit point, needlepoint, or tapestry with figural, floral, scenic, or Persian-carpet designs. We also buy jeweled vanity or dance bags. These small, very fancy brass filigree purses are encrusted with beautiful colored jewels and pearls, and often contain a compact or lipstick. They have jeweled metal tassels and metal carrying chains or silk cords, and may be marked Trinity Plate. We also buy unusual metal mesh bags. Purses should be in excellent to mint condition — no holes in body of bags or no missing sections of fringe. Missing jewels are acceptable. We do not buy leather or alligator bags or purses of average quality or design. Offers should include a photograph or photocopy and price. Shipping and insurance charges paid. I have been collecting for fifteen years.

Victorian Touch
Valerie Roberts
P.O. Box 4
Micanopy, FL 32667
904-466-4022

We Pay

Jeweled Brass Vanity Bag, with jeweled tassel & metal chain, interior silk pockets **175.00**
Needlepoint w/Figures, ornate jeweled frame & clasp, chain, France **225.00**
Beaded Reticule, floral design, beaded tassle, drawstring **95.00**
Mesh Bag, aqua color design, ornate openwork frame, blue glass jewels ... **135.00**
Woven Tapestry Purse, brown w/flowers & bird, ormolu frame, 1900s... **155.00**
Fine Petit Point, woman standing by rosebush, jeweled handle w/chain **165.00**
Cut Steel Beaded, jewel encrusted frame, muted carpet design, 9x16", mint condition **275.00**
Beaded, rose garlands, openwork frame w/flowers, chain handle **145.00**
Beaded Scenic, Venetian Canal, elaborate jeweled frame, lg, ca 1910s.... **300.00**
Metallic Gold Thread, seed pearls & prong-set rhinestones, chain **85.00**
Rose-Colored Velvet, with gold metallic beads & sequins, pearls purple jewels **115.00**
Beaded, unusual Egyptian motif, celluloid handle & link chain, fringed ... **165.00**

Cut Steel Beaded, colorful pattern, ornate net fringe, jewel encrusted, chain handle **285.00**

We collect **metal mesh purses painted with multicolored designs**. These bags were made by the Whiting & Davis Co. and the Mandalian Manufacturing Co. in the 1920s and early 1930s. There are three basic types of mesh: Dresden or chain-link type, Armor-Mesh or flat-link type, and Bead-Lite which is a flat link-and-bubble mesh.

Other metal mesh purses with painted designs circa 1920 through 1930 by these manufacturers are wanted as well: Evans, Napier-Bliss, R.&G. Co., F.&B. Co., and others. Especially wanted are purses featuring figural designs, scenic or landscape designs, elaborate geometric or floral patterns, ornate frames with polished stones, faux jewels or enameled decorations, painted frames, and Art Deco frames with painted inserts. Contact us about metal mesh purses in poor condition that are suitable as parts for repairing other purses. We do not collect the plain gold or plain silver clutch-type bags made in the 1940s and 1950s. Request a detailed want list of specific purses.

We are interested only in purses in mint or near-mint condition. The uniqueness of the design and condition of the paint on the mesh are the most important factors in determining desirability. Bags in mint condition must have virtually perfect paint. Near-mint purses will have a few or no missing fringe chains or drops and will show only minor paint wear. See also Compacts in this book. **Other related wants include**:

Advertisements, for mesh purses from vintage magazines circa 1920 through 1930
Jewelry Catalogs or Other Catalogs, circa 1920 through 1930 with color pages showing mesh purses
Photos, circa 1920 through 1930 showing women carrying mesh bags

Sherry and Mike Miller
303 Holiday Dr.
Tuscola, IL 61953
217-253-4991

Painted Metal Mesh Purses	**We Pay**
Child's Size (2¼x3", 2½x3½", or 3x4¾")	**40.00-75.00**
Small Size (3¼x5¾", 3½x6¼", or 4x7")	**60.00-95.00**
Medium Size (4½x7¾", 5x6¼", or 5¼x8")	**75.00-150.00**
Large Size (4½x10", 5x9", or 6x9¾")	**100.00-175.00**
Extra-Large Size (7x12", 8x9" or 9¼x12")	**200.00+**

Compact & Mesh Combination Vanity Bag.................................**160.00-500.00**
Celebrity Bag (Clark Gable, Marion Davies, Charlie Chaplin)......**400.00-600.00**

Looking to buy **old Victorian-type beaded, needlepoint, mesh, or silver evening bags from before 1950** — any condition wanted. Will pay for shipping costs. Please call first for price before sending.

Jan Alpert
800-341-8583

I buy **colorful mesh and fine beaded purses, Art Deco styles, enameled purses, novelties, purses with gadgetry, and especially compact and purse combinations. I will pay $200 and up for compact and purse combinations made before 1940.**

Lori Landgrebe
2331 E Main St.
Decatur, IL 62521
271-423-2254

Wanted: **beaded purses with landscape, geometric, or floral designs** in good condition. Also I am crazy about **shoes from 1890 through 1970**. Button shoes must be complete with original buttons. I love shoes with cutouts, beadwork, or embroidery. I buy any size, any color ladies shoes in good condition but especially wanted are Victorian, wide size 9-10 (circa 1925 through 1945), and platforms of the 1970s. I will consider other Victorian shoes. Please send photo and description. Please see Prints in this book for other wants.

Cracker Hill
P.O. Box 403
Waldo, FL 32694-0403

PUZZLES

I would like to buy **advertising jigsaw puzzles that were given away by companies or sold at a nominal price**. There must be advertising on the face of the puzzle, a picture of the product advertised, or the name cut out as a piece of the puzzle. I would like to have the original envelope or box the puzzle came in. I will accept incomplete puzzles at a greatly reduced price (about 50% less). Regional brands or local store puzzles are more desirable than the nationally advertised products. I will pay a premium for regional brands or local store puzzles. I will buy one puzzle or quantities of the same puzzle. I am also interested in buying **any World's Fair, celebrity, or comic character jigsaw puzzle**. See also Paperweights and Locks in this book for other wants.

Don Friedman
660 W Grand, Apt. 4E
Chicago, IL 60610
312-226-4741

	We Pay
Essolube, illustrated by Dr Seuss	**50.00**
Victrola, record shaped w/pictures of artists	**55.00**
Shell Oil, view of Airport	**35.00**
South Bend Watch Company	**40.00**
1933 Nash at the Century of Progress	**45.00**
Minneapolis Shoe Company	**40.00**
Movie-land Cut UPS, Wilder Mfg Co	**35.00**
Goodrich Tire Co, Akron, Ohio	**30.00**
RCA Victor, His Master's Voice	**50.00**

We buy **all puzzles made through the 1950s**. You need not check to be sure all pieces are there, but the puzzle(s) should be nearly complete. Types wanted include Tuco, Picture Perfect, Crosley, Jig of the Week, Puzzle of the Week, wooden puzzles, etc. Prices vary due to many factors and subject matter.

Bob and Gail Spicer
R.D. 1 Ashgrove Rd., Box 82
Cambridge, NY 12816
518-677-5139

RADIOS

I buy **transistor radios**. All models and makes are wanted as well as novelties and figural advertising characters. I prefer radios with civil defense marks. All radios must be in excellent condition, but I will consider some radios for parts. When sending a description of your radio, send information on color and manufacturer, and carefully remove back to see model number and make. I pay postage, so send by UPS for my offer.

Mickey Starr
2722 340th
Keokuk, IA 52632
319-524-1601

	We Pay
Regency, all models	**75.00+**
Mitchell	**75.00+**
Bulova	**20.00+**

Specific models wanted include:

Emerson 849-999
Layfayette FS-91
Seminole 601
Sony TR-63-86-55

Wanted to buy: **novelty radios**, if reasonably priced. I would like to buy a Commodore 'adding machine' radio or any of the six model 'doll' novelty radios. Please call or write.

Larry Brock
111 Mattie Ree Ln.
Jacksonville, AL 36265
205-435-6848

RAILROADIANA

I buy the following tall **globe lantern frames and globes** which are marked with embossed (raised) letters. All such items must be old and in excellent condition. The globes must be at least five inches tall with an extended base (lip) on the bottom. Higher prices paid for colored globes with these embossed markings. Will also pay top dollar for other marked brass top lanterns and/or embossed extended globes from other Western railroads.

Bill Cunningham
3629 Candelaria
Plano, TX 75023
214-596-9646

Lantern Frames	We Pay
AT&SFRR, w/steel top	300.00+
AT&SFRR, w/brass top	650.00+
CB&QRR, w/brass top	500.00+
CRI&PRR, w/brass top	550.00+
Santa Fe Route, w/steel top	200.00+
UPRW, w/brass top	650.00+
UPRR, w/brass top	600.00+
UPRW-U, w/brass top	650.00+
UPRW-SP, w/brass top	650.00+
Union Pacific, w/brass top	450.00+

Lantern Globes	We Pay
AT&SFRR	650.00+
AT&SF	500.00+
CB&QRR	300.00+
CRI&P	450.00+
CRI&PRR	600.00+
UPRW	650.00+
UPRR	600.00+
UPRW-U	650.00+
UPRW-SP	650.00+
Union Pacific	300.00+
Santa Fe Route	200.00+

The term railroadiana is meant to cover all collecting facets of the golden age of railroading. Depending upon the collector's interest, items such as lanterns, tools, locks and keys, dining car wares (china, glass, silver, linen), advertising timetables, signs, and other items are eagerly sought.

Our particular area of interest is **authenticated patterns of dining car china**. We prefer those pieces which have a top or side logo (design or mark) and/or a designated railroad's name on the underside of the piece. In addition, we seek to buy railroad station restaurant and eating housewares, examples of china and silver from street and electric railways, and also pieces from railroad-related ferryboat and steamship systems. This listing represents only a sampling of railroadiana items we seek to buy. We respond to all offerings. Other interests include **Shelley (see our listing in this book), Buffalo Pottery, butter pats, buttons and buckles, and Hummels**.

Fred and Lila Shrader
2025 Hwy. 199 (Hiouchi)
Crescent City, CA 95531
707-458-3525

Railroad China	**We Pay**
Alaska RR, anything	**100.00+**
Baltimore & Ohio RR, cups & saucers	**75.00+**
Butter Pats, any railroad	**25.00+**
Chesapeake & Ohio RR, Chessie, anything	**75.00+**
Denver & Rio Grande, Curecanti, anything	**200.00+**
Fred Harvey, Cactus logo, anything	**25.00+**
Great Northern, Glory of the West, anything	**50.00+**
Great Northern, Mountains & Flowers, anything	**50.00+**
Missouri, Kansas, Texas RR, Bluebonnet, anything	**100.00+**
Southern Pacific, Prairie Mountain Wildflower, anything	**45.00+**
Southern Pacific, Sunset, anything	**50.00+**
Union Pacific, Historical, anything	**100.00+**
Union Pacific, Portland Rose, anything	**100.00+**
Unitah Railway, Mesa, anything	**200.00+**
Western Pacific, Feather River, anything	**50.00+**

Glassware	**We Pay**
Cordials, any railroad	**25.00+**
Carafe, any railroad, w/o or w/silver holder	**50.00+**
Wine, stem; any railroad	**15.00+**

Linen	**We Pay**
Blanket, w/RR logo in weave, any railroad	**25.00+**
Headrest, w/RR logo, any railroad	**10.00+**
Napkin, white on white or colored	**10.00+**
Placemat	**10.00+**
Tablecloth	**15.00+**
Towel	**10.00**

RAZORS

I collect early **unusual safety razors, blade banks, mechanical blade sharpeners, and stroppers**, as well as shaving-related catalogs, instruction sheets and booklets, window and counter advertising, display materials, and manufacturer giveaways. I no longer collect the following brands: Rolls, Durham, Valet, Gillette, Kriss Kross, Twinplex, or Listerine.

Prices will vary depending on the particular item, its age and condition, as well as its container. But my price will reflect a collector's interest and not a dealer's — who might expect to pay less in order to be able to resell. The following are brand names of some early safety razors which might command prices in excess of $100 and in some cases several hundreds of dollars:

A-C Specialty
Dr Scott Electric
Home
Mohican
Wanie
Wilbert
Yale
Collins Wind-Up
Fox
Modern Deluxe
U-Magnet
Witch
Winner
Zinn

Lester Dequaine
155 Brewster St.
Bridgeport, CT 06605
203-335-6833

RECORDS

I am a collector interesting in purchasing **Vogue picture records** produced by Sav-Way Industries in Detroit, Michigan, between 1946 and 1947. **I will pay a minimum of $25 for any Vogue record in good condition and will pay in the range of $100 to $500 for the following records**:

R711
R712
R713
R715
R723
R725
R726
R747
R748
R750
R784
S100

John T. Coates
324 Woodland Dr.
Stevens Point, WI 54481
715-341-6113

RED WING

I am a collector of **Red Wing stoneware** and would like to hear from anyone who may have any of the following items for sale. Also would especially be interested in any piece with advertising. Pieces wanted include: churns, jugs, beater jars, spongeware items, pitchers, bean pots, etc. I am *not* interested in dinnerware items. Prices paid depend on condition, size, marks, scarcity, and if the piece is needed for my collection. Thank you for your consideration. Call collect if you wish.

R.V. Chase
121 2nd Ave. N
Onalaska, WI, 54650
608-783-3014

RHODE ISLAND EPHEMERA

Buying Rhode Island paper collectibles: billheads (especially illustrated), trade cards, calendars, blotters, certificates, scrapbook items, postcards, postal history items (deltiology and philatelics), etc.

Gordon Carr
Ephemera
67 Chapel St.
Lincoln, RI 02865-2101

	We Pay
Billheads, ea	**2.00-5.00**
Blotters, ea	**1.00-5.00**
Calendars, ea	**2.00-10.00**
Checks, ea	**1.50-8.00**
Postal Commemoratives, ea	**1.00-20.00**
Real Photo Postcards, ea	**1.00-20.00**
Trade Cards, ea	**1.00-3.00**
Other Ephemera Items, ea	**1.00-20.00+**

ROSEVILLE POTTERY

We buy **jardinieres and pedestals in most patterns**. These do not need to be paired. Prices are influenced by the pattern, as the most popular patterns command a higher price. Some of those patterns would be Blackberry, Sunflower, Baneda, Cherry Blossom, Fuchsia, Pine Cone, and Wisteria. After the pattern, the size and color affect the price range with blues more valuable than browns in most patterns, and browns more valuable than greens in most patterns. The sizes available vary by pattern, but the prices are higher for the larger pieces. If the piece is not in mint condition or if the sharpness in the mold or color is less than perfect, the price will drop. We reimburse actual UPS and insurance charges. There are over one hundred size/color/pattern combinations. If you don't find yours here or if you have other pieces, please call or write!

M.J. Mahoney
5506 Fir Ave.
Erie, CO 80516
303-666-0366

	We Pay
Baneda, 8" jardiniere w/pedestal, pink/blue	**1,200.00+**
Blackberry, 12" jardiniere w/pedestal, green	**2,000.00+**
Bushberry, jardiniere 657-8", blue	**225.00+**
Cherry Blossom, jardiniere, brown, 8"	**400.00+**
Fuchsia, jardiniere 645-8", blue	**400.00+**
Fuchsia, pedestal for 645-10" jardiniere, brown	**300.00+**
Magnolia, jardiniere 465-8", blue	**200.00+**
Pine Cone, pedestal for 632-8" jardiniere, blue	**400.00+**
Pine Cone, jardiniere 402-8", blue	**600.00+**
Pine Cone, pedestal for 406-10" jardiniere, brown	**300.00+**
Pine Cone, pedestal for 632-12" jardiniere, brown	**400.00+**
Pine Cone, 12" jardiniere w/pedestal, blue	**1,500.00+**
Snowberry, jardiniere IJ-8", brown	**200.00+**
Sunflower, jardiniere, green, 8"	**350.00+**
Water Lily, jardiniere 663-8", blue	**200.00+**
White Rose, pedestal for 653-8" jardiniere, brown,	**175.00+**
Wisteria, jardiniere, blue, 8"	**400.00+**

ROYCROFT

We are the largest buyer of Roycroft, Elbert Hubbard, and related items. We will buy **any Roycroft product**, regardless of condition, but avidly seek out rare items and one-of-a-kind items not made to be sold. If you even think your item might be Roycroft, call us! We travel to see! No one will beat our offer for items we want. Association items wanted include:

- Cordova Leather Products
- Alex Fournier Paintings
- Eleanor Douglas Paintings
- Raymond Nott Artwork
- Toothacher Artwork
- Dard Hunter Artwork
- Books by Louis Kinder
- Cooper & Silver by Walter Jennings
- Schiedmantle Leather Products
- Sandor Landeau Paintings
- Carl Ahrens Paintings
- Samuel Warner Artwork
- WW Denslow Artwork
- Books by John Grabeau
- Copper & Silver by Karl Kipp
- Copper by Avon

Roycroft Arts Museum
Boice Lydell
341 E Fairmount Ave.
Lakewood, NY 14750
716-763-1111 or 716-763-5555

	We Pay
Books	up to 20,000.00
Copper	up to 20,000.00
Lamps	up to 200,000.00
Furniture	up to 50,000.00
Leather	up to 5,000.00
Artwork	up to 20,000.00
China (Buffalo)	up to 2,000.00

RUSSEL WRIGHT

I am looking to buy Russel Wright in both **Iroquois and American Modern**. I am interested in original boxed sets and children's pieces. Please let me make you an offer.

Kim Kimler
P.O. Box 154
Ripton, VT 05766

SALESMAN'S SAMPLES AND MINIATURES

We buy any **old miniatures or salesman's samples** that are in reasonably good condition. We will reimburse for actual shipping costs. If you send a photo along with description and price, we will return your photo.

R. Ouellette
3510 Stanton Rd.
Oxford, MI 48371

I am looking for a **salesman's sample coal-burning stove from the late 1800s**. Please write, describing your item. Thank you.

Elenore D. Chaya
4003 S Indian River Dr.
Ft. Pierce, FL 34982
407-465-1789

SALT AND PEPPER SHAKERS

I buy **all types of novelty figural salt and pepper shakers**. I'll buy one set or an entire collection. Favored categories include recognizable characters and personalities (Felix the Cat, Ghandi, Martin and Lewis, Nancy and Sluggo, etc.); figural nodders (two shakers which rock back and forth inserted in a stationary base); Black Americana (Coon Chicken Inn, Luzianna Mammy, etc.); advertising figurals (Happy Homer, Hershey Bean Babies, etc.); plastic gas pumps; condiment sets (pair of shakers and little covered mustard cruet with spoon, usually on a tray) in characters such as Popeye, Katzenjammer Kids and Pinocchio; Ceramic Arts Studio sets such as Disney or nursery rhyme characters; anthropomorphic sets (fruit and vegetable people, inanimate objects or animals dressed as people); German, Goebel and figural lustreware sets; mermaids; and naughties. Price paid is determined by condition, desirablity, quality, and rarity. I don't buy nonfigural glass or wood sets. There are hundreds more I want to buy besides what are listed here. Please supply description, price, and/or photos when offering shakers to me.

Judy Posner
R.D. 1, Box 273 HW
Effort, PA 18330
717-629-6583 or FAX 717-629-0521

Shaker Sets	**We Pay**
Al Capp Shmoo, various	**50.00-100.00**
Black People, w/graduate caps	**75.00**
Ceramic Arts Studio Brown Bear, on all fours	**150.00**
Ceramic Arts Studio Camel	**125.00**
Cowboy Nodder	**200.00-225.00**
Disney's Tweedledee & Tweedledum	**250.00**
Fruit & Vegetable People	**15.00-25.00**
Felix the Cat, Germany	**250.00-350.00**
Felix the Cat, Japan	**150.00-200.00**
Hershey Chocolate Bean Babies	**100.00-125.00**
Inanimate Objects, dressed as people	**15.00-45.00**
Little Black Girl in Bathtub	**150.00**
Little Black Sambo & Tiger	**175.00**
Mermaids, various	**15.00-45.00**
Mickey Mouse Condiment Set, Germany	**250.00-350.00**
Pinocchio & Jiminy Cricket	**75.00-85.00**
Popeye Condiment Set, lustreware	**300.00-325.00**
Sad Sack	**95.00-125.00**

We buy **pre-1980 novelty shakers** and will pay top dollar for items that are needed to add to our collection. We buy one shaker or many and travel all over the US in search of large, unusual collections. We also collect **American Goldscheider, pie birds, and razor blade banks**.

Vera and Steve Skorupski
What's Shaking
P.O. Box 572
Plainville, CT 06062

Shaker Sets	**We Pay**
Advertinsing	**5.00-200.00**
Mr Peanut, tan & black	**5.00**
Mr Peanut, ceramic	**35.00+**
Blue Nun	**50.00+**
Ceramic Arts Studio	**10.00-200.00+**
Ceramic Arts Studio, Black Sambo & Tiger	**200.00+**

Ceramic Arts Studio, Donkeys ....50.00+
Ceramic Arts Studio, Rabbits ....45.00+
Ceramic Arts Studio, Mouse & Cheese 10.00
Poinsetta Studio ....10.00-45.00+
Poinsetta Studio, Lamp, 2-piece 10.00
Poinsetta Studio, Black Couple ....45.00+
Poinsetta Studio, Hare & Tortoise ....20.00+
Sorcha Boru ....20.00-100.00+
Sorcha Boru, King & Queen ....100.00+
Sorcha Boru, Sailors ....75.00+
Sorcha Boru, Lambs 20.00
Character ....20.00-1,000.00+
Felix the Cat ....100.00+
Shmoos ....75.00+
Popeye Condiment, complete ....200.00+
Mickey Mouse Condiment, Germany, 1920s, complete ....1,000.00+
Nodders ....100.00+

Plastic figural gasoline pump salt and pepper shaker sets that stand approximately 2½" tall are just one example of the many specialty versions of novelty salt shaker collectibles. Produced for and distributed free by service stations from the early 1950s through the 1970s, these miniature replicas of actual gas pumps were made for almost every brand of gasoline during that era. Brands representing those with the most service stations thus are the most common and are less desirable, such as Esso, Texaco, and Phillips 66.

I'm seeking to buy sets representing the gasoline brands listed below. Many may still be in their original boxes; others will be unpackaged. Write with your find, and I'll respond immediately to your inquiry. Also see my listing under Thermometers in this book. **Prices paid range from $10 to $85 a pair for these brand names:**

Aetna	APCO	Amlico
Ashland	B/A	Bay
Boron	CALSO	Carter
Clark	Cliff Brice	Comet
Crystal Flash	Derby	Dixie
Fleet-Wing	FS (Farm Service)	Frontier
Getty	Hancock	Hudson
Hi-Speed	Imperial	Jet
Keystone	Kayo	Leonard
Lion	MFA	Martin
Pan-Am	Paraland	Rocket
Site	Speedway 79	SOC
Tenneco	UTOCO	Vickers
Zephyr		

Peter Capell
1838 W Grace St.
Chicago, IL 60613-2724
312-871-8735

I buy **Japanese silver salt and pepper shakers**, preferably as pairs. They are usually of Japanese subjects such as pagodas, Buddahs, fans, musical instruments, shoes, boats, dieties, parasols, etc. These are usually marked 925, 950, or sterling. Please send a photo or drawing with a description, dimensions, condition, and the price you are asking. Please include a telephone number and the best time to call along with your address. I can not return your photo unless you provide a SASE. Please do not send the shakers to me without first receiving confirmation and mailing instructions.

Mark Weseloh
2-3905 E Cliff Dr.
Santa Cruz, CA 95062

SCOUTING COLLECTIBLES

I am buying scouting items for display. Needed are many **Boy and Girl Scout pieces from 1911 through the 1950s**. Listed below is a sample of materials needed. Contact me with other items you have for sale for fair and quick service.

Edward J. Quirk, Jr.
46 Kelsey Ave.
W Haven, CT 06516
203-933-2714

	We Pay
Arm Band, guide, 1953	**25.00+**
Patch, 369/WWW, felt	**50.00+**
Patch, rank, pre-1950	**3.00+**
Patch, Order of the Arrow, pocket	**2.00+**
Patch, Camp Sequassen, felt	**5.00+**
Merit Badge Sash	**10.00+**
Medal, Eagle Scout	**25.00+**
National Jamboree Ring, 1935 or 1937, ea	**25.00+**

National Jamboree Flag, 1935 or 1937, ea .... **50.00+**
National Jamboree Shoulder Tab, NJ, 1935, felt .... **25.00+**
National Jamboree Shoulder Tab, 1937 .... **10.00+**
National Jamboree Stickers .... **5.00+**
Jamboree Arm Band .... **8.00+**
Jamboree Baggage Tag .... **1.00+**
Jamboree Pennant .... **5.00+**
Jamboree Pillow Covers, ea .... **5.00+**
Jamboree Printed Material .... **2.00+**
Jamboree Souvenir Item .... **2.00+**
Jamboree Troop Flag .... **10.00+**
NOAC Button, 1946 .... **10.00+**
NOAC Patch, 1948, felt **20.00**
NOAC Chorus, staff material .... **15.00+**
World Jamboree Medal, 1920 .... **100.00+**
World Jamboree Patch, pre-1967 .... **20.00+**
World Jamboree, any other item .... **5.00+**

I collect **old Boy Scout items**. I am interested in old manuals, Jubilee items, and anything bearing the Boy Scout emblem. I am a private collector and am currently working on my eagle project, so I would also be interested in **anything having an eagle**. Please send information and asking price.

Tyler Lininger
2205 2nd Ave. W
Seattle, WA 98119

SEWING PATTERNS

Patterns are one of the few historical records that women had a part in producing. The evolution from early printed patterns to modern instructions for sewing shows not only the changes in clothing styles but also the introduction of machines to improve the process of creating a wardrobe for a woman and her family.

The earliest patterns were gotten by responding to a newspaper or magazine ad and the pattern was sent through the mail. Some of the earlier pattern companies were DuBarry, Advance, Hollywood, Superior, and Vogart. Also wanted are Simplicity, McCall's, Vogue, Butterick, Folkwear, and Past Patterns.

I collect all sizes of vintage patterns dating before 1960. I am also interested in some craft patterns. Please respond with list of patterns and prices desired. Purchase depends on condition, completeness, and rarity of pattern.

Lori Hughes
253 Magda Way
Pacheco, CA 94553
510-687-1029

SHAVING MUGS

Collector seeks **all types of old shaving mugs** and is particularly interested in shaving mugs with name/occupation depicted. Also wanted are shaving mugs with fraternal organization designs, with name and artwork, or name only. Any shaving mugs other than these are also wanted. Collector will consider damaged, chipped, and cracked pieces, if designs and artwork is intact. Please send complete description of mug, any maker's marks, and damage. Photos of mugs would be appreciated.

John J. Bellew
15243 Profit Ave.
Baton Rouge, LA 70817
504-756-4875

SHAWNEE

I collect **Corn King and Corn Queen**. This delightful pottery resembles, more or less, ears of corn, with the surface of the clay molded into low-relief kernels and leafy husks. The Corn King pattern was decorated with a field-fresh yellow and green glaze. Corn Queen is considered to be more modern with cream-colored kernels and forest-green husks. This pottery was produced from 1941 to 1961, and I consider it to be art pottery for the masses.

The price I will pay varies, depending on the pattern, color, and condition of each piece. Cracks, scratches, staining, or other signs of heavy wear will lower the value of a piece. Some wear, however, is to be expected. The following is a guide for pieces in excellent to mint condition. I will pay fair prices and will reimburse actual UPS and insurance charges. Send color photos and/or description of what you have along with the price. All letters will be answered and calls returned without delay.

Rebecca S. Thomas
7760 E Montebellow Ave.
Scottsdale, AZ 85250-6164
602-947-5693

	We Pay
Cookie Jar	**150.00-200.00**
Casserole, sm	**40.00-50.00**
Vegetable Bowl	**30.00-35.00**
Mug	**35.00-45.00**
Pitcher	**50.00-65.00**
Sugar Shaker	**50.00-60.00**
Salt & Pepper Shakers, Indian corn, pr	**50.00-65.00**
Teapot, 30-oz	**50.00-75.00**

SHELLEY

We wish to buy Shelley china (or the earlier Wileman pieces) to accommodate our Shelley china replacement service. We particularly wish to buy the Dainty shape (6-flute), Ludlow (14-flute), Oleander shape and the more 'modern' shapes of Eve, Mode, Regent, Vogue, and the graceful Queen Anne. Individual pieces, luncheon sets, dessert sets, and full dinner sets are sought. We respond to all offerings.

Fred and Lila Shrader
2025 Hwy. 199 (Hiouchi)
Crescent City, CA 95531
707-458-3525

	We Pay
Bowl, vegetable; oval or round, open, 9" to 10½", ea	**60.00+**
Bowl, vegetable; oval, w/lid, ea	**100.00+**
Butter Pat	**20.00+**
Cake Plate, pedestal, 3½" tall	**85.00+**
Chamber Set (pitcher, bowl & accessories)	**150.00+**
Children's Ware (cup & saucer, plate, egg cup, etc), ea	**35.00+**
Coffeepot or Teapot, various sizes, ea	**100.00+**
Cup & Saucer Set, various sizes, per set	**35.00+**
Napkin Ring, Place Card Holder, Etc, ea	**35.00+**
Platter or Chop Plate, various sizes, ea	**65.00+**
Shakers, individual or sets, ea	**35.00+**
Anything Not Listed Above	**Please Call**

SHOT GLASSES

The Shot Glass Club of America is buying shot glasses! If you have extras that you would like to sell, either send them directly to us (we will pay return postage if we decline to offer or if our offer is refused) or send us a detailed description of what you have to sell, and we will provide you with a quote. Listed below is a general guide of prices we usually pay for glasses.

Certain glasses will command higher prices such as carnival patterns, fancy art designs (i.e., Mary Gregory or Tiffany), rare sample glasses, etc. Please note that all glasses must be in good condition with no chips, cracks, or significant fading or worn designs. Also glasses should be true shot glasses — 3" or under in height, 1- to 2-oz capacity, no handles or separate bases, and no toothpicks or candle holders. No plain shot glasses (without a design) wanted.

For large collections (over 100), we usually pay 50 to 60 cents a glass. Remember that you are welcome to send us an eighth-page ad for our newsletter for collections that are for sale; we will publish it free in a newsletter. If you are interested in trading, let us know what you have to offer (catalog numbers and/or detailed descriptions) as well as what you are looking for! Send your inquiries to:

The Shot Glass Club of America
P.O. Box 90404
Flint, MI 48509

We Pay

Taiwan Tourist, local advertising, ea....................**50¢**
US Tourist, frosted, college, black porcelain replicas, enameled designs, or national advertising, ea....................**1.00**
Etched, pewter, 22K gold, square w/designs, turquoise & gold tourist, tall Depression designs, or barrel-shaped w/design, ea....................**2.00**
Soda or Pop Advertising (Coca-Cola, Pepsi, 7-Up, etc), 2-tone bronze & pewter, square w/pewter, or nude shots, ea....................**5.00**
Certain Depression patterns, ruby red or flashed glasses w/lettering, pre-prohibition sample glasses, or cut glass patterns, ea....................**10.00**

SILHOUETTES

Silhouettes on glass are wanted that were made from the 1920s through the 1950s. I am not interested in the newer ones. These are **convex or flat glass with painted-on silhouettes**. The silhouettes made on convex glass were of black, red, rose, blue, white, or yellow colors. Any color, shape, or size is wanted. Related items such as ashtrays, books with silhouette illustrations, china, lamps, jewelry or boxes, trays, wastebaskets, etc., are sought as well. I am also looking for **old catalogs, salesmen's samples, or anyone with information about Fisher** (they made pictures and trays with wildflower backgrounds). Other wants include **butterfly wing pictures and jewelry**. Prices will depend on condition and rarity. I will accept collect calls, but photographs or photocopies are very helpful.

Shirley Mace
P.O. Box 1602
Mesilla Park, NM 88047-1602
505-524-6717

SILVER AND SILVERPLATE

I've been **buying and selling silver (not silverplate)** for over fifteen years and will always try to pay the most for your silver. To prove this is my policy, if you send your silver to me (remember to pack it securely and insure) I will send you my offer in the form of a check. If you accept, just cash the check; if you are not happy with my offer, just return my check, and I will return your silver plus your postage costs. So it costs you nothing to try — so far over 99% of my offers have been accepted!

The following is a brief listing of the prices that I will pay. Please keep in mind that these are minimums for bent or damaged pieces. I will pay more (often much more) for rarer, nicer, or more unusual pieces. See also my listing under Coins in this book.

B - 4 Your Time
Attention: Phil Townsend
15 Tabar Ave.
Lee, MA 01238

	We Pay
Forks or Spoons, sm, ea	**1.00-50.00**
Forks or Spoons, lg, ea	**2.00-100.00**
Thimbles, ea	**1.00-50.00**
Salt & Pepper Shakers, pr	**5.00-100.00**
Candlesticks, pr	**5.00-1,000.00+**

Silver and Silverplate

I buy **only silver-plated holloware and flatware manufactured by**:

Bray, Redfield & Co. (1852-1857)
Bancroft, Redfield & Rice (1857-1863)
Redfield & Rice (1863-1873)
Redfield & Rice Manufacturing Co. (1863-1873)

These names will appear stamped on the bottom of holloware pieces or on raised discs on the bases of pieces. On flatware pieces the marks will be Bancroft R & R or Redfield & Rice. If you find any other marks on flatware that you think may belong to these companies, let me know.

All pieces must be complete, with no missing parts and no cracks. Glass inserts with small, no-harm chips okay if noted. Minor dents and worn plating are not a problem if the pieces are priced fairly for their condition. *Never* replate a piece before offering it to me. Send a detailed description, including condition and your price for the piece. A photo or Xerox would also be helpful.

Also wanted are **paper items related to these silver-plate companies**. I am interested in all types of original paper items such as letterheads, billheads, advertisements, brochures, price lists, catalogs, etc. I would consider both items sent out by the companies and items addressed to the companies. Please give a detailed description of each piece, including its condition, your price, and a Xerox of a sample.

Judy Redfield
2507 Old 63 South
Columbia, MO 65201
314-449-8523

Holloware	**We Pay**
Teapot, Coffeepot, etc, ea	**60.00+**
Table Castor Set, w/3 to 7 original glass bottles, ea	**80.00+**
Table Castor Frame, ea	**40.00+**
Pickle Castor Set, w/1 to 2 original glass containers & glass lids, ea	**80.00+**
Pickle Castor Frame, ea	**40.00+**
Cake Basket, ea	**60.00+**
Creamer, Sugar, Waste Bowl or Spooner, ea	**25.00+**
Creamer, Sugar, Celery, etc, w/original glass liner, ea	**50.00+**
Butter Dish, Syrup Pitcher, ea	**30.00+**
Toast Rack, Muffineer or Figural Knife Rest, ea	**30.00+**
Mug, Goblet, Vase or Individual Salt, ea	**15.00+**
Napkin Ring, plain, ea	**15.00+**
Napkin Ring, figural, ea	**60.00+**
Tray, ea	**50.00+**
Pitcher, ice water; stationary, ea	**80.00+**
Pitcher, ice water; on stand, ea	**150.00+**
Coffee Urn, w/burner, ea	**150.00**
Other Pieces	**Call or Write**

Flatware **We Pay**

Teaspoon or Table Fork, ea 3.00-5.00
Dessert Fork or Nut Pick, ea 10.00
Olive Fork, Oyster Fork, or Pickle Fork, ea 12.00-15.00
Table Knife, Butter Knife, Ladle (sm), or Salt Spoon, ea 12.00-15.00
Other Serving Pieces, ea ....20.00+

Original Paper Relating to Redfield Companies **We Pay**

Letterheads, Billheads, or Advertisements, ea ....5.00+
Brochures, or Price Lists, ea ....10.00+
Catalogs, ea..200.00+

SNOWDOMES

I buy the following types of **plastic snowdomes**: souvenirs of small, obscure tourist attractions and cities anywhere in the world (*not* large cities, states and the major tourist sites); souvenirs from exotic, faraway places (especially if the place name is in a foreign language); advertisements for products, hotels, and railroads; commemoratives of special events; and those inspired by Disney movies of the 1960s. They can be in any shape — the traditional half-oval, a red base with flat sides, a bottle (usually found on its side), a rectangle — but *they must have visible words: a place or product name written on either a plaque inside or on the front of the base.* I don't care about the water level or condition of the snowdome, as long as the words are visible and legible. I **also want figurals** — 5" high plastic figurines with plastic water balls in their middle — including both animals and characters. Water level is not important in these either, and most of them don't have place names.

Nancy McMichael
P.O. Box 53132
Washington, DC 20000
202-234-7484

We Pay

Albany, New York State Capitol 40.00
Angel, figural..75.00
Flagship Hotel, advertising..40.00
Batman, tall plastic dome 75.00
Black Cat, figural..60.00
Bozo the Clown 50.00

Snowdomes

Grim Reaper, figural **75.00**
Greek God, figural **80.00**
Indian Chief, figural **75.00**
Jello, advertising, plastic **60.00**
Letchworth State Park **30.00**
Owl, figural **60.00**
Panda Bear, figural **60.00**
Pine Creek Railroad, Allaire, NJ **30.00**
Pinocchio, w/Disney & Marx Toy trademarks on bottom, lg **50.00**
Playland, Rye, NY **30.00**
S Fallsburg, NY **25.00**
Valley Fair **20.00**
Yankee Stadium, Home of the New York Yankees, red base **50.00**
Souvenirs From Faraway Exotic Places, English language used on place plaque, such as Fiji Islands, Krakow, Durban, Kuwait, etc, ea **30.00**
Souvenirs w/Foreign Languages, used on place plaque, especially want Middle East & Orient, ea **40.00**

We buy **plastic souvenir snowdomes from the late 1960s through the late 1980s that name a location**. We do *not* purchase Lucite scenes screened inside on plastic disks or domes with location names printed on the outside of base. Condition effects value, however domes need not be in perfect condition. Amusement parks, Los Angeles area, and foreign domes are particularly wanted. Figural domes, if they name a location, are also sought. One dome or a collection bought. We will pay shipping. All sizes and shapes are of interest.

Chloe Ross
7553 W Norton Ave. #4
Los Angeles, C 90046-5523
213-874-3044

Snowdomes	**We Pay**
Small Oval	**3.00+**
Large Oval	**5.00+**
Calendar Base	**8.00+**
Pedestal Base	**6.00+**
Figural	**8.00+**
Bottle	**3.00+**

SODA FOUNTAIN COLLECTIBLES

We are new **soda fountain glass** collectors. We are looking for Donald Duck, Major Cola, Green River, Grapette, Orange Crush, Cleo Cola, Dr. Pepper, Seven-Up, Hire's Root Beer, Nesbitt's, Bireley's, Dad's Root Beer, Bubble-Up, Cheer-Up, B-1 Lemon-Lime Soda, Vess, Dr. Wells, Teem, Like, Kist, Kickapoo, Moxie, Squirt, Whistle, etc. If it is a soda fountain glass and you have it for sale, we are interested! We will pay fair prices for any glasses. We are not interested in any mugs at this time. We do want glasses with no fading and good color.

Dee and Connie Mondey
P.O. Box 272
Haslet, TX 76052-0272
817-439-4807

SOUVENIR CHINA

Wanted: **rolled edge 10" souvenir/historical plates from Staffordshire,** England, and imported by Rowland and Marsellus, Royal Fenton, and A.C. Bosselman, as well any other souvenirs with scenes of cities or towns that have any of these importers' marks. We buy all unusual Rowland and Marsellus souvenir china. Their back-stamp mark may be written in full or be shown as R&M in a diamond. (R&M was a New York importer from Staffordshire, England.) Blue transfers on white are of cities, towns, or personalities and were produced from 1900 through 1930. **Also wanted are German white porcelain divided dishes that usually have a large gold or orange and red lobster handle**. Please write or call. All calls and letters answered.

David Ringering
1480 Tumalo Dr. SE
Salem, OR 97301-9278

	We Pay
Rolled-Edge Plate	**50.00+**
Coupe Plate, 10"	**45.00+**
Fruit & Flower Bordered Plate, 9½"	**35.00+**
Souvenir Plate, 9"	**25.00+**
Tumbler	**40.00+**
Cup & Saucer	**50.00+**

Vase .... **150.00+**
Pitcher .... **150.00+**
Miscellaneous Piece .... **90% of book value**
Divided Lobster Dish, German .... **50.00+**
Souvenir Tumbler, German, metal w/North American scene .... **10.00+**

We buy **old pictorial souvenir china depicting places in the United States**. These include porcelain creamers, cups, tumblers, vases, plates, containers, toothpick holders, and a wide variety of figurals such as baskets, hearts, animals, autos, etc. These pieces were usually imported from Germany or England in the early 1900s and have scenes of buildings, streets, or locally historic places pictured on them. Small town scenes are of greatest interest. We do *not* want anything that is chipped or cracked. Also buying **mauchline (wooden transfer ware), postcards, and other older souvenir items**. We do *not* want souvenir plates from the 1950s or '60s.

Gary Leveille
Antique Souvenir Collector
P.O. Box 562
Great Barrington, MA 01230

	We Pay
Creamer	**20.00-35.00**
Cup	**15.00-30.00**
Plate	**10.00-20.00**
Figural	**25.00-45.00**

Made in Germany, these small plates, dishes, vases, etc., usually had a **black transfer scene of towns in the US along with a local merchant's name on the back**. I will pay $3 and up for all pieces plus postage charges. Souvenirs of certain Western states such as Colorado, Wyoming, Arizona, and Utah are more desirable; I will pay $8 and up for these. Items must be perfect. Nobody usually wants these souvenirs, so here's a buyer.

My collecting interest is varied — from **all character-related items to militaria to World's Fairs** — just drop me a note or call with what you have and your asking price. I will pay fair prices. I pay postage.

Mickey Starr
2722 340th
Keokuk, IA 52632
319-524-1601

SPICE SETS

Spice sets of all types are wanted. Sets may consist of four containers to twenty or more. They may be metal, glass, plastic, or ceramic with wood lids, and they may be in various types of original holders. Lower-priced ceramic hand-painted under the glaze sets from the 1930s to 1960s are the type most desired. Ceramic sets may have fruit, flowers, figures, Pennsylvania Dutch, or abstract designs. Old metal cans from McCormick, Schilling, Cains, and other companies should be complete and have little paint loss. Prices of Depression glass sets will depend on color, manufacturer, quantity, and desirability. Send complete description, including measurements, number of containers, and photos. **Canister and cruet sets** will also be considered. No pattern glass or crystal sets are wanted. I will answer all correspondence. Please, do not call collect.

Janet Hume
11000 S Bryant
Oklahoma City, OK 73160
405-794-7493

	We Pay
Ceramic Sets, unmarked or Japan, per set	5.00-10.00
Ceramic Sets, marked Made in USA, per set	5.00-20.00
Manufacturer Cans, ea	50¢-2.00
European China or Pottery Sets, per set	10.00+
Hoosier Cabinet Sets, per set	20.00+
Depression Glass Sets, per set	10.00+

SPORTING COLLECTIBLES

I have been collecting **baseball and football cards (pre-1975)** since 1948 and am newly into **other sports collectibles and memorabilia**. No balls or bats are wanted. **Photos, stadium pins, and especially Brooklyn Dodger items** are wanted. I collect newer items or repros but only if they are Brooklyn Dodger. I do much trading and will travel to purchase larger collections. My husband is a devout sports fan and collects just about anything. Examples of typical prices paid are listed here. Thank you.

Nancy Pinto
159 SW 97th Terrace
Coral Springs, FL 33071
305-341-8718

Sporting Collectibles

	We Pay
Football Cards, pre-1975, ea	**up to 60% of current Beckett**
Sports Cards, pre-1975, ea	**up to 80% of current Beckett**
Pin-Back Buttons, ea	**up to 50.00**
Photos, ea	**10.00-30.00**

We buy the following sporting-related items. All items must be in good condition. Other wants include **advertising pocket mirrors, Santa pins with department store names (given when a child visited Santa), and Hubley dog figural paperweights.**

Dean Dashner
349 S Green Bay Rd.
Neenah, WI 54956
414-725-4350

	We Pay
Ducks Unlimited Pin-Backs, ea	**35.00+**
Duck-a-Nickel Collection Donation Tins, ea	**50.00+**
Hazelton Books, ea	**65.00+**
Old Duck Hunting Books, ea	**10.00+**
Wisconsin Live Decoy Tags, ea	**10.00+**
Live Decoy Holders, ea	**10.00+**
Wisconsin Decoys, ea	**35.00+**
Mason Decoys, ea	**35.00+**
Sporting Magazines, prior to 1940, ea	**1.00+**
Wisconsin Game Warden Badges, ea	**50.00+**
Wisconsin Hunting Regulations, ea	**1.00+**
Shot Shell Boxes, 2-pc cardboard style, ea	**10.00+**
Shot Shell Boxes, wood	**10.00+**

Other Wants	**We Pay**
Pocket Mirrors, w/advertising, ea	**10.00+**
Santa Pins, ea	**5.00+**
Dog Figural Paperweights, marked Hubley, ea	**10.00+**

Wanted: **pre-1974 hockey trading cards in sets or single cards as well as post-1973 singles in bulk**. Send description of cards and asking price.

Cal Hackeman
8865 Olde Mill Run
Manassas, VA 22110
703-368-6982

STAMPS

I am interested in buying **United States and foreign postage stamps and covers**. Below are some examples of buying prices. All items must be clean and undamaged. I have other numerous and diverse collecting interests. See a partial listing here, or send for my buy list on other items wanted. Your list of items for sale is also welcome. **A partial listing of wants include**:

Advertising
Aviation
Banks
Buckles
Dolls
Figurines
Law Enforcement
Political Items
Postcards
Razors
Stock Certificates
Tokens
Watches & Watch Fobs
World's Fairs
Automobilia
Badges
Bottles
Coins & Currency
Expostions
Hummels
Militaria
Pocketknives
Railroadiana
Sterling Items
Tobacciana
Toys
Weapons

Ivan Platnick
2506 Cliffmont
Bluefield, WV 24701

	We Pay
Stamps, US Mint (no postage dues, official or special delivery), ea	**80% face**
First Day Covers, US, w/cachet, unaddressed, ea	**15¢**
First Day Covers, US, w/cachet, addressed, ea	**5¢**
Postcards, before 1920, w/clear postmarks, ea	**10¢+**

STONEWARE

I'm actively buying **Illinois marked stoneware items** such as crocks, jugs, jars, animal figurines, snake jugs, face jugs, pig bottles, and flasks. Also of interested are unmarked salt-glazed crocks, jugs, and unusual or odd items. Especially interested in dug pottery, even broken pieces, as well as other dug artifacts, bottles, or what have you — I buy by the piece, handful, or bucket full. I will travel for a load of plain old salt-glazed stoneware or dug artifacts and bottles. The following is a list of the marked items and prices paid. For unmarked pottery and dug pieces, please call or write for a quick reply. Also feel free to send me a list or photos of the stoneware or other items you're looking for, and I'll be glad to help you in your search. Don't forget prices!

Jonn Light
2324 Sanford Ave.
Alton, IL 62002
618-465-0276 or 618-465-0292

Stoneware Marked:	**We Pay**
Anna Ill Pottery	**25.00-5,000.00**
AD Ruckels & Son	**25.00-100.00**
Alton, Ill	**100.00-500.00**
Upper Alton, Ill	**100.00-500.00**
Brighton, IL	**100.00-500.00**
Blue Band Stoneware	**25.00-100.00**
Carrolton, Ill	**100.00-500.00**
Dow, Ill	**100.00-500.00**
Grafton, Ill	**100.00-500.00**
Jerseyville, Ill	**100.00-500.00**
Western Stoneware (Plant No 5)	**25.00-100.00**
White Hall, Ill	**25.00-100.00**

I am buying **blue and white stoneware, and crocks and jugs with blue decoration**. Also wanted is a **Dazey butter churn**. It must be marked Dazey on both the churn lid and the glass jar. Nothing broken or cracked wanted. Other types of butter churns will also be considered.

Lynda Mitchell
35900 Deersville Rd.
Cadiz, OH 43907

SWANKY SWIGS

We buy all Swanky Swigs which are in fair to excellent condition. These glasses were originally manufactured by the Kraft Food company from 1933 to 1978. They have various designs and motifs painted on the exterior. They vary in size from 3³⁄₁₆" to 4⅝" and come in a wide spectrum of colors with the main colors being black, red, yellow, brown and blue.

We ask that you send us a photograph of your offering in order for us to better evaluate the condition and suitability of your merchandise. We will reimburse for any actual expenses incurred.

Curt Johnson
Box 811
Aberdeen, SD 57401

	We Pay
Band Pattern #5, ea	3.50+
Bicentennial Tulip, ea	10.00+
Checkerboard, sm, ea	15.00+
Checkerboard, lg, ea	18.00+
Checkers, sm, ea	8.00+
Checkers, lg, ea	15.00+
Circles & Dots, sm, ea	4.50+
Circles & Dots, lg, ea	8.00+
Dots Forming Diamonds, ea	15.00+
Ethnic Series, ea	10.00+
Fleur-de-Lis, ea	18.00+
Galleon, ea	8.00+
Lattice & Vine, ea	18.00+
Provincial Crests, ea	8.00+
Sailboat #1, ea	10.00+
Sailboat #2, ea	15.00+
Stars #1, sm, ea	4.50+
Stars #1, lg, ea	8.00-15.00+
Stars #2, ea	3.50+
Sportsman Series, ea	10.00+
Texas Centennial, ea	20.00+
Wildlife Series, ea	10.00+

TEDDY BEARS

We buy teddy bears. We are looking for all the **Muffy Vanderbears** from 1984 and will buy older Vanderbear families as well. We buy **antique as well as reproductions by Steiff Teddy Bear Co.**, **Hermann**, and **Schuco Toy Co.**. We also buy some older artist-made bears. The price we will pay is commensurate with condition of the bear. Please send photos. Specific bears wanted include:

Vanderbears:
Christening I & II
Red Flannel
Valentine I & II
Cruisewear
Taffeta
Day in the Country
Halloween Witch
Nutcracker
Skating 'Furrier & Ives'
Tree Trimming

Steiff Teddy Bear Company:
All Bears, dating to 1950
Margaret Strong Series
Disney World Convention
Limited Editions, w/white tag in ear

Schuco Toy Company:
Yes/No Bears, 1920s, any size

Gebruder Hermann
Bears, 1950 or older, any size

Dolores Ingraham
9570 S Tropical Trail
Merrit Island, FL 32952
407-777-2578

TELEGRAPH MEMORABILIA

Keys, sounders, and relays are the most frequently found **telegraph instruments**. And while many were made as late as the 1950s, earlier 19th-century items may be quite valuable. I particularly seek the earlier makers, but it's sometimes difficult to determine age. A photo or sketch or just a name may be all that's needed. Condition is not critical. Other telegraph-related items are also sought: registers (these embossed dots and dashes or printed characters on paper tape), stock tickers, signs, peg-type switchboards, forms boxes, glavanomets, messenger call boxes — just about any telegraph hardware. **Telegraph ephemera** is also wanted such as trade catalogues of instrument makers, messenger caps and cap badges, pre-1900 telegrams other than Western Union and Postal Telegraph, watch fobs or tie tacks of miniature telegraph keys, franks (cards authorizing free messages), or other early telegraph advertising. Photographs of telegraph offices or employees are needed too. There were over 100 makers of instruments in the 1800s, so the list below is not complete but may help in identification. *Please note* that instruments marked Signal or Menominee are not wanted, nor are keys marked J-37 or J-38 (World War II surplus).

Roger W. Reinke
5301 Neville Ct.
Alexandria, VA 22310
800-348-0294

Instruments Marked:	**We Pay**
JH Bunnell & Co	**10.00-75.00**
Foote, Pierson & Co	**20.00-100.00**
ES Greeley	**50.00-200.00+**
MESCO	**10.00-75.00**
LG Tillotson	**50.00-200.00+**
Western Electric Co (later)	**20.00-100.00**

Other early makers' instruments are valued at $100 to $2,500 and up, depending on type and rarity. These include:

Dr L Bradley
MA Buell
Caton Instrument Shop
Charles T or JN Chester
James J or William Clark
WB Cleveland
AS Chubbuck
William E Davis or Davis & Watts
Electrical Construction Co
Thomas Hall
David Hughes
CE Jones
AB Lyman
Patrick & Bunnell or Patrick & Carter
George M or WP Phelps

Telegraph Memorabilia

PRR-Altoona Shops
Jerome Redding
Western Electric Mfg Co
Charles Williams

TELEPHONES

We buy accumulations, sweepings, collections, leftcovers, singles of **many types of telephones, parts, literature, and related items** in most any condition. Please see listing here for examples. We pay from $25 to $100 for pay phones that are incomplete or in any condition. These or remnants can be ragged, tattered, droopy, have been charged and stampeded by buffalo, eaten by moths, trampled on by ants or torn by strife.

We are also interested in contacting members of the following families: Eckerdt, Schutz, Anapolsky from Noworosijsk, Neuheim (Krasnodar area), Vadlmir Anapolsky decendants, and Sapagina from Moscow.

Phoneco
Ron and Mary Knappen
207 E Mill Rd., P.O. Box 70
Galesville, WI 54630

	We Pay
Airplane Telephones	**5.00-50.00**
Candlestick Telephones, black plastic	**5.00-15.00**
Decorator Telephones	**1.00-50.00**
European Telephones or Parts	**35.00-400.00**
Ericafones	**1.00-10.00**
Pay Phones (any condition or incomplete)	**25.00-100.00**
Pay Phone Signs (may be torn, worn or bent)	**5.00-100.00**
Spacesaver Telephones	**1.00-15.00**
Telephones w/3" Dials	**1.00-3.00**
Wall Telephones, wood w/crank, incomplete	**5.00-15.00**
Nameplates, ea	**1.00-5.00**

Paper Items, Prior to 1900	**We Pay**
Books, by Knappen or Hadler	**1.00-20.00**
Catalogs	**1.00-75.00**
Charts	**up to 40.00**
Magazines	**up to 8.00**

Periodicals .... **up to 8.00**
Postcards .... **10¢-3.00**
Prints **1.00-60.00**
Posters .... **up to 40.00**
Signs .... **up to 40.00**

THERMOMETERS

I collect a specialized type of **advertising thermometer in plastic, shaped like old gasoline station pole signs**. Almost 7" tall, these thermometers are imbedded under the gasoline sign's support column and often had the dealer/distributor's name and location stamped on the base alongside a small paper calendar. These were given away by gasoline stations as a premium/gift item in the late 1950s and through the mid-1960s. I am seeking regional and local gasoline brand thermometers such as those listed below. No national or more common brands such as Esso, Texaco, Mobil, etc., are wanted. Let me hear from you if you have one; I'll respond immediately. **Prices paid range from $10 to $30 each.**

APCO
Ashland
Billups
Barnsdall
Bay
CALSO
Clark
Deep Rock
Derby
ENCO
Fleet-Wing
Frontier
FS (Farm Service)
Getty
Hi-Speed
Hudson
Humble
Husky
Imperial
Ingram
Keystone
Martin
M-F-A
Pan-Am
Richfield
Rio Grande
Shamrock
Signal
SOC
Speed-Wing
Spur
Sunray
Tenneco
Total
United
UTOCO
Vickers
Wareco
White Rose
Zenith
Zephyr

Peter Cappell
1838 W Grace St.
Chicago, IL 60613-2724
312-871-8735

TIFFANY

I buy **Tiffany items signed LCT or Tiffany Studios, New York**. I buy all pieces no matter what condition. I buy lamps, vases, desk sets, bronzes — anything signed Tiffany. We reimburse for UPS and insurance charges. You will be paid with US postal money order. Also I'm buying **quality signed oil paintings**. Price depends on artist and evaluation of painting.

Storms Fine Art Gallery + Liquidations
704 Center St.
Jim Thorpe, PA 18229
717-325-8053

	We Pay
Bowl	**150.00-500.00**
Candy Dish	**50.00**
Compote	**150.00-500.00**
Desk Set	**250.00-1,000.00**
Inkwell	**200.00-800.00**
Lamp	**200.00-4,000.00**
Silver	**100.00-800.00**
Vase	**200.00-800.00**

TIRE ASHTRAYS

Although I'm interested in buying most tire ashtrays, I'm especially interested in obtaining those listed below. The prices shown are what I'll pay for these examples in good, complete condition without defects such as burn marks on the tire or incomplete (or missing) painted advertising imprints/stickers on the ashtray insert. Whether your tire ashtray is listed below or not, please contact me prior to shipment and provide a complete description in your first letter. I also have tire ashtrays available for sale, as well as *The Tire Ashtray Collector's Guide*©. I'll reply to all inquiries which include SASE.

Jeff McVey
1810 W State St. #427
Boise, ID 83702

	We Pay
Armstrong Air Coaster 6.00-16 Deluxe Streamline, w/white tire	**30.00**
Atlas Bucron	**35.00**
Bridgestone Super Speed Radial II	**20.00**
Diamond Deep Cleat HB	**20.00**
Dunlop Fieldmaster	**25.00**
Dunlop 25 Jahre Reifen-Kiotz Wabern-Kassel	**25.00**
Firestone Heavy Duty High Speed Gum-Dipped Balloon 6.00-18 (made in Canada)	**25.00**
Firestone Made in Africa (English on one side, French on other)	**30.00**
Firestone 32 x 4½ RMC	**50.00**
Firestone Sport 200 (made in France)	**20.00**
Firestone Deluxe Champion (made in South Africa)	**20.00**
Firestone Transporte (made in South Africa)	**20.00**
Firestone Champion Ground Grip (made in South Africa)	**20.00**
Fisk (any)	**40.00**
Gates (any)	**25.00**
Goodyear 32 x 10 Super Cushion 250/660 X-8989	**40.00**
Hood Farm Service Open Center	**20.00**
India Super Service 31-6.00, w/electric lighter	**80.00**
Made in Soviet Union (any so marked)	**30.00**
McCreary (any)	**30.00**
Mitsuboshi (any)	**20.00**
Mobil (any)	**20.00**
Noyes (any)	**30.00**
Overman, w/statue of devil in center	**100.00**
Pennsylvania Vacuum Cup, all glass	**60.00**
Red River Army Depot	**40.00**
United (any)	**20.00**
United States Tires Are Good Tires, glass & metal w/removable wheel	**75.00**
US Royal Fleet Carrier	**30.00**

TOASTERS

Electric toasters had to wait their turn in history. First came the wire, invented by Albert L. Marsh in 1905. This wire could withstand the heat required to toast bread. From 1906 to 1908 several toasters were invented using Marsh's wire. In 1908 General Electric produced a D-12 Model toaster. Several versions were made. This perch-type toaster had bread slices positioned so that they leaned into the toaster. The model had a porcelain base.

Some were black with white floral decoration — considered to be the first issue. Very soon after the D-12, many, many companies came up with numerous styles trying to beat paying fees for patents. I will list a few toasters, but these are by no means all toasters that were made.

To be collectible, a toaster should be clean, free of rust, and complete. A cord helps (if there originally was one with that particular model). I will purchase toasters in decent condition or if repairable. A good, clear picture should accompany a note describing the toaster along with any writing or label information. I buy **toasters circa 1905 through 1940**. All types wanted! If it produces toast, I want it! Prices depend on condition and rarity.

Oscar P. Barkhurst
3910 Brookside Dr.
Rapid City, SD 57702-2219
605-348-1354

	We Pay
Bersted Electric Toaster	30.00-40.00
El Tosto	50.00-80.00
Excelsior Twin Reversible	40.00-80.00
Electroweld	30.00-40.00
General Electric D-12	80.00-100.00
Marion Giant Flip-Flop Toaster Model 67	60.00-80.00
Pelouze	40.00-50.00
Simplex T-211	60.00-100.00
Star Elect Toaster	20.00-30.00
Star Elect Toaster Model 75000	40.00-50.00
Toast Stove	60.00-80.00
Toast-O-Lator	60.00-100.00
Toaster, w/china or porcelain cover	250.00-400.00
Tresco	30.00-50.00
Universal E-941	50.00-60.00
Universal E-9419	100.00-200.00
Westinghouse Turnover Toaster Model 231571	40.00-80.00

TOBACCIANA

I am buying **cigar advertising items** of various kinds. Note: I do *not* want cigar signs, tins, boxes, box labels or cigar bands.

The Cigar Man
Mike Schwimmer
325 E Blodgett
Lake Bluff, IL 60044-2112
708-295-1901

	We Pay
Advertising Mirrors	**20.00-50.00**
Ashtrays	**10.00-20.00**
Change Mats, any material	**15.00-35.00**
Change Receivers, glass	**35.00-75.00**
Cigar Cutters, Piercers or Trimmers	**15.00-35.00**
Cigar Box Openers	**10.00-20.00**
Corkscrews	**10.00-20.00**
Pin-Back Buttons	**20.00-50.00**
Pocketknives	**10.00-20.00**
Pocket Match Safes, Matchboxes or Book Holders	**15.00-45.00**
Pocket Pouches, leather, cloth or metal	**5.00-15.00**
Tip Trays or Serving Trays	**40.00-100.00**
Trade Cards or Business Cards	**4.00-8.00**
Watch Fobs	**15.00-40.00**
Other Unusual, Small Items	**Call or Write**

I buy **all types of antique smoking pipes** — those produced for tobacco as well as opium consumption. Pipes must be at least 100 years old and be in fine to very fine condition. The material is as important as the condition, and I have interest in all the following: meerschaum, porcelain, carved wood, metal, and other materials. One category that is most unusual is the opium pipe from China, and my interest is especially keen about these and other Oriental smoking implements such as Japanese kiseru, tabako-bons, tabako-ire, and tonkotsu. I will make offers on all pipes submitted to me with a photograph and accompanying data that states condition, dimensions (length and height), and maker's marks in the carrying cases (if present). Examples of prices paid follow here.

Also of interest are **rare and out-of-print domestic and foreign-language literature** on the following categories of tobacco: cigar, snuff, pipe, accessories, associated paraphernalia, related prose or poetry, history, and other pro-nicotine works. Illustrated books and late 19th-century manufacturers' catalogs are especially in demand. Price is wholly contingent on subject matter and the book's condition and is subject to negotiation.

Ben Rapaport
11505 Turnbridge Ln.
Reston, VA 22094-1220
703-435-8133

	We Pay
Meerschaum Pipe, carved w/unique motif, lg	**1,000.00+**
Porcelain Pipe, figural, Bohemian	**250.00+**
Carved Wood Pipe, circa early 18th through 19th centuries	**350.00+**
Opium Pipe, jade or ivory w/damper	**750.00+**
Unusual Ethnographic Pipes, from Africa or the Americas	**250.00+**
Japanese Kiseru, w/inlay, overlay shakudo, shibuichi	**300.00+**

TOOLS

I collect and use **wooden moulding planes**. Plane makers sometimes stamped their name and location on the front of the plane. Not all markings are makers, sometimes owners' marks appear. Planes with no makers' marks are purchased depending on size and shape. The earliest planes measure more than 9½" long and have a round wedge shape and flat chamfers. Most wanted are complex moulders that are 1½" wide and greater. Really wide planes are called cornice planes; these are 4" and wider. Also wanted to purchase are panel raisers; these are 2" to 4" wide, and the blade is skewed or set at an angle to the body of the plane. These were used to make raised panel doors.

Write with a description including size, wedge shape (an outline is helpful), and any marking on the plane and blade. Photos are helpful; all letters will be answered and photos returned.

Robert W. Moore
71 Kenoza St.
Haverhill, MA 01830

TOOTHBRUSH HOLDERS

These figural holders have been made depicting animals, people, storybook personalities, and Disney characters. They have been made of plastic, bisque, and ceramic material and date from the 1930s. Please describe or send a photo. **I will pay $35 and up** depending on the subject.

Joyce Wolford
1050 Spriggs Dr.
Lander, WY 82520

TOYS

We specialize in **collectible memorabilia from the 1950s through today, primarily '50s and '60s**. We are especially interested in buying character products. We are not limited to just toys; we will also buy board games, lunch boxes, movie and TV character toys, comic books, comic strips, original art, toy soldiers, toy weapons, action figures, playsets, View-Master items, robots, space toys, non-sports cards, drinking glass, cereal premiums, and so on. We are always interested in **original packaging, instruction sheets, and catalogs**.

Toy Scouts
137 Casterton Ave.
Akron, OH 44303
216-836-0668 or FAX 216-869-8668

	We Pay
Character Rings, 1940s, ea	**Call**
Comic Books, 1960s, ea	**Call**
Doll, Batgirl Super Queen, Ideal, 1967	**500.00**
Doll, GI Joe Female Nurse, Hasbro, 1967	**1,000.00**
Figurine, Superman or Captain Marvel, wood, 1940s, ea	**500.00-1,000.00**
Gun, Lost in Space Roto-Jet, Mattel, 1966	**1,000.00**
Jewelry, MAD's Alfred E. Newman, 1960s	**100.00+**
Outfit, Captain Action or Spider Man, Ideal, 1967, ea	**1,000.00**
Outfit, MAD's Alfred E. Newman Straight Jacket, 1960s	**500.00**
Outfit Accessory, Batman Utility Belt, Ideal, 1966	**500.00**
Playset, Batman, Ideal, 1966	**1,000.00**
Playset, Justice League of America, Ideal, 1967	**1,500.00**
Model Kit, King Kong's Thronester, Aurora, 1966	**1,500.00**
Model Kit, Godzilla's Go-Kart, Aurora, 1966	**1,500.00**

Wanted: banks that lock with keys. **Goebel, character, robot, still, tin, and iron banks** are wanted in mint condition. Also **trade cards that feature banks. Toys made prior to 1960** such as Japan tin toys, robots, cast-iron toys, battery-operated toys, and character-related toys as well as circa pre-1960 dolls are wanted. I buy mint to near-mint condition items and will pay fair prices for items that interest me. Condition is very important, so please describe any flaws the item has when you write. If possible, send a photo of the item along with your price.

Doris Caloggero
2 Charles St.
P.O. Box 961
Methuen, MA 01844

	We Pay
Goebel Banks	**15.00+**
Tin Banks	**20.00+**
Trade Cards	**10.00+**
Robots	**50.00+**
Japan Tin Toys	**20.00+**
Dolls	**20.00+**

I am looking for **Fisher-Price pull toys and playsets from 1932 to 1986**. I am especially interested in The Castle, Hospital, and Sesame Steet playsets or pieces. The paper litho on the toys must be intact with little to no edge wear. I am also looking for any wooden people in very good condition. I would also like to invite anyone interested in joining our Fisher-Price Collector's Club with a current membership of 250 strong nationwide and still growing. Below are just a few of the prices I am willing to pay for your Fisher-Price toys. Please call or write to me for more information on any of these areas.

Brad Cassity
1350 Stanwix
Toledo, OH 43614
419-385-9910

	We Pay
Any Castle, Hospital, or Sesame Street People or Pieces, ea	**1.50**
Wooden People, like-new condition, ea	**1.00**
Castle, Hospital or Sesame Street House, w/no pieces	**10.00**
Pull Toy, 1970-1980, ea	**10.00-20.00**
Pull Toy, 1960-1970, ea	**20.00-30.00**

Pull Toy, 1950-1960, ea **30.00-125.00**
Pull Toy, 1931-1950, ea **30.00-600.00**
Fisher-Price Catalogs, ea **5.00-25.00**

Wanted: **tin toy globes produced by Ohio Art, Chein, Repogle and others**. I prefer globes that are 7" or smaller; these must be in good condition with no rust and minimal dents. Globes with red and yellow oceans, foreign languages, and game bases are particularly wanted as are globes depicting Mars, the moon, or other planets. Banks are okay. I will also pay postage. **Free-standing models of the Eiffel Tower in any material** are also wanted.

Chloe Ross
7553 W Norton Ave. #4
Los Angeles, CA 90046-5523
213-874-3044

We Pay

Tin Toy Globes, ea .... **5.00+**
Eiffel Tower Models, ea .... **5.00+**

I buy **Pound Pur-r-ries (stuffed toy cats) by Tonka in the 12" size only**. I prefer colors other than white. I also buy Pound Pur-r-ries clothing, especially denim jackets. I'm also interested in **Stays-Stuffed cats by Schaper**, preferably with accessories. **I pay from $1 to $10** depending on condition, etc.

Linda Toivainen
R.R. 1, Box 128
Waterboro, ME 04087
207-247-3993

Wanted: **old toy sewing machines**. For prices, see my book *Toy and Miniature Sewing Machines* by Glenda Thomas, published by Collector Books. Of particular interest is a red, blue, or green metal Singer toy sewing machine from the 1950s. Also I would like to buy old magazine or catalog advertisements about toy sewing machines. Good copies are acceptable.

Glenda Thomas
P.O. Box 893
Electra, TX 76360

If it's a **boy's toy made prior to 1970** and it's still in excellent shape, chances are that I'll want to buy it from you. I'll pay you a fair price for GI Joe figures (painted hair, no flocked hair) and equipment, Captain Action figures and equipment, Aurora monster models, tin wind-up and battery-operated toys. I also buy **TV and comic character-related lunch boxes**. Buying almost anything related to **Lost in Space, Green Hornet** and **Rat Fink**. If you have a large or small GI Joe collection, please drop me a note. Listed below is a sampling of typical amounts paid for those toys in excellent or better condition in their original boxes. Please send me a list of what you have (letting me know what you want for it helps) — I'll promptly answer all inquiries and return all photos.

Bob Cummings
5669 Chelsea Ave.
La Jolla, CA 92037
619-456-2556

	We Pay
Aurora, monster model, mint in box	**150.00+**
Ben Cooper Costume, Rat Fink, Green Hornet, or Lost in Space, w/original box, ea	**75.00+**
Corgi, Yellow Submarine, w/original box	**200.00+**
Hasbro, GI Joe Action Soldier, Sailor, Marine or Pilot, w/original box, ea	**150.00+**
Hasbro, GI Joe Action Soldier, Black version, w/original box	**700.00+**
Ideal, Captain Action, w/original box	**200.00+**
Ideal, Action Boy, w/original box	**300.00+**
Mattel, Matt Mason Scorpio figure, w/original box	**300.00+**
Mattel, Hot Wheels, in original blister package	**30.00+**
Mattel, Lost in Space Switch 'n' Go Playset	**500.00+**
Japanese Robot, battery operated, w/original box	**200.00+**
Jetson's or Star Trek Lunch Box, ea	**300.00+**
Green Hornet's Black Beauty Car, tin	**200.00+**

We are seeking **older 1/24th and 1/25th scale plastic model cars**. These can be the kits that kids put together in the 1950s and '60s or the dealership-issued promotionals. The years of interest are 1955 through 1974 issues. Although we prefer sealed, unbuilt kits, we will consider any and all. We will be glad to make an offer on what you have, if you can send a detailed list with photos. You can also send model(s) on approval, and if we do not purchase them, we will return them postpaid. We will travel for large collections.

Trader Rick's
Collectible Toy Cars
P.O. Box 161
Newark, IL 60541
815-695-5135

	We Pay
Unbuilt Kit, depending on condition & issue	2.00-100.00
Built Kit, depending on condition & rarity	1.00-50.00
Dealer Promotional Car, depending on condition	15.00+
Model Car Magazine	2.00+
Empty Box	2.00+
Unused Decal Sheet	1.00+

We buy **toy soldiers, civilian figures, and animals manufactured between the 1890s and the 1960s**. Figures can be made of metal or composition material; however, we also buy plastic figures made during the 1950s and 1960s. In addition to military figures, we purchase **farm, zoo, and circus figures and any trucks or other vehicles related to toy soldiers**. In all cases, the condition of the figure is very important. We do *not* buy broken figures or those with severe paint damage.

Dave Francis
One Park Centre, Ste. 207
Wadsworth, OH 44281
216-335-3717

	We Pay
Britains Ltd, individual soldiers, ea	10.00+
Britains Ltd, complete set	100.00+
Britains Ltd Farm Figure	5.00+
Britains Ltd Zoo Figure	10.00+
Other English Figures	5.00+
American Dime Store Figure	10.00+
German Solid Lead Figure	10.00+

French Lead Figure .... **10.00+**
German Composition Figure .... **10.00+**
Other Figures .... **5.00+**

Never having outgrown my childhood, I am still buying toys. I buy **all kinds of vintage toys** but am especially interested in lithographed tin, cast-iron, celluloid, and character toys. I also buy old board games, dolls, doll-house furniture, children's dishes, and accessories.

Judith Katz-Schwartz
222 E 93rd St. 42D
New York, NY 10128
212-876-3512

We Pay

Battery-Operated Toys .... **10.00-1,000.00+**
Board Games .... **20.00-500.00+**
Character Toys .... **25.00-5,000.00+**
Children's Dishes .... **10.00-500.00+**
Disney Toys .... **25.00-5,000.00+**
Dollhouse Furniture .... **5.00-200.00+**
Doll Head, old bisque .... **50.00-2,000.00+**
Friction Toys .... **20.00-500.00+**
Lithographed Tin Toys .... **15.00-1,000.00+**
Toy or Salesman's Sample Stoves, cast iron .... **50.00-1,000.00+**

Wanted: **French bulldog pull toy** made circa 1880 to about 1900. This wheeled toy has a red ruff around his neck, nods, and barks when a string on his back is pulled. Also wanted is any Pug dog toy of any period.

Elenore D. Chaya
4003 S Indian River Dr.
Ft. Pierce, FL 34982
407-465-1789

I am interested in buying **slot race cars and model race sets from the 1960s and 1970s**. This hobby was also known as model motoring or model car racing. Slot car racing allowed hobbyists the excitement of real racing around a plastic electric-powered racetrack. The cars were powered by a small electric motor and equipped with what was called a guide. The guide is plastic and extends out from the bottom of the car into the narrow groove in the racetrack surface. The slot keeps the car on the electrified track and determines the direction. Model cars and accessories were available in four popular sizes: HO scale, 1/32, 1/24, and 1/25 scale. HO is the smallest scale with cars approximately 3" in size while 1/25th scale measures almost 12" in size.

As a rule of thumb, car bodies that were fastened to the chasis with screws (rather than bodies that snapped together) are older and worth more money. Please write and describe: make, model, color, condition, year (if known), and any missing or broken parts. Be sure the car body wheel wells have not been damaged or carved out. If you have an item call me at 206-935-0245 (Western Standard Time) or send the cars, photographs, or complete description for my offer. All offers will be made within 72 hours of receipt — check or items returned by UPS. Please include your phone number. I also buy **books or catalogs from manufactures listed below on slot cars or model motoring from the 1960s and 1970s**.

Below are prices for cars in new, almost new, or in-the-box condition. **Note**: Aurora and Tyco HO must be from the 1960s and 1970s.

Gary Pollastro
4156 Beach Dr. SW
Seattle, WA 98116
206-935-0245

	We Pay
AC Gilbert's Auto-Rama, all scales, individual car	**10.00-100.00**
AC Gilbert's Auto-Rama, all scales, boxed set	**10.00-200.00**
Allstate, Marx, all scales, individual car	**10.00-100.00**
Allstate, Marx, all scales, boxed set	**10.00-100.00**
AMT Corporation, 1/25 scale, individual car	**10.00-100.00**
AMT Corporation, 1/25 scale, boxed set	**10.00-300.00**
AMT Corporation, 1/24 scale, most cars, ea	**40.00**
Atlas, all scales, individual car	**5.00-50.00**
Atlas, all scales, boxed set	**5.00-75.00**
Aurora, all scales, no TOMY Aurora, individual car, from 1960s or 1970s only	**5.00-100.00**
Aurora, all scales, no TOMY Aurora, boxed set, 1960s or 1970s only	**10.00-150.00**
Aurora, boxed set, 1960s	**50.00-250.00**
Aurora Vibrators, #1554 Hot Rod Coupe	**50.00**
Aurora T-Jet, #1347 Maserati	**30.00**
Cox (LM Cox), all scales, individual car	**5.00-50.00**
Cox (LM Cox), all scales, boxed set	**10.00-75.00**
Eldon Industries, 1/32 scale, individual car	**5.00-50.00**
Eldon Industries, 1/32 scale, boxed set	**10.00-100.00**

Eldon Industries, 1/32 scale, Cheetah **40.00**
Lionel, all scales, individual car **5.00-50.00**
Lionel, all scales, boxed set **10.00-100.00**
Monogram, 1/24 or 1/25 scale, individual car **5.00-50.00**
Monogram, 1/24 or 1/25 scale, boxed set **10.00-100.00**
Revell, all scales, individual car **5.00-50.00**
Revell, all scales, boxed set **10.00-100.00**
Revell, boxed set, from 1960s **30.00-200.00**
Scalextric, Tri-Ang of England, all scales, individual car **10.00-100.00**
Scalextric, Tri-Ang of England, all scales, boxed set **10.00-100.00**
Strombecker, all scales, individual car **5.00-50.00**
Strombecker, 1/32 scale, Cheetah **40.00**
Strombecker, all scales, boxed set **10.00-100.00**
Testors, all scales, individual car **5.00-50.00**
Testors, all scales, boxed set **10.00-100.00**
Tyco, HO scale, gold chasis, individual car, 1960s or 1970s only **5.00-40.00**
Tyco, HO scale, gold chasis, boxed set, 1960s or 1970s only **10.00-100.00**
Victory Industries, all scales, individual car **10.00-100.00**
Victory Industries, all scales, boxed set **10.00-100.00**

I buy **old toy trucks, cars, and construction vehicles from the 1890s to the 1960s**. These can be in any condition, as I need parts also. You can send me a picture or the item by US mail or UPS. I will then call you and negotiate a price or return your item. I prefer toys with no plastic parts, but missing wheels are okay.

C.L. Chaussee
1001 5th St.
Calhan, CO 80808
719-347-2000

We buy **any metal or rubber toy plane, train, or auto you can hold in the palm of your hand made before 1960**. It helps if the item has a name printed on it. The toy must have at least 60% original paint, parts, etc. We also duplicate metal and rubber parts. High and fair prices paid for better items in excellent condition. Original box is a big plus. **Paying up to 90% of book values for items wanted**. Try us — you'll like us!

Bob Cimino
921 S Webster Ave.
Scranton, PA 18505
717-344-3751

I am known for my fair dealings and for paying top prices for **windups, robots, space toys, toys made by TPS, Japanese/German/English motorcycles, Japanese tin cars, clowns, character toys, celluloid, Disney, boats, airplanes, and battery-operated toys**. Of special interest are **pre-1950s holiday items, especially Halloween and Christmas**. On a number of occasions I have paid over $20,000 for a single toy. What do you have?

Mark Bergin
P.O. Box 1555
Hollis, NH 03049-1555
603-465-7727 or FAX 603-465-3771

We Pay

Character Toys (any character, any type) .... **up to 15,000.00**
Christmas Items (candy containers, Santa figures, old ornaments, figural bulbs, blocks, games, feather trees, figures of any Christmas character, etc) .... **up to 1,500.00**
Halloween Items (candy containers, diecuts, jack-o'-lanterns, crepe paper goods, figures, etc), vintage only .... **up to 1,500.00**
Robots or Space Toys, tin, Japanese, circa 1950s, w/original box...... **up to 24,000.00**
Motorcycles, tin, German or Japanese .... **up to 5,000.00**
Cars, tin, Japanese **200.00-8,000.00**
Windup Toys, all types wanted .... **up to 7,500.00**

I am interested in buying **all windup and battery-operated toys (working or not working)** — the older, the better! And remember, broken is okay. Price paid will depend on the toy and the extent of its defects. No rusted klunkers, please. I am interested in quantity. Call the Toy Doctor.

Leo E. Rishty, The Toy Doc
77 Alan Loop
Staten Island, NY 10304
718-727-9477 or FAX 718-727-2151

I am interested in purchasing **tin windup toys made in America, Japan, and Germany**. Makers include Louis Marx, Chein, Strauss, Modern Toy, Unique, etc. All tin windups should be in excellent to mint condition. Also interested in purchasing **cast-iron toys** such as Arcade, Hubley, Dent, Stevens, etc.

I am interested in **Black American toys and transportation toys** such as cars, trucks, airplanes, and motorcycles. Also buying **comic character toys** including Mickey Mouse, Donald Duck, Popeye, Felix, Uncle Wiggly, etc. **I will pay 65% of book price.**

Jacquie Henry
Antique Treasures and Toys
P.O. Box 17
2240 Academy St.
Walworth, NY 14658
315-986-1424

We are interested in purchasing **any pressed steel or cast-iron toys such as cars, trucks, construction vehicles, pedal vehicles, tractors, scooters, trikes, ride-ons, and wagons, as well as gas station-related toys — especially anything related to Texaco**. We prefer original condition above 8+ but will also buy items which need to be restored. Please send photos which help us give you a better price and better ability to identify your item. We are mainly wanting items from 1980 or older (except Texaco collector series diecast banks which started in 1984). Let us know if your items are in their original boxes.

Merle J. Von Drasek
Mid City Auto-Antiques-Collectibles
409 N Hampton Rd.
DeSoto, TX 75115
214-223-6770 or
214-223-4087 (7 pm to 9 pm)

I am interested in buying **tin windup toys from the 1950s through the early 1970s** that were made in the US, Germany, England, and Japan; **trains** made by Marx, Marklin, and American Flyer; **GI Joes; vintage Barbies and clothes; and Walt Disney items**. Please send detailed description, price, and a photocopy if possible.

D. Lerch
P.O. Box 586
N White Plains, NY 10603

TRANSPORTATION MEMORABILIA

I collect **all kinds of items related to transportation circa the late 1800s to the 1960s**. Motorcycle, auto, and racing-related memorabilia that shows the history of transportation including advertising artwork to zany items to many others in between — books, sales literature, sculptures (i.e., inkwells or desk sets in shape of cars or motorcycles), china with motoring scenes, advertising signs and showroom sales items, racing posters of all kinds, tire advertising, oil cans with cars or people, advertising clocks or figural desk clocks, racing trophies, figural cookie and biscuit tins, toys with advertising, and even actual motorcycles and racing cars. There are way too many items to list, but I would welcome hearing from anyone on these and other items they might have for sale.

Randy Sykes
20 Pond St.
Nashua, NH 03060
603-889-5924

	We Pay
Biscuit or Cookie Tins, figurals such as cars or motorcycles, ea	**200.00+**
Child's Tea Set, tin or china w/motoring scenes	**150.00**
Dealer Sign, Indian Motorcycles	**1,000.00**
Dealer Sign, Packard	**500.00**
Desk Set, w/auto scene	**250.00**
Gas Pump Globes	**300.00**
Inkwell, car figural	**300.00**
Oil Can, Oilzum Oil, w/goofy kid face on can	**300.00**
Oil Can, Henderson Motorcycle	**300.00**
Oil Sign, for aircraft	**300.00**
Postcard, auto racing or motorcycle, ea	**5.00-15.00**
Racing Helmets, ca 1930s to 1940s, ea	**125.00**
Sales Literature, Porsche, Ferrari or other European makes	**25.00-100.00**
Thermometers, early, ea	**50.00**
Toy Race Car, gas powered	**up to 500.00**

Wanted: **transportation passes from the 1800s** issued by American Express, American Merchant Union Express, Merchant Union Express, Pacific Express, Wells Fargo, United American Express, Railway Express, and various steamboat passes. Also looking for **Western Union passes and credit cards that date before 1930**.

Walt Thompson
P.O. Box 2541-W
Yakima, WA 98907-2541

	We Pay
American Express Pass, before 1920	**4.00+**
American Merchant Union Express Pass	**6.00+**
Merchant Union Express Pass	**8.00+**
Pacific Express Pass	**10.00+**
Railway Express Pass, before 1920	**6.00+**
United American Express Pass	**10.00+**
Wells Fargo Pass	**10.00+**
Any Railroad Pass, before 1800	**125.00+**
Any Railroad Pass, before 1860	**20.00+**
Any Railroad Pass, before 1900	**7.00+**

TYPEWRITER RIBBON TINS

I am buying **typewriter ribbon tins**. Tins should be in good condition. Please contact me about any tin that you may have.

Conrad Hamil
615 Grandridge
Grandview, WA 98930
509-882-3617

	We Pay
Tin w/Picture	**2.00-10.00+**
Tin w/Lettering	**2.00+**
Tin, tall size	**5.00-15.00+**

TYPEWRITERS

Antique typewriters wanted. Listed below are some of their names. Please contact me about any old typewriters that you may have.

Conrad Hamil
615 Grandridge
Grandview, WA 98930
509-882-3617

	We Pay
American	200.00+
Bennett	200.00+
Blickensderfer Electric	500.00+
Brooks	500.00+
Burnett	500.00+
Caligraph	300.00+
Chicago	200.00+
Century	200.00+
Champion	500.00+
Columbia Bar-Lock	500.00+
Conover	500.00+
Crandall	500.00+
Crown	500.00+
Daugherty	500.00+
Densmore	200.00+
Edison	500.00+
Elliot Fisher	200.00+
Emerson	200.00+
Fay Sholes	500.00+
Fitch	500.00+
Fox	200.00+
Ford	500.00+
Franklin	500.00+
Hall	500.00+
Hammond Curved Keyboard	500.00+
Hartford	500.00+
International	500.00+
Jackson	500.00+
Jewett	500.00+
Junior	500.00+
Keystone	500.00+
Lambert	500.00+
Lincoln	500.00+
Mc-Cool	500.00+
Merritt	500.00+
Mignon	200.00+
Monarch	200.00+
Munson	500.00+
Molle	50.00+
Moon-Hopkins	500.00+
National	500.00+

Typewriters

Item	Price
North	500.00+
Odell	500.00+
Oliver 1-4-6-10-11	200.00+
Pearl	500.00+
Peerless	500.00+
Peoples	500.00+
Pittsburgh	500.00+
Postal	500.00+
Prouty	500.00+
Rapid	500.00+
Reliance	200.00+
Rem-Blick	200.00+
Rem-Sholes	500.00+
Remington 1-2-3-4-5-8-9	200.00+
Salter	500.00+
The Shimer	500.00+
Sholes	500.00+
Sholes & Glidden	500.00+
Sun	500.00+
Victor	500.00+
Virotype	200.00+
Webster	500.00+
Williams	500.00+
The World	200.00+
Yost	500.00+
Yu Ess	500.00+

VALENTINES

I buy **pre-1950s vintage valentine and other occasion greeting cards** and am interested in one item or a large collection. Condition is very important, and most should be in good to mint condition. However when buying a collection, some damaged cards may be acceptable. As both a dealer and collector of these beautiful old cards, I wish to see them properly preserved for the enjoyment of future generations. I am willing to pay a fair price. (Price depends on condition and age of cards.) Birthday, Christmas, Easter, Halloween, and other occasion cards are wanted, and I will consider postcards as well. Please send either a descriptive letter about your items or send your items on approval. I reimburse all mailing and insurance costs.

Gail Magnon
R.D. #1, Box 481
Palmyra, PA 17078

I buy **old valentines**: honeycomb, mechanical, three-dimensional, Victorian, etc. Old and large ones are preferred; they may be signed or unsigned and marked either Germany or Made in USA. Price is commensurate to size and condition (may not be ripped or torn).

Rhonda Hasse
566 Oak Terrace Dr.
Farmington, MO 63640

VERNON KILNS

I collect **Vernon Kilns dinnerware and pottery along with a number of other American dinnerware patterns**. Of particular interest are pieces manufactured from 1930 through the 1950s. Vernon Kilns produced a wide variety of items with distinctive styling. Some of the Vernon Kilns designers and patterns I collect are:

Jane F Bennison — bowls, candlesticks, planters, vases, etc
Harry Bird — various dinnerware patterns
Don Blanding — Aquarium, Coral Reef, & Honolulu patterns; children's pieces or sets
Walt Disney — all dinnerware, figurines, & hand-decorated bowls & vases
May & Vieve Hamilton — dinnerware & pottery
Rockwell Kent — Moby Dick, Our America, & Salamina patterns
Janice Pettee — Sally Rand & other figurines
Gale Turnbull — various dinnerware patterns
Winchester 73/Frontier Days pattern, most pieces

Please send description, price, and condition of your piece. Photographs are helpful and will be returned. I may be interested in other items also. No phone calls, please. Thank you.

Ray Vlach, Jr.
5364 N Magnet Ave.
Chicago, IL 60630-1216

Vernon Kilns

We are interested in purchasing **Vernon Kilns pottery by the following designers: Harry Bird, Rockwell Kent, Hamilton Sisters, and Gale Turnball**. We have a special interest in Harry Bird plates with floral, bird, or fish motifs. Please call with sizes and descriptions for prices.

Dave Lusty
Magazine Street Antiques
1829 Magazine St.
New Orleans, LA 70130
504-524-2807

VICTORIAN COLLECTIBLES

I purchase **anything from the Victorian era (1845-1900)**. I am especially looking for the unusual, unique items in excellent condition. I can not appraise your items or respond to requests for educational information. Please send picture, written description, and your price.

Gary and Rhonda Hallden
21958 Larkin Dr.
Saugus, CA 91350
805-259-7868

	We Pay
Bride's Baskets (also bowls or frames only)	**30.00+**
Books, illustrated children's or color-illustrated bindings	**8.00+**
Boxes, for gloves or collars, usually w/pictures of ladies	**40.00+**
China, hand painted (no decals wanted)	**25.00+**
Clothing, shoes, parasols, etc	**20.00+**
Cranberry Glass	**20.00+**
Dishes, blue & white floral or historic themes	**20.00+**
Flow Blue	**60.00+**
Paperweights	**15.00+**
Photo Albums, w/pictures on covers	**25.00+**
Pie Birds	**20.00+**
Postcards, unusual	**5.00+**
Purses, beaded, fancy forms or designs	**30.00**
Scrapbooks	**25.00+**
Silver	**35.00+**
Valentines	**25.00+**
Other Old Paper Items, depicting ladies, children or animals	**15.00+**

I have a passion for collecting **all Victorian items**. Nothing is too insignificant. Victorian items with cherubs, animals, children, and flowers are particular favorites. If it's monogrammed or slightly worn, that's okay. Price will depend on the item and its condition. Please send me a list of what you have and the price you are asking. Pictures are sometimes helpful. I buy full estates or individual pieces. Below is a partial listing. Victorians had many special pieces for a single use, and I crave them all — anything a Victorian man, woman, or child used is wanted.

Also wanted are **any items with cherubs (also angels or newts, cherubs without wings)** on them. Items can be almost anything of any material. The price I pay is dependent on the item and its condition. Please send a picture and description of what you have along with your asking price. Below is a partial listing of what I collect.

Cindi Lininger
2205 2nd Ave. W
Seattle, WA 98119

We Pay

Jewelry (cameos, lockets, brooches, pins, hair jewelry, rings, hatpins, hair combs, bracelets, charms, photography pins, hearts, chatelaines), ea **4.00-500.00**
Silverplate or Quadplate (serving pieces, utensils, castor sets, bride's baskets, candlesticks, purses, napkin rings, tea sets, trays, dresser sets, butter dishes, pickle castors, or boxes), ea **2.00-250.00**
Photo Albums, Scrapbooks, or Autograph Books, ea **5.00-50.00**
Pictures or Prints, children, animals, cherubs, & flowers, framed or unframed, lg or sm, ea .... **up to 200.00**
Parasols, Purses, or Fans (lace, tapestry, beaded, leather, sequin, or fabric), ea .... **up to 75.00**
Boxes (celluloid, silver, velvet, leather, china), ea .... **up to 75.00**
Baby Items (jewelry, clothes, toys, shoes, rattles, dishes, pictures, furniture), ea .... **up to 50.00**
Card Cases, Match Safes, or Calling Card Receivers, ea .... **up to 75.00**
Dresser Items (combs, brushes, buttonhooks, perfume bottles, hair receivers), ea .... **up to 50.00**
Sewing Items & Accessories (needle cases, scissors, tape measures, thimbles, & seam gauges), ea .... **up to 50.00**
Yard Long Prints, ea .... **up to 50.00**
Clothing (camisoles, slips, or hats), ea .... **up to 50.00**
Linens & Lace **1.00-100.00**
Colored Glass Items (fancy Victorian), ea .... **up to 500.00**
China (complete sets or individual pots, tureens, bowls, etc) .... **up to 500.00**
Buttons, ea .... **up to 5.00**
Calling Cards or Greeting Cards, old, ea .... **up to 5.00**

Items with Angels, Cherubs or Newts — **We Pay**

Candlesticks, porcelain, silver, or gilt, pr **5.00-100.00**

Dishes, ea .... **up to 100.00**
Frames, ea .... **up to 100.00**
Jewelry, ea.. **up to 200.00**
Silver Items, ea .... **up to 200.00**
Boxes, ea .... **up to 50.00**
Prints, ea .... **up to 300.00**
Paintings, ea.. **up to 300.00**

Wanted: **elegant and unusual hats of the Victorian era through the 1940s**. I especially collect ones with feather plumes, jewels, or beads. These hats are for my personal collection. Also of interest are **hat stands, hatpins, gloves, cameos, and other accessory pieces**. As I also collect and repair old dolls, I need **antique infants' clothing and accessories** to dress up dolls. Please send a photo or detailed description and SASE. Ship items only after getting approval.

Joyce Andresen
P.O. Box 1
Keystone, IA 52249

We Pay

Hats, ea .... **2.00-20.00+**
Gloves, pr .... **1.00+**
Hat Stands, ea.. **3.00+**
Hatpins, ea... **5.00+**
Cameos, ea... **3.00+**
Doll or Children's Items, ea .... **3.00+**

I collect **pre-1920s hats, hatpins, hat pin holders, and feathers that may be used on hats, hat boxes, and hair accessories**. Anything that a hat maker would have been used is wanted. I'm interested in **any type of hair jewelry** that would have used prior to the 1920s. Along with these items, **old hair receivers or complete dresser sets** are wanted. Please send information and asking price.

Tiffany Lininger
2205 2nd Ave. W
Seattle, WA 98119

VIEW-MASTER AND OTHER 3-D PHOTOGRAPHICA

View-Master, the invention of William Gruber, was first introduced to the public at the 19309-1940 New York World's Fair and at the same time at the Golden Gate Exposition in California. Since then thousands of different reels and packets have been produced on subjects as diverse as life itself. Sawyers View-Master even made two different cameras for the general public, enabling people to make their own personal reels, and then offered a stereo projector to project the pictures they took on a silver screen in full color 3-D.

View-Master has been owned by five different companies: the original Sawyers Company, G.A.F. (in October 1966), View-Master International (in 1981), Ideal Toy Company, and Tyco Toy Company (the present owners).

Unfortunately, after G.A.F. sold View-Master in 1981, neither View-Master International, Ideal, nor Tyco Toy Company have had any intention of making the products anything but toy items, selling mostly cartoons. This, of course, has made the early non-cartoon single reels and three-reel packets desirable items.

The earlist single reels from 1939-1945 were not white in color but were originally dark blue with a gold sticker in the center and came in attractive gold-colored envelopes. Then they were made in a blue and tan combination. These early reels are more desirable, as the print runs were low.

From 1946-1957 most white single reels are very common, as they were produced in the millions. There are exceptions, however, such as commercial reels promoting a product or obscure scenic attractions, as these would have had smaller print runs. In 1952 a European division of View-Master was established in Belgium. Most reels and items made in Belgium are more valuable to a collector, since they are harder to find in this country.

In 1955 View-Master came up with the novel idea of selling packets of three reels in one colorful envelope with a picture or photo on the front. Many times a story booklet was included. These became very popular and single reels were slowly discontinued. Most three-reel packets are desirable, whether Sawyers or G.A.F., as long as they are in nice condition. Nearly all viewers are common and have little value, except the very early ones, such as Model A and Model B. These viewers had to be opened to insert the reels. The blue and brown versions of the Model B are rare. Another desirable viewer is the Model D, which is the only focusing viewer that View-Master Made.

Condition is very important to the value of all View-Master items, as it is with most collectibles. I buy most all desirable and scarce View-Master material in very good to mint condition.

Also wanted are **Tru-Vue** items. Tru-Vue, a subsiderary of the Rock Island Bridge and Iron Works in Rock Island, Illinois, was first introduced to the public at the 1933 Century of Progress Exposition in Chicago, Illinois. With their popular black and white 3-D filmstrips and viewers, Tru-Vue quickly became the successor to the Stereoscope and stereocards of the 1800s and early 1900s. They made many stereo views of cities, national parks, scenic attractions, and even some foreign countries. They also produced children's stories, some that featured personalities and nightclubs, and many commercial and instructional filmstrips.

By the late 1940s, Sawyers View-Master had become a very strong competitor. Their full-color 7-scene stereo reels were very popular with the public and had cut into Tru-Vue's sales considerably. So it was a tempting offer when Sawyers made a bid to buy out the company in 1951. Sawyers needed Tru-Vue, not only to eliminate competition, but because Tru-Vue owned the rights to photograph Disney characters and the Disneyland theme park in California.

Sawyers View-Master continued to carry Tru-Vue products but ceased production of the 3-D filmstrips and viewers. Instead, they produced a new format of 7-scene 3-D cards with a new viewer to see the pictures in 3-D. These new Tru-Vue cards were sold mostly in toy stores, and today they have little value. All of the pictures used a cheaper Eastman color slide film, which today has mostly faded into a magenta color. Many cards also came apart, as the glue that was used tends to easily separate. The value of these, therefore, is low and many cards were later remade as View-Master reels with better Kodachrome film. When G.A.F. bought View-Master in 1966, they slowly faded out the Tru-Vue format through the next years.

Walter Sigg
P.O. Box 208
Swartswood, NJ 07877

View-Master **We Pay**

Camera, Mark II, w/case **100.00**
Camera, Personal Stereo, w/case **100.00**
Close-Up Lens, for Personal Camera **100.00**
Film Cutter, for cameras **100.00**
Packet, scenic, 3-reel set **1.00-25.00**
Packet, TV or movie, 3-reel set **2.00-50.00**
Packet, Addams Family or Munsters, 3-reel set, ea **50.00**
Packet, Belgium made, 3-reel set **4.00-35.00**
Packet, miscellaneous subject, 3-reel set **3.00-50.00**
Projector, Stereo-Matic 500 .... **200.00**
Reel, gold center, gold-colored package **10.00**
Reel, blue **2.50-10.00**
Reel, Sawyers, white, early .... **25¢-5.00**
Reel, commercial, brand-name product (Coca-Cola, auto makers, etc)... **5.00-50.00**
Reel, 3-D movie preview (House of Wax, Kiss Me Kate, etc) **50.00**
Reel, Belgium made **1.00-10.00**
Viewer, Model B, blue or brown, ea **100.00**
Viewer, Model D, focusing type **30.00**
Any Advertising Literature, dealer displays, etc (items not meant to be sold to

the public) .... **Write**
Original Factory Items .... **Write**

Tru-Vue **We Pay**

Card **1.00-3.00**
Filmstrip, children's story **1.00-3.00**
Filmstrip, commercial (promoting products) **20.00-50.00**
Filmstrip, instructional **5.00-15.00**
Filmstrip, personality (Sally Rand, Gypsy Rose Lee, etc) **15.00-20.00**
Filmstrip, ocean liner **15.00**
Filmstrip, scenic **1.00-5.00**
Filmstrip, World's Fair **7.50**
Viewer **5.00**
Any Advertising Literature, dealer displays, etc (items not meant to be sold to the public) .... **Write**

I buy **all kinds of 3-dimensional items:** stereocards, cameras, Tru-Vue filmstrips, View-Master, magazines, comics, projectors, viewers, movies, any store displays for 3-D products, stereoscopes, movie memorabilia, lenticular pictures, etc. I do not want any Nishika or Nimslo cameras. I do not want stereocards that are color prints. My favorite areas of stereocards are pictures of Hollywood, movie stars, movie theaters, other movie-related items, World's Fairs after 1920, autos, trains, store fronts, street scenes, hand-tinted photos, and most everything from 1920 to 1940. I do not want Tru-Vue cards or View-Master viewers made after the 1950s. I do not want the View-Master Model D viewer which is battery operated and has a focusing knob above the right eye piece. I am especially wanting advertising or promotional Tru-Vue filmstrips and View-Master reels. I want 3-D slides from before 1960 and am especially looking for 3-D product store displays. If it's 3-D, I want it.

Chris Perry, Doctor 3-D
7470 Church St. #A
Yucca Valley, CA 92284
619-365-0475

We Pay

Airquipt Stereo Theater **100.00**
3-D Movie Magazine **18.00**
Projector, Compco Triad **100.00**
Projector, Nord 3-D **90.00**
Projector, TDC 116 Vivid **180.00**
Projector, Realist 81 or Realist 82, ea **350.00**

Reel, military **7.00**
Stereocards, movie related, ea **25.00**
Stereocards, 1933 or 1939 World's Fair, full size, ea **10.00**
Tru-Vue Dealer Display **200.00**
Tru-Vue Filmstrip, advertising **25.00**
Tru-Vue Filmstrip, TV-1 through TV-6, ea **30.00**
Tru-Vue Filmstrip, World's Fair **10.00**
Tru-Vue Viewer, Century of Progress **40.00**
View-Master Dealer Display **180.00**
View-Master Reel, advertising promotion **20.00**
View-Master Reel, movie preview **75.00**
View-Master Stereomatic 500 .... **230.00**
View-Master Viewer, Model D **45.00**
View-Master Viewing Cabinet **200.00**
Viewer, Kodaslide **50.00**
Viewer, Realist Red Button **55.00**
Viewer, Roto-Viewer **120.00**

I am an avid **3-D stereo photo** collector. In the five years I have been seriously collecting, I have amassed a sizable collection. I've paid as much as $2,000 for a single collection. Having a great desire to continue building my collection, **all types are of interest but older (prior to 1980) US and foreign-made reels and packets** are wanted. Besides scenics, I am especially interested in 'Made in Belgium' reels, military training reels, and medical reels. Personal or amateur-made reels, whatever subject, are wanted also. Please list your collection by reel or packet number when writing me and indicate condition. I am a collector, not a dealer. Your collection will find a good home with me.

I also collect **3-D stereo slides** (4x1⅝"). These are predominately amateur slides made from personal 3-D cameras popular in the 1950s. All subject matter is of interest, but I especially desire scenic and travel topics — US and foreign. I also want stereo viewers and cases. Please write with a brief description of what you have including approximate number of slides and subject matter.

Kyle Spain
620 Brightside Ln.
Pasadena, CA 91107

We Pay

Packet, complete .... **3.00+**
Made in Belgium Reel **4.00**
Military Training Reel **4.00**
Medical Reel **4.00**
Non-White Reel .... **2.00+**

Personal Reel 1.00
Advertising Reel 5.00

WATCHES

They say: The 'first' watch made was in the year 1500 A.D. The minute hand did not appear until 1687 A.D. Watches with movable figures date back to 1790 A.D. There are 195,000 watches sold per day.

We say: Dig out those watches and turn them into money. **Watches need not be working** or in good shape. Our policy is to return your watch that day if you don't like our offer. In all these years, we are proud to say that we haven't returned one watch! Examples of prices are lised below. Depending on condition, gold, diamonds, etc., prices may be much more.

James Lindon
5267 W Cholla St.
Glendale, AZ 85304
602-878-2409

We Pay

Audemars Piquet 350.00
Benrus 20.00
Breitling 100.00
Bucherer 20.00
Bulova 20.00
Cyma 20.00
Ebel 30.00
Gruen 30.00
Hamilton 30.00
Heuer 40.00
Hyde Park 20.00
Illinois 30.00
Le Coultre 100.00
Longines 50.00
Mido 30.00
Movado 80.00
Omega 50.00
Patek Philippe 1,200.00
Rolex 300.00
Tiffany 100.00
Ulysse Nardin 80.00
Universal Geneva 100.00

Vacheron Constantin **1,000.00**
Wittnauer........ **30.00**
Any Character Watches........ **Call or Write**
Any Advertising Watches .... **Call or Write**
Any Watch-Related Advertising........ **Call or Write**

I buy **older working watches**. Depending on condition, gold, diamonds, etc., prices may be much higher. Better offers made for unusual watches in original box with papers. Contact us with a photo and what you feel is a fair price. I also purchase **Swatch watches**. Other interests include **motion and lava lamps and figurals from the 1940s and '50s**.

C.E. Nolte
2979 S 15 Pl.
Milwaukee, WI 53215

	We Pay
Benrus	**20.00**
Beecheron	**20.00**
Bulova	**20.00**
Green	**35.00**
Hamilton	**35.00**
Le Coultre	**100.00**
Longines	**50.00**
Omega	**50.00**
Swatch, plastic band, before 1985	**10.00**
Swatch, plastic band, before 1990	**6.00**
Swatch, leather band, before 1985	**15.00**
Swatch, leather band, before 1990	**10.00**
Swatch, Universal Geneva	**100.00**

WATT POTTERY

We buy **unusual and regular Watt pieces** and are willing to pay top prices for canister and casserole lids, cookie jars, ice buckets, salt and pepper shakers, etc. We are interested in all Watt; call for quote.

Cleo Hunter
4197 Haywood Dr.
Horse Shoe, NC 28742
704-891-4807 or 704-877-3455

	We Pay
Pitcher, Fruit & Flower	**60.00+**
Bowl	**25.00+**
Casserole, w/lid	**60.00+**
Canister Set	**200.00-1,000.00+**
Canister Lids, Dutch Tulip, complete set	**200.00+**
Plate	**50.00+**
Salt & Pepper Shakers, Fruit & Flower, pr	**100.00+**
Coffeepot	**600.00+**
Teapot	**600.00+**

We buy **all Watt pottery pieces** in all the hand-painted patterns. Prices we are willing to pay will depend on condition, quality of the piece, and its rarity. We do not buy pieces with signs of use (i.e., minor cracks, tiny chips, etc.) but will pay more for mint-condition items. Let us know what you have, your asking price, and send photo of pieces if you can.

Randy and Jane Wright
Jane's Collectibles and Stuff
Rt. 2, Box 372 I, Hill St.
Erin, TN 37061
615-289-4068 or
615-289-4096

WEATHER VANES AND ARROWS

I am a collector of lightning rod weather vanes, arrows, and balls. I will buy full-body animal vanes, glass tail arrows, and metal tail arrows. I will also buy lightning rod tips. Please send picture and description along with price desired.

Also wanted are **lightning rod balls, shooting gallery targets, and windmill weights**.

Bob Claybrook
68701 D St.
Cathedral City, CA 92234
619-324-7872

WEDGWOOD

I buy **all Wedgwood's Jasperware produced before World War II, and select pieces of post-World War II production**. Almost all pieces of Wedgwood Jasperware should have Wedgwood incised (generally) on their base. Most pre-war Wedgwood will be dark blue with white raised relief decor, but I am especially interested in the more unusual colors such as crimson, black, yellow, brick, lavender, and pieces which were made using three or more colors of Jasper (such as green and lavender on white). Please, very carefully examine pieces for any damage, including chips, cracks, staining, or missing pieces of relief work, and describe the condition of the piece fully. Include in your description any and all markings found on the base of the piece.

Larry D. Cook
P.O. Box 211
Walnut, IA 51577-0211

	We Pay
Bisuit Barrels, ea	100.00-400.00
Cheese Dishes, ea	100.00-300.00
Chess Pieces, ea	25.00-150.00
Covered Vases or Urns, ea	125.00-500.00
Figural Candlesticks or Bough Pots, ea	500.00-1,000.00
Pitchers, ea	25.00-300.00
Plaques, ea	75.00-500.00
Plates, ea	25.00-200.00
Salad Sets (salad bowl w/spoon & fork)	100.00-200.00
Salt & Pepper Shakers, pr	50.00-150.00
Sugar Shakers, ea	75.00-200.00
Tea Caddies, ea	75.00-200.00
Tobacco Jars, ea	50.00-200.00

I am interested in buying **Wedgwood Jasperware**. I will buy modern pieces marked Made in England in colors other than blue or green such as lilac, black, taupe, pink, teal, terra cotta, etc. I am interested in old pieces marked Wedgwood or Wedgwood England in any color. Items must be in mint condition. The following is an example of prices I might pay. Please price and describe your item and enclose SASE for reply.

Ellen R. Rubell
58 Kingsland Ave.
Wallingford, CT 06492
203-284-9090 or FAX 203-265-0069

We Pay

Dish, 4" .... **10.00+**
Creamer .... **20.00+**
Sugar .... **20.00+**
Vase .... **25.00+**
Candlestick .... **25.00+**

WESTERN COLLECTIBLES

We buy **all types of Western items** which includes items made of leather, metal, wood, paper, glass, ivory, or other materials. Listed below are some of the things we will buy. Some may require a photo or a photocopy before a price can be given.

Bill Shaw
801 Duval Dr.
Opp, AL 36467

Authentic, Old Western Items **We Pay**

Ammunition, in boxes .... **5.00+**
Badges, Police, US Marshal, Texas Ranger, Deputy, DEA, FBI, etc, ea .... **30.00+**
Cowboy Clothing, hats, chaps, old holsters, etc, ea .... **25.00+**
China & Dinnerware Pieces, w/western logos, ea .... **5.00+**
Dice, ivory or bone, pr .... **5.00+**
Playing Cards, circa 1880s to early 1900s .... **10.00+**
Other Gambling Items, ea .... **30.00+**
Gold Coins, ea .... **75.00+**
Gold Scales, pocket type or counter scales, ea .... **40.00+**
Handcuffs, circa 1880s-1950s .... **30.00+**
Jewelry, such as bolos, belt buckles, etc, w/western theme, ea .... **5.00+**
Match Safes, ea .... **20.00+**
Pocket Watches, ea .... **30.00+**
Photos, original only of cowboys, saloons, etc, ea .... **5.00+**
Revolver, Colt .45 .... **300.00+**
Derringer, pocket types such as Colt .41, Remington .41, etc, ea .... **100.00+**
Sheath Knives, hunting, bowie, daggers, etc, ea .... **25.00+**
Spurs, American, Mexican, etc, pr .... **50.00+**
Saddle Bags, ea .... **40.00+**
Whiskey Bottles, w/labels under glass, ea .... **25.00+**

We are **buying, selling, and restoring all kinds of old cowboy items**: colorful boots, spurs, horsehair items, bits, cuffs, Western badges, leather gun holsters, old West and saloon items, guns, advertising, Indian items, chaps, horn furniture, photos, etc.

Cowboy Collectibles
218 Country Wood
San Antonio, TX 78216
210-490-2433 or FAX 210-490-3433

	We Pay
Chaps, batwing	**100.00+**
Chaps, wooly	**200.00+**
Gun Holsters or Rigs	**50.00+**
Badges, Western	**25.00+**
Boots, colorful	**35.00+**
Spurs	**50.00-2,000.00**
Photos	**25.00+**
Cuffs	**20.00+**
Horsehair Hatbands, Belts, Bridles	**35.00+**

We are now buying **any old (pre-1955) Western collectibles** in good or better condition in brass, iron, cast iron, aluminum, silver, and bronze. **Items wanted include**:

- Arrow Heads
- Bead Work
- Brand Books
- Branding Irons
- Clothing
- Cuffs
- Bows
- Hatchets
- Kerchiefs
- Knives
- Horse Bits
- Moccasins
- Padlocks
- Saddles
- Saddle Horns
- Spurs
- Stirrups, metal
- Head Stalls
- Watch Fobs
- Wells Fargo Items
- Winchester Rifles
- Small Safes
- Safe Banks

Many other related items wanted as well. Note that stirrups do not have to be in pairs — singles will do as well. Thank you.

c/o W.L. Barnes
1137 Frank Ave. SE
Huron, SD 57350

WESTMORELAND

I buy **all unusual and rare Westmoreland glass pieces** in the Paneled Grape, Old Quilt, Beaded Grape, Cherry patterns, as well as others. I am also interested in buying Westmoreland covered animal dishes, children's pieces, baskets, glass animals, collector plates, wedding bowls, etc. Special interest in milk-glass pieces that are hand-painted with the Roses and Bows decoration. Unusual items in purple marble, brown marble, and green marble are bought. I prefer items that are clearly marked (mold marked) with WG; however, I will consider all items. Chipped, cracked, or factory-defective pieces are not purchased. Only mint-condition pieces are purchased. Actual UPS and insurance charges will be reimbursed. Phone calls accepted after 6:30 pm (CST) weekdays and all day weekends. Below is only an example of items purchased. All items considered.

Memories by Michele
12026 Ibis St., NW
Coon Rapids, MN 55433
612-754-2848

	We Pay
Paneled Grape Epergne	**210.00**
Paneled Grape Belled Vase, 11½"	**60.00**
Paneled Grape Parfait	**25.00**
Paneled Grape Banana Bowl	**95.00**
Paneled Grape Bowl, oblong, 12"	**95.00**
Paneled Grape Cake Salver, 10x4"	**75.00**
Paneled Grape Canisters	**85% of book value**
Old Quilt Bowl	**80% of book value**
Old Quilt Plate	**80% of book value**
Old Quilt Saucer	**80% of book value**
Old Quilt Cup	**80% of book value**

Wanted: any item related to Westmoreland Glass Co., Westmoreland Speciality Co., and Speciality Glass Works located in Grapeville, Jeannette, and Westmoreland, Pennsylvania, respectively. These companies existed from about 1890 through 1980. **Ephemeral items** such as ads, brochures, postcards, and sales literature as well as glass products are wanted. Specific **items wanted are crystal with ruby stain in these patterns**:

#1058 Della Robbia
#1855 Ashburton
#1881 Paneled Grape
#1967 Rose & Lattice
#1932 Waterford (Irish Waterford)

Daniel Sperry
P.O. Box 5487
Hauppauge, NY 11788-0121

WORLD'S FAIRS AND EXPOSITIONS

I am looking for records sold at World's Fairs. **Any sound recordings** from World's Fairs would be of interest to me. I am also looking for **8mm, 16mm, and 35mm motion picture films** from any World's Fairs. I am especially looking for **3-D films shown at the 1939-1940 or any other World's Fair**. I buy **any Tru-Vue filmstrips** of World's Fairs as well as **View-Master reels and packets** of World's Fairs. I buy **stereocards of World's Fairs after 1920**. I prefer full-size views of World's Fairs as opposed to Keystone Jr. views which are smaller. I want **any 3-D photo of World's Fairs after 1920**, but not ordinary photos. I prefer color movie films rather than black and white, but I will buy both if the quality is good. I also buy **anaglyph 3-D pictures** of World's Fairs. These pictures use two-color red/green glasses. I am also looking for sheet music from World's Fairs after 1920.

Chris Perry, Doctor 3-D
7470 Church St., Suite A
Yucca Valley, CA 92284
619-365-0475

	We Pay
Anaglyph 3-D Picture	**10.00**
Film, 35mm, per ft	**25¢**
Film, 16mm, per ft	**8¢**
Film, 8mm, per ft	**3¢**
Records, ea	**5.00+**
Sheet Music	**3.00+**
Stereocard, 1933 World's Fair, full size	**6.00**
Stereocard, 1939 World's Fair, full size	**6.00**
Tru-Vue Filmstrips, ea	**10.00**
View-Master Reels, ea	**5.00**
View-Master 3-Reel Packet	**10.00**

YARD LONGS

Yard long prints are lithographs. The ones we collect show **lovely ladies dressed in fashions of the early 1900s to the late 1920s**. Although called yard longs, few actually were exactly a yard long, and some have been trimmed to fit into smaller frames. Various yard longs range in width from 6" to 11" with lengths of around 27" to 37". Some have the artist's name on the front, and most have advertising and a small calendar on the back. A few of the companies whose advertising appears on the reverse of yard longs are Pompeian Beauty Products, Diamond Crystal Salt, Pabst Extract, Walk-Over Shoes, and Selz Shoes.

We collect only prints that are in excellent condition (meaning no highly visible creases, tears, or water stains). The colors must be bright, crisp, and not noticeably faded. We prefer untrimmed, original-length prints with the original frame and glass.

The following are examples of specific yard longs we would like to find for our collection. There are many others not listed that we would also like to have.

Also wanted are **German die-cut and embossed calendar tops showing pretty ladies, a Maxfield Parrish print entitled *Cleopatra* in large size (24½x28"), and Art Deco picture frames** of all metal or glass with painted designs and metal corners that range in size up to 12x14". (An illustrated flyer is available on request.) See also Boxes, Compacts, and Purses in this book.

Mike and Sherry Miller
303 Holiday Dr.
Tuscola, IL 61953
271-253-4991

We Pay

1913 Pabst, signed Stuart Travis **100.00-150.00**
1914 Pabst, signed Alfred Everitt Orr **110.00-165.00**
1926 Pompeian, signed Gene Pressler **90.00-125.00**
1925 Selz, unsigned **175.00-200.00**

OTHER INTERESTED BUYERS OF MISCELLANEOUS ITEMS

In this section of the book we have listed buyers of miscellaneous items and related material. When corresponding with these collectors, be sure to enclose a self-addressed stamped envelope if you want a reply. Do not send lists of items for appraisal. If you wish to sell your material, quote the price that you want or send a list of items you think they might be interested in and ask them to make you an offer. If you want the list back, be sure to send an SASE large enough for the listing to be returned.

ABC Plates
English
Sally Van Aller
140 Overlook Dr.
Queenstown, MD 21658
410-827-6097

Advertising
Elsie the Cow and Reddy Killowatt
Lee Garmon
1529 Whittier St.
Springfield, IL 62704

Cereal
Scott Bruce
P.O. Box 481
Cambridge, MA 02140
617-492-5004

Motorcycle
Bruce Kiper
2205 Sunset Ln.
Lutz, FL 33549
813-949-5060

Motorcycle
Tom Wilhelm
R.R. 1, Box 203
Eaton, NY 13334
315-684-9675

Pocket mirrors
Dean Dashner
349 S Green Bay Rd.
Neenah, WI 54956
414-725-4350

Spice, canister, or cruet sets
Janet Hume
11000 S Bryant
Oklahoma City, OK 73160
405-794-7493

Jewel T. Spice Tins
Kayla Conway
4500 Napal Ct.
Bakersfield, CA 93307
805-833-0291

Stoneware
Bruce and Nada Ferris
3094 Oakes Dr.
Hayward, CA 94542
510-581-5285

Refrigerator magnets
Yvonne Marle Holmberg
7229 Pine Island Dr., NE
Comstock Park, MI
49321-9534
616-784-1715

John and Margaret Kaduck
The Collection Builders
P.O. Box 26076
Cleveland, OH 44126
216-333-2958

Tobacco pocket tins
Dennis Schulte
8th Ave NW
Waukon, IA 52172
319-568-3628
(before 10 pm CST)

Also toys
Delores Lawson
6129 Misson Dr.
Orlando, FL 32810
407-298-4749

Cigar and match safes
Mike Schwimmer
325 E Blodgett
Lake Bluff, IL 60044-2112
708-295-1901

Coca-Cola and Pepsi
Terri Ivers
1104 Shirlee Ave.
Ponca City, OK 74601
405-762-8697 or
405-762-5174

Coca-Cola, Evening in Paris, and Camel Cigarettes
Betty Hornback
707 Sunrise Ln.
Elizabethtown, KY 42701
502-765-2441

Purse and compact ads
The Curiosity Shop
P.O. Box 964
Cheshire, CT 06410
203-271-0643

Phonograph
Hart Wesemann
600 N 800 W
W Bountiful, UT 84087
801-298-3499

Round Oak Stoves
Steve Saltzman
101 Spruce St.
Douagial, MI 49047
616-782-8052

Victrolas, phonographs, and music boxes
Brett and Cheryl Hurt
6000 Amber Oaks Ave.
Bakersfield, CA 93306
805-872-6296

Transportation, motorcycle, racing, etc.
Randy Sykes
20 Pond St.
Nashua, NH 03060
603-889-5924

Photographica
Harry E. Forsythe
3914 Beach Blvd.
Jacksonville, FL 32207

Appliances
Marked Porcellier
Susan Grindberg
6330 Doffing Ave. E
Inver Grove Hts., MN 55076
612-450-6770

Art Glass
Galle Cameo
Frank Bernhard
2791 Fiesta Dr.
Venice, FL 34293

Tiffany, Steuben, Sinclaire, etc.
Ms. Dulce Holt
504 Broadway
Chesterton, IN 46304
219-926-2838 or
219-926-4170

Art Pottery
Kandice and
Glenn Goodman
21575 Meriann Dr.
Clearlake Oaks, CA 95423
707-322-1082

Arts and Crafts
Roycroft
Roycroft Arts Museum
Boice Lydell
341 E Fairmount Ave.
Lakewood, NY 14750
716-763-1111 or
716-763-5555

Gary Struncius
P.O. Box 1374
Lakewood, NJ 08701
908-364-7580 or
800-272-2529

Ashtrays
Chrome airplane on pedestal
Dick Wallin
P.O. Box 1794
Springfield, IL 62705
217-498-9279

Atlantic City
Back Door Antiques
P.O. Box 1125
Island Hgts., NJ 08732
908-929-1112

Badges
PA Drivers
Ed Foley
P.O. Box 572
Adamstown, PA 19501-0572

Banks
Antique, complete or parts
Baker's International
Antiques & Collectibles
1421 Main St.
Oakdale, NY 11769
516-567-9295

Any that lock with a key
Doris Caloggero
2 Charles St. , P.O. Box 961
Methuen, MA 01844

Baseball Memorabilia
Bill Simmons
315 SW 77th Ave.
N Lauderdale, FL 33068-1200

Baseball Cards
Elva Hughs
26 Franklin Rd., Box 192
Hinsdale, MA 01235
413-655-2016

Billards and Pool
Also tables, books and ephemera
Tim Lawrence
2489 Bexford Pl.
Columbus, OH 43209-1710
614-235-9472

Black Americana
Arthur Boutiette
410 W 3rd St., Ste. 200
Little Rock, AR 72201
501-372-1995

Blade Banks
David Giese
1410 Aquia Dr.
Stafford, VA 22554

Also blade sharpeners and stroppers
Lester Dequaine
155 Brewster St.
Bridgeport, CT 06605
203-335-6833

Steve Skorupski
P.O. Box 572
Plainville, CT 06062

Blue Ridge
Crab Apple and Square Dance
The Cocklebur Antiques
2161 Pointer Rd.
W Branch, MI 48661
517-345-7242

Blue Willow
Elva Hughs
26 Franklin Rd., Box 192
Hinsdale, MA 01235
413-655-2016

Books
Arthur Boutiette
410 W 3rd St., Ste. 200
Little Rock, AR 72201
501-372-1995

Ann Rice, Ann Rampling, or A.N. Roquelaure hardcover first editions
Vicki Woodrow
2620 W Salem Church Rd.
Covington, IN 47932

Civil War
Stephen Edwards
Rt. 1, Box 1348
Mt. Philo Rd.
Charlotte, VT 05445
802-425-2006

Children's
Melanie Hewitt
2101 Beechwood
Little Rock, AR 72207
501-280-9600

Children's; Janice Holt Giles, Jesse Stuart, or Robert Penn Warren
Betty Hornback
707 Sunrise Ln.
Elizabethtown, KY 42701
502-765-2441

Billy Whiskers or goat-related items
Linda Toivainen
R.R. 1, Box 128 Middle Rd.
Waterboro, ME 04087

Glassware and pottery by Collector Books
Violet Moore
P.O. Box 637
Walker, LA 70785
504-665-3257

By Knappen or Hadler
Phoneco
Ron and Mary Knappen
207 E Mill Rd., P.O. Box 70
Galesville, WI 54630

By North Dakota authors or about North Dakota
Stan and Carrie Soderstrom
003-3rd St. SW
Rt. 2, Box 300
Bowman, ND 58623

Paperweights
Andrew Dohan
49 E Lancaster Ave.
Frazer, PA 19355
610-647-3310

Bride's Baskets
Gary and Rhonda Hallden
21958 Larkin Dr.
Saugus, CA 91350
805-259-7868

Bronzes
Melanie Hewitt
2101 Beechwood
Little Rock, AR 72207
501-280-9600

Also other metal items
Montage Magie
P.O. Box 3423
Veero Beach, FL
32964-3423
407-234-5409

Buffalo Pottery
Fred and Lila Shrader
2025 Hwy. 199 (Hiouchi)
Crescent City, CA 95531

Buttons
Gwen Daniel
18 Belleau Lake Ct.
O'Fallon, MO 63366
314-978-3190

Also buckles
Fred and Lila Shrader
2025 Hwy. 199 (Hiouchi)
Crescent City, CA 95531

California Perfume Company
Not common; marked Goetting Co., Marvel Electric Silver Cleaner, Easy-Day Automatic Clothes Washer, Savoi et Cie
Dick Pardini
3107 N El Dorado St.
Stockton, CA 95204-3412

California Raisins
Larry DeAngelo
516 King Arthur Dr.
Virginia Beach, VA 23464

Cameras
Michael Breedlove
15633 Cold Spring Ct.
Granger, IN 46530
800-858-3267

Harry E. Forsythe
3914 Beach Blvd.
Jacksonville, FL 32207

William Hoos
335 Ridge Ave.
Wilmette, IL 60091
708-256-6383

Candlewick
Michelle C. Ondrey
12026 Ibis St. NW
Coon Rapids, MN 55433
612-754-2848

Carnival Items
Tom Davis
147 Longleaf Dr.
Blackshear, GA 31626
912-449-6243

Radio lamps of plaster
Tom Morris
P.O. Box 8307
Medford, OR 97504
503-779-3164

Carnival Glass
Also carnival glass buttons and Depression glass
Reyne Hogan
67 Park W
Houston, TX 77072

Cat Collectibles
Kitty Cucumber and Kilban Cat
Pamela Wiggins
6025 Sunnycrest St.
Houston, TX 77087

Crystal figurines
Glenna Moore
440 Lewers St., #205
Honolulu, HI 96815-2445

Catalogs
Fisher-Price
Brad Cassity
1350 Stanwix
Toledo, OH 43614
419-385-9910

Gambling supplies
John Benedict
P.O. Drawer 1423
Loxahatchee, FL 33470
Phone/FAX 407-798-2520

Glass insulators
Mike Bruner
6980 Walnut Lake Rd.
W Bloomfield, MI 48323

Jewelry; circa 1920-30
Sherry and Mike Miller
303 Holiday Dr.
Tuscola, IL 61953
217-253-4991

Mission, Arts and Crafts
Gary Struncius
P.O. Box 1374
Lakewood, NJ 08701
908-364-7580 or
800-272-2529

Silhouettes on glass, circa 1920s-'50s
Shirley Mace
P.O. Box 1602
Mesilla Park, NM
88047-1602
505-524-6717

Toy sewing machines
Glenda Thomas
P.O. Box 893
Electra, TX 76360

Slot cars or model cars
Gary Pollastro
4156 Beach Dr. SW
Seattle, WA 98116
206-935-0245

Cereal Boxes and Premiums
Scott Bruce
P.O. Box 481
Cambridge, MA 02140
617-492-5004

Character and Promotional Drinking Glasses
Distributed or produced by Coca-Cola
Robert J. Bodendorf
379 Market St.
Rockland, MA 02370

Character Collectibles
Also any related collectibles
Bill Bruegman
Toy Scouts, Inc.
137 Casterton Ave.
Akron, OH 44303
216-838-0668 or
FAX 216-869-8668

Betty Boop
Leo A. Mallette
2309 Santa Anita Ave.
Arcadia, CA 91006-5154

Gumby
Mike Drollinger
1010 N Walnut
Veedersburg, IN 47987

Gumby
Colleen Garmon Barnes
114 E Locust
Chatham, IL 62629

Lil' Abner
Kenn Norris
P.O. Box 4830
Sanderson, TX 79848-4830

The Lone Ranger
Terry and Kay Klepey
The Silver Bullet Newsletter
P.O. Box 553
Forks, WA 98331

Peanuts comic strip
Freddi Margolin
P.O. Box 512P
Bay Shore, NY 11706

Mickey Mouse
Patty Durnell
703 Tilton Rd.
Danville, IL 61832
217-443-4201

Elvis Presley and Marilyn Monroe
Lee Garmon
1529 Whittier St.
Springfield, IL 62704

Marilyn Monroe
Joan Jenkins
45 Brown's Ln.
Old Lyme, CT 06371
203-434-1852

Disney; ceramic items
Calvin L. Hackeman
8865 Olde Mill Run
Manassas, VA 22110
703-368-6982

Also Disney, Elvis, Western Heroes
Terri Ivers
1104 Shirlee Ave.
Ponca City, OK 74601
405-762-8697 or
405-762-5174

Roy Rogers
Robert W. Phillips
1703 N Aster Pl.
Broken Arrow, OK
74012-1308

Uncle Wiggily
Audrey V. Buffington
2 Old Farm Rd.
Wayland, MA 01778
6508-358-2644

Wizard of Oz; also W.W. Denslow
Michael Gessel
P.O. Box 748
Arlington, VA 22216
703-532-4261

Wizard of Oz
Gwen Daniel
18 Belleau Lake Ct.
O'Fallon, MO 63366
314-978-3190

Chase
Carl Ratner
550 Lamoka Ave.
Staten Island, NY 10312
718-317-1838

Children's Things
Sandy Blair
Box 1409
Forney, TX 75126

China and glassware
Diane Genicola
25 E Adams Ave.
Pleasantville, NJ 08232
609-646-6140

Russel Wright child's set
Kim Kimler
P.O. Box 154
Ripton, VT 05766

T. Rodrick
R.R. #2, Box 163
Sumner, IL 62466

Cigarette Lighters
Clayton V. Vecellio
Box 298
Lewis Run, PA 16738
814-368-5294

Linda Peris
261 Bonnie Brae
Elmhurst, IL 60126
708-782-5369

Sterling silver and table models
Bill Simmons
315 SW 77th Ave.
N Lauderdale, FL
33068-1220
305-726-3381

Civil War Memorabilia
D. Lerch
P.O. Box 586
N White Plains, NY 10603
Phone/FAX 914-761-8903

Clocks
Art Deco
Carl Ratner
550 Lamoka Ave.
Staten Island, NY 10312
718-317-1838

Novelty pendulettes
Jim and Kaye Whitaker
Eclectic Antiques
P.O. Box 475, WB
Lynnwood, WA 98046
206-774-6910

Antique
Norma Wadler
The Whale's Tale
P.O. Box 1520A
Long Beach, WA 98631
360-642-3455

Clothing
Hats, circa 1930s-40s
Ann Warner
363 Day Dr.
Elkton, OR 97436
503-584-2109

Infants
Joyce Andresen
P.O. Box 1
Keystone, IA 52249

Motorcycle
Bruce Kiper
2205 Sunset Ln.
Lutz, FL 33549
813-949-5060

Shoes, circa 1890-1970s
Cracker Hill
P.O. Box 403
Waldo, FL 32694-0403

Coca-Cola
T. Rodrick
R.R. #2, Box 163
Sumner, IL 62466

Coins
Also paper money and exonumia
Dempsey and Baxter
1009 E 38th St.
Erie, PA 16504

Elongated, rolled-out; buy, sell or trade
Doug Fairbanks, Sr.
5937 Beadle Dr.
Jamesville, NY 13078
315-469-4682

David E. French
P.O. Box 18924
Fairfield, OH 45018
513-829-1226

Also gold, silver, and diamonds
San Juan Precious Metals Corp.
4818 San Juan Ave.
Jacksonville, FL 32210
904-387-3466

Comic Books
Also any character or related collectibles
Toy Scouts, Inc.
137 Casterton Ave.
Akron, OH 44303
216-838-0668 or
FAX 216-869-8668

Compacts
Sandra Norrell
P.O. Box 439
Aransas Pass, TX 78335
512-758-8254

Connie Yore
814 State St.
St. Joseph, MI 49085
616-983-4144

Cookbooks
Also old kitchen utensils
Noreen Stayton
2414-107th Ave
Oakland, CA 94603

Country Store Collectibles
Randy Wright
Rt. 2, Box 372I, Hill St.
Erin, TN 37061
615-289-4068 or
615-289-4096

Credit Cards
Circa before 1930
Walt Thompson
P.O. Box 2541-W
Yakima, WA 98907-2541

Cuff Links and Men's Jewelry
The National Cuff Link Society
Eugene R. Klompus
P.O. Box 346
Prospect Hgts., IL 60070
Phone/FAX 708-632-0561

Czechoslovakian Collectibles
Bill and Carolyn Price
P.O. Box 1622
Cottonwood, CA 96022
916-347-0692

Dog Collectibles
Figurines, books, jewelry, etc.
D. Matnis
P.O. Box 9341
Tulsa, OK 74157-0341
918-585-1282

Collies, old, new or unusual; also Lassie
J. Neidhardt
428 Philadelphia Rd.
Joppa, MD 21085
410-679-7224

Dolls
Betsy McCall and friends
Marci Van Ausdall
P.O. Box 946
Quincy, CA 95971

Especially vintage Barbies
Aylene Krichinsky
5910 Bent Pine Dr., Apt. 209
Orlando, FL 32822
407-468-9148

From the 1950s
Linda Melanson
33 Maguire Rd.
Brockton, MA 02402
508-588-7784

Barbie and others
Edna Moon
2199 Bold Springs Rd.
Dacula, GA 30211
404-822-5987

My Child
Linda Toivainen
R.R. 1, Box 128 Middle Rd.
Waterboro, ME 04087

Nancy Ann Storybook
Noreen Stayton
2414-107th Ave
Oakland, CA 94603

Doorstops
Bulldog
Memories by Michele
12026 Inbis St., NW
Coon Rapids, MN 55423
612-754-2848

Dresser Sets
Also hair receivers
Tiffany Lininger
2205 2nd Ave. W
Seattle WA 98119

Easter
Rick Scott
49 Mersereau Ave.
Staten Island, NY 10303
718-981-2514

Egg Cups
Ann Warner
363 Day Dr.
Elkton, OR 97436
503-584-2109

Enameled Items on Silver or Sterling
Pat Cavoli
3001 Ave. U
Brooklyn, NY 11229
718-434-5426

Ephemera
Barber shop and razor
Lester Dequaine
155 Brewster St.
Bridgeport, CT 06605
203-335-6833

Civil War; especially diaries, letters, and photos
Stephen Edwards
Rt. 1, Box 1348
Mt. Philo Rd.
Charlotte, VT 05445
802-425-2006

Mesh purses
Sherry and Mike Miller
303 Holiday Dr.
Tuscola, IL 61953
217-253-4991

Also postcards and trade cards
John and Margaret Kaduck
The Collection Builders
P.O. Box 26076
Cleveland, OH 44126
216-333-2958

Motorcycle
Bruce Kiper
2205 Sunset Ln.
Lutz, FL 33549
813-949-5060

Motorcycle
Tom Wilhelm
R.R. 1, Box 203
Eaton, NY 13334
315-684-9675

Golf
Richard Regan
293 Winter St., #5
Hanover, MA 02339
617-826-3537

Match holders or match safes
George Sparacio
P.O. Box 791
Malaga, NJ 08328
609-694-4167

Any Redfield silverplate company
Judy Redfield
2507 Old 63 South
Columbia, MO 65201
314-449-8523

Judith Katz-Schwartz
222 E 93rd St. 42D
New York, NY 10128
212-876-3512

Rhode Island
Gordon Carr
Ephemera
67 Chapel St.
Lincoln, RI 02865-2101

Telegraph
Roger W. Reinke
5301 Neville Ct.
Alexandria, VA 22310
800-348-0294

Telephone
Phoneco
Ron and Mary Knappen
207 E Mill Rd., P.O. Box 70
Galesville, WI 54630

Transportation, motorcycle, etc.
Randy Sykes
20 Pond St.
Nashua, NH 03060
603-889-5924

Victorian
Gary and Rhonda Hallden
21958 Larkin Dr.
Saugus, CA 91350
805-259-7868

Westmoreland Glass Company
Daniel Sperry
P.O. Box 5487
Hauppauge, NY
11788-0121

Fast-Food Collectibles
Delores Lawson
6129 Misson Dr.
Orlando, FL 32810
407-298-4749

Older McDonald's® items
Betty Hornback
707 Sunrise Ln.
Elizabethtown, KY 42701
502-765-2441

Fiesta
Don Williams
150 E Lakeview Ave.
Columbus, OH 43202-1217
614-261-8549

Figurines
Any Victorian, Florence Ceramics, Dresden, German, bronze, marble, porcelain, etc.
Mrs. Dee Dee McAlexander
409 Lakewood Ave.
Tampa, FL 33613-1830
813-963-5814

Fire-King
Wendy Seamons
614 N Main
Lewiston, UT 84320
801-258-2852

Fishing
Also hunting
Back Door Antiques
P.O. Box 1125
Island Hgts., NJ 08732
908-929-1112

Especially lures and live bait containers
The Olde Outdoorsman
George H. Mace
P.O. Box 388
Paw Paw, IL 61353
815-497-2407

Old hunting and fishing licenses
Dennis Schulte
8th Ave NW
Waukon, IA 52172
319-568-3628
(before 10 pm CST)

Old wooden lures
Art Pietrasfewski, Jr.
60 Grant St.
Depew, NY 14043
716-681-2339 (4 pm-10 pm)

Flow Blue
Gary R. Smith
517 Laurel Ave.
Modesto, CA 95351

Flower Frogs
Figurals of any material
Linda Peris
261 Bonnie Brae
Elmhurst, IL 60126
708-782-5369

Fostoria
American
Betty Hornback
707 Sunrise Ln.
Elizabethtown, KY 42701
502-765-2441

Fountain Pens
Also related items
M. Jane Crane
132 Dillon Dr.
Lemont Furnace, PA 15456
412-437-1209

Deborah and James Golden
3182 Twin Pine Rd.
Grayling, MI 49738
517-348-2610

Antique
Norma Wadler
The Whale's Tale
P.O. Box 1520A
Long Beach, WA 98631
360-642-3455

Fruit Kids
Ceramic items
Michelle Carey
2512 Balmoral Blvd.
Kokomo, IN 46902
317-455-3970

Furniture
Oak in rough condition
Mark and Darlene Fish
P.O. Box 236
Lake Benton, MN 56149
507-368-4310

Mission, Arts and Crafts
Gary Struncius
P.O. Box 1374
Lakewood, NJ 08701
908-364-7580 or
800-272-2529

Gasoline Globes and Signs
Oil Co. Collectibles
Scott Benjamin
411 Forest St.
La Grange, OH 44050
216-355-6608

German China
Divided dishes with lobster handles
David Ringering
1480 Tumalo Dr. SE
Salem, OR 97301-9278

Glass Animals
R. Kuhne
Box 636
New Suffolk, NY 11956
516-765-5809

Blown; circa 1940s-50s
Celie's Pretty Things
2942 Lynda Ln.
Columbus, GA 31906

Glassware
Van Borough crystal by Royal Doulton
Cal Hackeman
8865 Olde Mill Run
Manassas, VA 22110
703-368-6982

Circa 1930s-40s
Jim Kirkpatrick
Rt. 1, Box 22
Mineola, TX 75773
903-569-6518

Bubble in red or green
Violet Moore
P.O. Box 637
Walker, LA 70785
504-665-3257

Cranberry, but not new Fenton
Rhonda Hasse
566 Oak Terrace Dr.
Farmington, MO 63640

Any ruby or red
Loretta Woodrow
1828 W Snoddy Rd.
Covington, IN 47932

Boopies in red
Twila Zackmire
1405 E Bonebrake Rd.
Veedersburg, IN 47987

Beakers and other items marked Eastman Kodak
Kathy Nascimbeni
609 Laundry St.
Kannapolis, NC 28083
704-933-5810

Shot glasses; no plain
The Shot Glass Club of America
P.O. Box 90404
Flint, MI 48509

Spice, canister, or cruet sets
Janet Hume
11000 S Bryant
Oklahoma City, OK 73160
405-794-7493

Swanky Swigs
Curt Johnson
Box 811
Aberdeen, SD 57401

Goldscheider
American
Vera Skorupski
P.O. Box 572
Plainville, CT 06062

Figurines
Gene A. Underwood
909 N Sierra Bonita Ave., Apt. 9
Los Angeles, CA 90046-6551
213-850-6276

Hall
Carousel Antiques
1006 Meyer at Fourth
Seabrook, TX 77586

Red Poppy
Mark and Darlene Fish
P.O. Box 236
Lake Benton, MN 56149
507-368-4310

Haviland
France, unusual floral pieces
Susan Correa
1236 Shirley St.
Omaha, NE 68144
402-333-7425

Holiday Memorabilia
Gail Magnon
R.D. #1, Box 481
Palmyra, PA 17078

Rick Scott
49 Mersereau Ave.
Staten Island, NY 10303
718-981-2514

Before 1950s
Mark Bergin
P.O. Box 1555
Hollis, NH 03049-1555
603-465-7727 or
FAX 603-465-3771

Homer Laughlin Art Pottery
James E. Nelson
1211 56th Ave., Ter. E
Bradenton, FL 34203
813-756-7337

Hull Pottery
Sharon L. Wilder
Rte. 5, Box 92 B
Mankato, MN 56001
507-625-7544

Hummels
Fred and Lila Shrader
2025 Hwy. 199 (Hiouchi)
Crescent City, CA 95531

Incense Burners
Linda Peris
261 Bonnie Brae
Elmhurst, IL 60126
708-782-5369

Jewelry
Czechoslovakian; jeweled brass or glass
Victorian Touch
Valerie Roberts
P.O. Box 4
Micanopy, FL 32667
904-466-4022

Made of hair
Tiffany Lininger
2205 2nd Ave. W
Seattle WA 98119

Made of butterfly wings; also pictures
Shirley Mace
P.O. Box 1602
Mesilla Park, NM 88047-1602
505-524-6717

Gail S. Magnon
R.D. #1, Box 481
Palmyra, PA 17078

Keen Kutter
Dennis Schulte
8th Ave NW
Waukon, IA 52172
319-568-3628
(before 10 pm CST)

Key Chains
DAV and BF Goodrich licenses
Dennis Schulte
8th Ave NW
Waukon, IA 52172
319-568-3628
(before 10 pm CST)

DAV and BF Goodrich Licenses
Kayla Conway
4500 Napal Ct.
Bakersfield, CA 93307
895-833-0291

Kitchen Collectibles
Dazey butter churn
Lynda Mitchell
35900 Deersville Rd.
Cadiz, OH 43907

Pea-Sheller, green handle, circa 1930s
Marilyn Busby
64 Country Club Dr.
Danville, IL 61832
217-446-6669

Plastic Aunt Jemima wares
Ival Maxwell
2501 S Market St.
Marion, IL 62959
618-997-2182

Yelloware, butter stamps, rolling pins, Cornish kitchen ware, and advertising teapots
Sally Van Aller
140 Overlook Dr.
Queenstown, MD 21658
410-827-6097

Glassware
Pamela Wiggins
6025 Sunnycrest St.
Houston, TX 77087
713-649-6603

Knives
Clayton V. Vecellio
Box 298
Lewis Run, PA 16738
814-368-5294

Kayla Conway
4500 Napal Ct.
Bakersfield, CA 93307
895-833-0291

Ladies' Accessories
Fans, perfumes, compacts, etc.
The Curiosity Shop
P.O. Box 964
Cheshire, CT 06410
203-271-0643

Lamps
Bill and Treva Courter
3935 Kelley Rd.
Kevil, KY 42053
502-488-2116

Miniature oil
Mrs. Thomas Tierney
231 Hearth Ct. W
Lakewood, NJ 08701
908-870-5691

Lava
C.E. Nolte
2979 S 15 Pl.
Milwaukee, WI 53215

Electric or oil Moon and Star pattern by L.G. Wright or L.E. Smith
Linda Holycross
109 N Sterling Ave., WB
Veedersburg, IN 47987

License Plates
Motorcycle, circa 1900-1965
Tom Wilhelm
R.R. 1, Box 203
Eaton, NY 13334
315-684-9675

Limited Edition Plates
Featuring cats
Glenna Moore
440 Lewers St., #205
Honolulu, HI 96815-2445

Lightning Rod Balls
Larry D. Cook
P.O. Box 211
Walnut, IA 51577-0211

Macerated Money Items
William J. Skelton
Highland Coin and Jewelry
P.O. Box 55448
Birmingham, AL 35255
205-939-3166, extension 3

Marbles
Frank Bernhard
2791 Fiesta Dr.
Venice, FL 34293

Daria A. Canino
HC 73, Box 991
Locust Grove, VA 22508
703-972-1525

Gerry Colman
4501 Palmyra NW
Albuquerque, NM 87115
505-897-3116

M. Jane Crane
132 Dillon Dr.
Lemont Furnace, PA 15456
412-437-1209

David E. French
P.O. Box 18924
Fairfield, OH 45018
513-829-1226

Ron Riley
2212 28th St.
Lubbock, TX 79411-1409
806-744-6460

Marriage Certificates
Decorative; framed or unframed
A. Solomon
P.O. Box 23
Ebensburg, PA 15931

Mauchline (Wooden Transfer Ware)
Gary Leveille
Antique Souvenir Collector
P.O. Box 562
Great Barrington, MA 01230

McCoy Pottery
Tiffany Buoni
P.O. Box 114
Analomink, PA 18320
717-420-1311

Also cookie jars
Jim Kirkpatrick
Rt. 1, Box 22
Mineola, TX 75773
903-569-6518

Mrs. Dee Dee McAlexander
409 Lakewood Ave.
Tampa, FL 33613-1830
813-963-5814

Militaria
John and Margaret Kaduck
The Collection Builders
P.O. Box 26076
Cleveland, OH 44126
216-333-2958

Mining Memorabilia
John W. Coons
9757 S. Isabel Ct.
Highlands Ranch, CO 80216
303-791-6496

Miscellaneous
Nearly anything
Cardillo Sales Co.
#62-4th Ave.
P.O. Box 792
Midvale, UT 84047

Nearly anything
Ronald Fitch
315 Market St.
Ste. 2G
Portsmouth, OH 45662
614-353-6879

Nearly anything
The Glass Packrat
Pat and Bill Ogden
3050 Colorado Ave.
Grand Junction, CO 81504

Nearly anything
Judith Katz-Schwartz
222 E 93rd St. 42D
New York, NY 10128
212-876-3512

Nearly anything
Ivan Platnick
2506 Cliffmont
Bluefield, WV 24701

Small collectibles such as tokens, medals, coins, etc.
David Smies
Box 522
Manhattan, KS 66052
913-776-1433

Nearly anything
Mickey Starr
2722 340th
Keokuk, IA 52632
319-524-1601

Models
Travel agency planes
Dick Wallin
P.O. Box 1794
Springfield, IL 62705
217-498-9279

Movie Memorabilia
Reyne Hogan
67 Park W
Houston, TX 77072

Also autographs
Bill Simmons
315 SW 77th Ave.
N Lauderdale, FL
33068-1220
305-726-3381

Music Boxes
Deborah and James Golden
3182 Twin Pine Rd.
Grayling, MI 49738
517-348-2610

Brett and Cheryl Hurt
6000 Amber Oaks Ave.
Bakersfield, CA 93306
805-872-6296

Dawn Persky
10070 SW 17 Ct.
Davie, FL 33324
305-424-5826

Nippon
Robert Greenwood
201 E Hatfield St.
Massena, NY 13662
315-769-8130

E.J. Hansen
49 Bianca Ln. #305
Watsonville, CA 95076
408-761-1202

Betty Hornback
707 Sunrise Ln.
Elizabethtown, KY 42701
502-765-2441

Nutcrackers
William Hoos
335 Ridge Ave.
Wilmette, IL 60091
708-256-6383

Ocean Liner
Rosie O'Grady's Antiques
& Fine Gifts
32 S Palm Ave.
Sarasota, FL 34236
800-793-4193

Oil Paintings
Storms Fine Art Gallery +
Liquidations
704 Center St.
Jim Thorpe, PA 18229

Optical Eyewear
Kayla Conway
4500 Napal Ct.
Bakersfield, CA 93307
805-833-0291

Optical Instruments
Telescopes and microscopes
Michael Breedlove
15633 Cold Spring Ct.
Granger, IN 46530
800-858-3267

Orientalia
Rosie O'Grady's Antiques
& Fine Gifts
32 S Palm Ave.
Sarasota, FL 34236
800-793-4193

Old Chinese snuff bottles
Andrew Hsueh
P.O. Box 233
Lake Lure, NC 28746
704-625-0600

Paper Dolls
Sandy Blair
Box 1409
Forney, TX 75126

Rhonda Hasse
566 Oak Terrace Dr.
Farmington, MO 63640

Framed and dressed in fabric
Miki Pfeffer
1961-1 Hwy. 308
Thibodaux, LA 70301
504-446-5122

Paperweights
Frank Bernhard
2791 Fiesta Dr.
Venice, FL 34293

Daria A. Canino
HC 73, Box 991
Locust Grove, VA 22508
703-972-1525

Cast iron dogs by Hubley
Dean Dashner
349 S Green Bay Rd.
Neenah, WI 54956
414-725-4350

Peanuts Comics and Charles Schulz
Freddi Margolin
P.O. Box 5124P
Bay Shore, NY 11706

Pepsi-Cola
Kelly Wilson
P.O. Box 41006
Winnipeg, Manitoba
Canada R3T 5T1
Phone/FAX 204-275-6438

Craig and Donna Sifter
511 Aurora Ave., #117
Naperville, IL 60540

Peasant Art Pottery
Delores Saar
45 Fifth Ave. NW
Hutchinson, MN 55350
612-587-2002

Phoenix Bird
Nancy Young
128 Mohican Rd.
Blairstown, NJ 07825
908-362-8757

Photo Albums
Circa early 1900s
Dawn Persky
10070 SW 17 Ct.
Davie, FL 33324
305-424-5826

Photographs
Hand-tinted
Gary R. Smith
517 Laurel Ave.
Modesto, CA 95351

Robert Moore
1076 Charles Ave.
St. Paul, MN 55104
612-644-4090

Pie Birds
Stephen Skorupski
P.O. Box 572
Plainville, CT 06062

Portrait Miniatures
Sender's
23500 Mercantile Rd.
Beachwood, OH 44122

Postcards
Gary Leveille
Antique Souvenir Collector
P.O. Box 562
Great Barrington, MA 01230

Especially with children
Pat Lockerby
885 Beltrees St., Apt. 2
Dunedin, FL 34698
813-733-9144

Related to Culver, IN
Mark A. Roeder
305 Akron St.
Culver, IN 46511

Gail Magnon
R.D. #1, Box 481
Palmyra, PA 17078

Gary R. Smith
517 Laurel Ave.
Modesto, CA 95351

Posters
Soviet political and satirical
Michael Gessel
P.O. Box 748
Arlington, VA 22216
703-532-4261

Pot Lids
Sally Van Aller
140 Overlook Dr.
Queenstown, MD 21658
410-827-6097

Pottery
Montage Magie
P.O. Box 3423
Veero Beach, FL
32964-3423
407-234-5409

McCoy with floral designs and Van Briggle
Betty Hornback
707 Sunrise Ln.
Elizabethtown, KY 42701
502-765-2441

Pressed Wood Items
By Syrocowood, Ornawood, Durawood, etc.
Carole Kaifer
P.O. Box 232
Bethania, NC 27010
910-924-9672

Primitives
The Cocklebur Antiques
2161 Pointer Rd.
W Branch, MI 48661
517-345-7242

Kris Grimes
5705 Lawndale Ln.
Plymouth, MA 55446
612-557-1426

P.T. Barnum and His Museum
Gary Bagnall
3090 McMillan Rd.
San Luis Obispo, CA
93401
805-542-9988 or
805-481-3847

Purses
Jan Alpert
4820 Fairview
Keego Harbor, MI 48322
810-737-6999

Beaded
Michael Cohen
2312 Gulf Gate Dr.
Sarasota, FL 34231
813-925-7355

Beaded
Kayla Conway
4500 Napal Ct.
Bakersfield, CA 93307
805-833-0291

Beaded
Sandra Norrell
P.O. Box 439
Aransas Pass, TX 78335
512-758-8254

Beaded
Connie Yore
814 State St.
St. Joseph, MI 49085
616-983-4144

The Curiosity Shop
Lynell Schwartz
P.O. Box 964
Cheshire, CT 06410
203-271-0643

Jeweled brass or jeweled frames
Victorian Touch
Valerie Roberts
P.O. Box 4
Micanopy, FL 32667
904-466-4022

Radios
Catalin
Richard O. Gates
P.O. Box 187
Chesterfield, VA 23832
804-748-0382 or
804-794-5146

Shortwave and ham; also equipment
Hirsch's
219 California Dr.
Williamsville, NY 14221
716-632-1189

Mickey Starr
2722 340th
Keokuk, IA 52632

Records
Elvis' Sun Label, 45rpm
Dwayne Caldwell
2600 NE Lawrance Rd.
Claremore, OK 74017

Red Wing Stoneware
Bruce and Nada Ferris
3094 Oakes Dr.
Hayward, CA 94542
510-581-5285

Rookwood
Frank Bernhard
2791 Fiesta Dr.
Venice, FL 34293

Bruce E. Thulin
P.O. Box 121
Ellsworth, ME 04605
207-667-5226

Rose Bowls
Kathy Langley
P.O. Box 159
Ft. Deposit, AL
36032-0159
205-227-8678

Roseville
Frank Bernhard
2791 Fiesta Dr.
Venice, FL 34293

Rowland and Marsellus
David Ringering
1480 Tumalo Dr. SE
Salem, OR 97301-9278
503-585-8253

Royal Doulton
Figurines
Robert W. Atkins
1950 Lawndale Dr.
Valparaiso, IN 46383-6617
219-462-7588

R.S. Prussia
Robert Greenwood
201 E Hatfield St.
Massena, NY 13662
315-769-8130

Salt and Pepper Shakers
Figurals
Michelle Carey
2512 Balmoral Blvd.
Kokomo, IN 46902
317-455-3970

Stan and Carrie Soderstrom
003-3rd St. SW
Rt. 2, Box 300
Bowman, ND 58623

Samplers
Jeane N. Trauger
1776 Division St.
New London, WI 54961
414-982-4366

Scales
Robert W. Atkins
1950 Lawndale Dr.
Valparaiso, IN 46383-6617
219-462-7588

Sewing Items
Kayla Conway
4500 Napal Ct.
Bakersfield, CA 93307
805-833-0291

Shawnee Pottery
Also cookie jars
Jim Kirkpatrick
Rt. 1, Box 22
Mineola, TX 75773
903-569-6518

Sandra Norrell
P.O. Box 439
Aransas Pass, TX 78335
512-758-8254

Also other potteries
Bill and Carolyn Price
P.O. Box 1622
Cottonwood, CA 96022
916-347-0692

Shelley
Mrs. Thomas Tierney
231 Hearth Ct. W
Lakewood, NJ 08701
908-870-5691

Shirley Temple
Irene F. Brockman
27 Ward Rd.
Blairstown, NJ 07825
908-362-6730

Shooting Gallery Targets
Larry D. Cook
P.O. Box 211
Walnut, IA 51577-0211

Silhouettes
Sender's
23500 Mercantile Rd.
Beachwood, OH 44122

Smokey Bear
Elva Hughs
26 Franklin Rd., Box 192
Hinsdale, MA 01235
413-655-2016

Snow Domes
Nancy McMichael
P.O. Box 53132
Washington, DC 20009
202-234-7484

Soda Fountain
Also ice cream molds
Robert W. Atkins
1950 Lawndale Dr.
Valparaiso, IN 46383-6617
219-462-7588

Souvenir Items
Robert W. Atkins
1950 Lawndale Dr.
Valparaiso, IN 46383-6617
219-462-7588

Gary Leveille
Antique Souvenir Collector
P.O. Box 562
Great Barrington, MA 01230

Engraved ruby-flashed crystal
George Belden
1224 N Mantua
Kent, OH 44240

Spoons
John W. Coons
9757 S. Isabel Ct.
Highlands Ranch, CO 80216
303-791-6496

Sports Memorabilia
Baseball
Bill Simmons
315 SW 77th Ave.
N Lauderdale, FL
33068-1220
305-726-3381

Most items; especially Brooklyn Dodger
Nancy Pinto
159 SW 97th Terrace
Coral Springs, FL 33071
305-341-8718

Billiards
Tim Lawrence
2489 Bexford Pl.
Columbus, OH
43209-1710

University of California, Berkeley
Alan Davis
P.O. Box 1083
Ashland, OR 97520
503-488-0027

Golf
Richard Regan
293 Winter St., #5
Hanover, MA 02339
617-826-3537

Stamps
San Juan Precious Metals
4818 San Juan Ave.
Jacksonville, FL 32210
904-387-3466

Stangl Pottery
James E. Nelson
1211 56th Ave., Ter. E
Bradenton, FL 34203
813-756-7337

State Farm Insurance Memorabilia
Denny Kaufman
5918 S Columbia Ave.
Tulsa, OK 74105
918-747-8211

Sterling Silver
Bill Simmons
315 SW 77th Ave.
N Lauderdale, FL
33068-1200

Michael Cohen
2312 Gulf Gate Dr.
Sarasota, FL 34231
813-925-7355

Stoneware
John Light
2324 Sanford Ave.
Alton, IL 62002
618-465-0292

Tapestries
Most (except religious ones)
Joyce Stratton
RFD #4, Box 550
Augusta, ME 04330
207-622-1001

Teddy Bears
Also monkeys
Gwen Daniel
18 Belleau Lake Ct.
O'Fallon, MO 63366
314-978-3190

Tools
David Barth
Box 81
Elk, WA 99009
509-292-2600

Toys
Lead soldiers
Frank Bernhard
2791 Fiesta Dr.
Venice, FL 34293

Tiffany Buoni
P.O. Box 114
Analomink, PA 18320
717-420-1311

Matchbox cars and all toy soldiers
Barry L. Evans
111 Deer Ave.
Pearisburg, VA 24134
703-921-2443 or
FAX 703-921-2786

Raggedy Ann dolls, books, music boxes, etc.
Kim Avery
104 Longwood Rd.
St. Marys, GA 31558

Wooden boats and old tin windups
Richard Gronowski
140 N Garfield Ave.
Traverse City, MI 49686
616-491-2111

Tootsietoys
Nick Giordano
125 Newton Ave.
Gibbstown, NJ 08027
609-423-1449

Tonka, prior to 1960
Ken Lininger
2205 2nd Ave. W
Seattle, WA 98119
206-283-7336

Also trains
Jerry H. Morris
2411 Crofton Ln., Ste. 17
Crofton, MD 21114
800-373-6003

Tramp Art
Jeane N. Trauger
1776 Division St.
New London, WI 54961
414-982-4366

Typewriter Ribbon Tins
Kayla Conway
4500 Napal Ct.
Bakersfield, CA 93307
805-833-0291

Typewriters
Michael Breedlove
15633 Cold Spring Ct.
Granger, IN 46530
800-858-3267

Universal Pottery
Cattail and Red Poppy
Ken and Barbara Brooks
4121 Gladstone Ln.
Charlotte, NC 28205
704-568-5716

Vaseline Glass
Dwayne Caldwell
2600 NE Lawrance Rd.
Claremore, OK 74017

View-Master
Also other 3-D items
Chris 'Dr. 3-D' Perry
7470 Church St., Ste. A
Yucca Valley, CA 92284
619-365-0475

Wall Pockets
Kathy Langley
P.O. Box 159
Ft. Deposit, AL 36032-0159
205-227-8678

Watch Fobs
John and Margaret Kaduck
The Collection Builders
P.O. Box 26076
Cleveland, OH 44126
216-333-2958

Watches
Pocket
Kayla Conway
4500 Napal Ct.
Bakersfield, CA 93307
805-833-0291

Watt Pottery
Sandra Norrell
P.O. Box 439
Aransas Pass, TX 78335
512-758-8254

Wedding Memorabilia
Miki Pfeffer
1961-1 Hwy. 308
Thibodaux, LA 70301
504-446-5122

Weathervanes
Kris Grimes
5705 Lawndale Ln.
Plymouth, MA 55446
612-557-1426

Westmoreland
Michelle C. Ondrey
12026 Ibis St. NW
Coon Rapids, MN 55433
612-754-2848

Windmill Weights
Larry D. Cook
P.O. Box 211
Walnut, IA 51577-0211

World's Fair
Pat Cavoli
3001 Ave. U
Brooklyn, NY 11229
718-434-5426

St. Louis
Gwen Daniel
18 Belleau Lake Ct.
O'Fallon, MO 63366
314-978-3190

Also Expositions
John and Margaret Kaduck
The Collection Builders
P.O. Box 26076
Cleveland, OH 44126
216-333-2958

Yelloware
Tom Davis
147 Longleaf Dr.
Blackshear, GA 31626
912-449-6243

INDEX